Åsne Seierstad was born in 1970 and studied Russian, Spanish and the History of Philosophy at Oslo University. She worked as a correspondent in Russia between 1993 and 1996, and in China in 1997. Between 1998 and 2000 she reported on the war in Kosovo for Norwegian television, and in 2000 she published *With Their Backs to the Wall: Portraits from Serbia*. In autumn 2001 she spent three months in Afghanistan, reporting for a number of major Scandinavian newspapers. In spring 2003 she reported on the war in Iraq from Baghdad.

Åsne Seierstad has received numerous awards for her journalism. *The Bookseller of Kabul* is one of the bestselling Norwegian books of all time, and has been translated into many languages.

'Honestly and intelligently written . . . offers lessons to those who choose to heed it on the folly of trying to make simple diagnoses or to apply simple remedies in Afghanistan' Isabel Hilton, *Daily Telegraph*

'A colourful portrait of people struggling to survive in the most brutal circumstances . . . bears witness to the power of literature to withstand even the most repressive regime' Michael Arditti, *Daily Mail*

'A compelling picture of a country which tragically continues to tear itself apart' *Sunday Telegraph*

'A triumph. From the terrors and complexities of courtship through the perilous cross-country pilgrimage by a guilt-addled son to the agonising fate of a thieving carpenter, these are compelling little dramas, mined from the resource of "every day life" . . . and peopled by characters who bristle with life and emotion and individuality . . .while their stories delight with the freshness of something foreign, they are both universal and intimately personal . . . [the] work's outward simplicity is matched by a subtle and complex understanding: the quality of truth' *Scotsman*

'Magnificent . . . Beautifully written, it dares to bestride incompatible worlds. It is the best outsider tale I have read from within the bounds of Islamic life since Sarah Hobson's *Through Persia in Disguise*, published twenty-nine years ago' *Scotland on Sunday*

'A unique insight into another world' *Daily Mirror*

'Moving and utterly gripping' *Big Issue in the North*

'A closely observed, affecting account . . . an admirable, revealing portrait of daily life in a country that Washington claims to have liberated but does not begin to understand' *Washington Post*

'Astounding . . . an international bestseller, it will likely stand as one of the best books of reportage of Afghan life after the fall of the Taliban' *Publishers Weekly*

The Bookseller
of Kabul

Åsne Seierstad

Translated by
Ingrid Christophersen

Virago

A *Virago* Book

First published in 2002 by J.W. Cappelens Forlag
First published in Great Britain in 2003 by Little, Brown
First published in 2004 by Virago
Reprinted 2004 (nine times)

A CIP catalogue record for this book is available from the British Library.

ISBN 1 84408 047 1

Typeset in Perpetua by M Rules
Printed and bound in Great Britain by Clays Ltd, St Ives plc

Virago Press
An imprint of
Time Warner Book Group UK
Brettenham House
Lancaster Place
London WC2E 7EN

www.virago.co.uk

For my parents

Contents

Foreword

One of the first people I met when I arrived in Kabul in November 2001 was Sultan Khan. I had spent six weeks with the commandos of the Northern Alliance – in the desert by the Tajikistani border, in the mountains of the Hindu Kush, in the Panshir Valley, and on the steppes north of Kabul. I had followed their offensive against the Taliban, I had slept on stone floors, in mud huts, and at the front, travelled on the back of lorries, in military vehicles, on horseback and on foot.

When the Taliban fell, I made for Kabul with the Northern Alliance. In a bookshop I happened upon an elegant, grey-haired man. Having spent weeks amongst gunpowder and rubble, where conversations centred on the tactics of war and military advance, it was refreshing to leaf through books and talk about literature and history. Sultan Khan's shelves were weighed down by books in many languages; collections of poems, Afghan legends, history books, novels. He was a good salesman; when I left the shop after my first visit I was carrying seven books. I would often pop in when I had some spare time, to look at books and talk to the interesting bookseller, an Afghan patriot who felt let down by his country time and again.

'First the Communists burnt my books, then the Mujahedeen looted and pillaged, finally the Taliban burnt them all over again,' he told me.

I spent hours listening to the bookseller's stories about his battles against the different regimes and their censors, how he launched his personal fight, hiding books from the police, lending them out to others – and finally going to prison for it. He was a man who had tried to save the art and literature of his country, while a string of dictators did their best to destroy them. I realized that he was himself a living piece of Afghan cultural history: a history book on two feet.

One day he invited me home for an evening meal. His family – one of his wives, his sons, sisters, brother, mother, a few cousins – was seated on the floor round a sumptuous feast.

Sultan recounted stories, the sons laughed and joked. The atmosphere was unrestrained, and a huge contrast to the simple meals with the commandos in the mountains. But I soon noticed that the women said little. Sultan's beautiful teenage wife sat quietly by the door with the baby in her arms. His first wife was not present that evening. The other women answered questions put to them, accepted praise about the meal, but never initiated any conversation.

When I left I said to myself: 'This is Afghanistan. How interesting it would be to write a book about this family.'

The next day I called on Sultan in his bookshop and told him my idea.

'Thank you,' was all he said.

'But this means that I would have to come and live with you.'

'You are welcome.'

'I would have to go around with you, live the way you live. With you, your wives, sisters, sons.'

'You are welcome,' he repeated.

On a foggy day in February I moved in with the family. My only possessions were my computer, some notebooks and pens, a mobile phone and what I was wearing. Everything else had disappeared en route, somewhere in Uzbekistan. I was welcomed with open arms, and gradually felt comfortable in the Afghan clothes I was lent.

I was given a mattress on the floor next to Leila, Sultan's youngest sister, who had been assigned the task of looking after my well-being.

'You are my little baby,' the nineteen-year-old said the first evening. 'I will look after you,' she assured me and jumped to her feet every time I got up.

Sultan had ordered the family to supply me with whatever I wanted. I was later told that whoever did not comply with this demand would be punished.

All day long I was served food and tea. Slowly I was introduced into family life. They told me things when they felt like it, not when I asked. They were not necessarily in the mood to talk when my notebook was at hand, but rather during a trip to the bazaar, on a bus, or late at night on the mattress. Most of the answers came about spontaneously, answers to questions I would not have had the imagination to ask.

I have written this book in literary form, but it is based on real events or what was told me by people who took part in those events. When I describe thoughts and feelings, the point of departure is what people told me they thought or felt in any given situation. Readers have asked me: 'How do you know what goes on inside the heads of the various family members?' I am not, of course, an omniscient author. Internal dialogue and feelings are based entirely on what family members described to me.

I never mastered Dari, the Persian dialect spoken by the Khan family, but several family members spoke English. Unusual? Yes. But then my tale from Kabul is the tale of a most unusual Afghan family. A bookseller's family is unusual in a country where three quarters of the population can neither read nor write.

Sultan had picked up a colourful and verbose form of English while teaching a diplomat his own Dari dialect. His young sister Leila spoke excellent English, having attended Pakistani schools when she was a refugee, and evening classes in Afghanistan. Mansur, Sultan's oldest son, also spoke fluent English, after several years of schooling in Pakistan. He was able to tell me about his fears, loves, and his discussions with God. He described how he wanted to immerse himself in a religious cleansing process, and he allowed me to accompany him on the pilgrimage to Mazar, as an invisible fourth companion. I was included in the business trip to Peshawar and Lahore, the hunt for al-Qaida, the shopping trips in the bazaar, the hammam, the wedding and wedding preparations, visits to the school, the Ministry of Education, the police station and the prison.

I did not personally take part in Jamila's dramatic fate or Rahimullah's escapades. I heard about Sultan's proposal to Sonya from those involved in the story; Sultan, Sonya, his mother, sisters, brother and Sharifa.

Sultan didn't allow anyone else outside the family to live in his house, so he, Mansure and Leila acted as my interpreters. This of course gave them a large influence over their family story, but I double-checked the various versions and asked the same questions of all three interpreters, who between them represented the large contrasts within the family.

The whole family knew that the purpose of my stay was to write a book. If there was something they did not want me to write, they told me. Nevertheless, I have chosen to keep the Khan family and the other people I quote anonymous. No one asked me to, I just felt it was right.

My days were the family's days. I woke at the break of day to howling children and men's commands. I waited my turn for the bathroom, or stole in when everyone had done. On lucky days there was still some warm water left, but I soon learnt that a cup of cold water in the face could also be refreshing. For the remainder of the day I stayed at home with the women, visited relatives and went to the bazaar, or I accompanied Sultan and his sons to the shop, round town or on journeys. In the evenings I shared a meal with the family and drank green tea until bedtime.

I was a guest, but soon felt at home. I was incredibly well treated; the family was generous and open. We shared many good times, but I have rarely been as angry as I was with the Khan family, and I have rarely quarrelled so much as I did there. Nor have I had the urge to hit anyone as much as I did there. The same thing was continually provoking me: the manner in which men treated women. The belief in man's superiority was so ingrained that it was seldom questioned.

I imagine they regarded me as some sort of 'bi-gendered' creature. As a westerner I could mingle with both men and women. Had I been a man I would never have been able to live so close to the women of the household, without gossip circulating. At the same time there was no obstacle to my being a woman, in a man's world. When the feasts were split, men and women in separate rooms, I was the only one able to circulate freely between the groups.

I was spared having to adhere to the Afghan woman's strict dress code, and I could go wherever I wanted. Nevertheless, I often dressed in the burka, simply to be left alone. A western woman in the streets of Kabul attracts a lot of unwanted attention. Beneath the burka I could gaze around to my heart's content without being stared at in return. I could observe the other family members when we were out, without everyone's attention being directed at me. Anonymity became a release, the only place to which I could turn; in Kabul quiet places were in short supply.

I also wore the burka to discover for myself what it is like to be an Afghan woman; what it feels like to squash into the chock-a-block back rows reserved for women, when the rest of the bus is half empty, what it feels like to squeeze into the boot of a taxi because a man is occupying the back seat, what it feels like to be stared at as a tall and attractive burka and receive your first burka-compliment from a man in the street.

How in time I started to hate it. How it pinches the head and causes headaches, how difficult it is to see any-thing through the grille. How enclosed it is, how little air gets in, how quickly you start to perspire, how all the time you have to be aware of where you are walking because you cannot see your feet, what a lot of dirt it picks up, how dirty it is, how much in the way. How liberated you feel when you get home and can take it off.

I also wore the burka as a matter of precaution, when I travelled with Sultan on the unsafe road to Jalalabad; when we had to spend the night in a dirty border station; when we were out late at night. Afghan women do not normally travel with a bundle of dollar bills and a computer, so high-waymen usually leave the burka-clad women alone.

It is important to emphasise that this is the story of *one* Afghan family. There are many millions of others. My family is not even typical. It is kind of middle-class, if one can use that expression in Afghanistan. Some of them were educated, several of them could read and write. They had enough money and never went hungry.

If I were to live in a typical Afghan family it would have been with a family in the countryside, a large family where no one could read or write, and every day was a battle for survival. I did not choose my family because I wanted it to represent all other families, but because it inspired me.

I dwelt in Kabul during the spring following the Taliban's flight. That spring fragile expectations flickered. The Taliban's fall was welcomed – no longer was anyone frightened of being pestered on the streets by the religious police, women could once again go to town unaccompanied, they could study, girls could go to school. But the period was also characterised by the previous decade's disappointments. Why should anything change now?

In the course of the spring, following a period of comparative peace, a more vigorous optimism could be detected. Plans were laid, an increasing number of women left the burka at home, some took jobs, refugees returned home.

The Government vacillated – between the traditional and the modern, between warlords and local tribal chiefs. In the midst of the chaos the leader, Hamid Karzai, attempted a balancing act and tried to stake out a political course. He was popular but possessed neither army nor party – in a country awash with weapons and warring factions.

Conditions in Kabul were reasonably peaceful, in spite of the murder of two ministers and the attempted murder of another; the population continued to be harassed. Many put their trust in the foreign soldiers who patrolled the streets. 'Without them civil war will start up again,' they said.

I have written down what I saw and heard, and have tried to gather my impressions of a Kabul spring, of those who tried to throw winter off, grow and blossom, and others who felt condemned to go on 'eating dust', as Leila would have put it.

Åsne Seierstad
Oslo, 1 August 2002

Migozarad!
(It will pass)

GRAFFITO ON THE WALLS OF A KABUL TEAHOUSE

The Proposal

When Sultan Khan thought the time had come to find himself a new wife, no one wanted to help him. First he approached his mother.

'You will have to make do with the one you have,' she said.

Then he went to his oldest sister. 'I'm fond of your first wife,' she said. His other sisters replied in the same vein.

'It's shaming for Sharifa,' said his aunt.

Sultan needed help. A suitor cannot himself ask for a girl's hand. It is an Afghan custom that one of the women of the family conveys the proposal and gives the girl the once-over to assure herself that she is capable, well brought up and suitable wife-material. But none of Sultan's close female relations wanted to have anything to do with this offer of marriage.

Sultan had picked out three young girls he thought might fit the bill. They were all healthy and good-looking, and of his own tribe. In Sultan's family it was rare to marry outside the clan; it was considered prudent and safe to marry relatives, preferably cousins.

Sultan's first candidate was sixteen-year-old Sonya. Her eyes were dark and almond-shaped and her hair shining black. She was shapely, voluptuous, and it was said of her that she was a good worker. Her family was poor and they were reasonably closely related. Her mother's grandmother and Sultan's mother's grandmother were sisters.

While Sultan ruminated over how to ask for the hand of the chosen one without the help of family women, his first wife was blissfully ignorant that a mere chit of a girl, born the same year she and Sultan were married, was Sultan's constant preoccupation. Sharifa was getting old. Like Sultan, she was a few years over fifty. She had borne him three sons and a daughter. The time had come for a man of Sultan's standing to find a new wife.

'Do it yourself,' his brother said finally.

After some thought, Sultan realised that this was his only solution, and early one morning he made his way to the house of the sixteen-year-old. Her parents greeted him with open arms. Sultan was considered a generous man and a visit from him was always welcome. Sonya's mother boiled water and made tea. They reclined on flat cushions in the mud cottage and exchanged pleasantries until Sultan thought the time had come to make his proposal.

'A friend of mine would like to marry Sonya,' he told the parents.

It was not the first time someone had asked for their daughter's hand. She was beautiful and diligent, but they thought she was still a bit young. Sonya's father was no longer able to work. During a brawl a knife had severed some of the nerves in his back. His beautiful daughter could be used as a bargaining chip in the marriage stakes, and he and his wife were always expecting the next bid to be even higher.

'He is rich,' said Sultan. 'He's in the same business as I am. He is well educated and has three sons. But his wife is starting to grow old.'

'What's the state of his teeth,' the parents asked immediately, alluding to the friend's age.

'About like mine,' said Sultan. 'You be the judge.'

Old, the parents thought. But that was not necessarily a disadvantage. The older the man, the higher the price for their daughter. A bride's price is calculated according to age, beauty and skill and according to the status of the family.

When Sultan Khan had delivered his message, the parents said, as could be expected: 'She is too young.'

Anything else would be to sell short to this rich, unknown suitor whom Sultan recommended so warmly. It would not do to appear too keen. But they knew Sultan would return; Sonya was young and beautiful.

He returned the next day and repeated the proposal. The same conversation, the same answers. But this time he got to meet Sonya whom he had not seen since she was a young girl.

She kissed his hand, in the custom of showing respect for an elder relative, and he blessed the top of her head with a kiss. Sonya was aware of the charged atmosphere and flinched under Uncle Sultan's searching look.

'I have found you a rich man, what do you think of that?' he asked. Sonya looked down at the floor. A young girl has no right to have an opinion about a suitor.

Sultan returned the third day and this time he made known the suitor's proposition: a ring, a necklace, earrings and bracelet, all in red gold; as many clothes as she wanted; 300 kilos of rice, 150 kilos of cooking-oil, a cow, a few sheep and 15 million Afghani, approximately £300.

Sonya's father was more than satisfied with the price and asked to meet this mysterious man who was prepared to pay so much for his daughter. According to Sultan he even belonged to their tribe, in spite of their not being able to place him or remember that they had ever met him.

'Tomorrow,' said Sultan, 'I will show you a picture of him.'

The next day, fortified by a sweetener, Sultan's aunt agreed to reveal to Sonya's parents the identity of the suitor. She took a photograph with her – a picture of Sultan Khan himself – and with it the uncompromising message that they had no more than an hour to make up their minds. If the answer was yes, he would be very grateful, and if it was no there would be no bad blood between them. What he wanted to avoid at all costs was everlasting bargaining about maybe, maybe not.

The parents agreed within the hour. They were keen on Sultan Khan, his money and his position. Sonya sat in the attic and waited. When the mystery surrounding the suitor had been solved and the parents had decided to accept, her father's brother came up to the attic. 'Uncle Sultan is your wooer,' he said. 'Do you consent?'

Not a sound escaped Sonya's lips. With tearful eyes and bowed head, she hid behind her long shawl.

'Your parents have accepted the suitor,' her uncle said. 'Now is your only chance to express an opinion.'

She was petrified, paralysed by fear. She did not want the man but she knew she had to obey her parents. As Sultan's wife her standing in Afghan society would go up considerably. The bride money would solve many of her family's problems. The money would help her parents buy good wives for their sons.

Sonya held her tongue, and with that her fate was sealed. To say nothing means to give one's consent. The agreement was drawn up, the date fixed.

Sultan went home to inform his family of the news. His wife Sharifa, his mother and sisters were seated around a dish of rice and spinach. Sharifa thought he was joking and laughed and cracked some jokes in return. His mother too laughed at Sultan's joke. She could not believe that he had entered into a proposal of marriage without her blessing. The sisters were dumbfounded.

No one believed him, not until he showed them the kerchief and sweetmeats the parents of a bride give the suitor as proof of the engagement.

Sharifa cried for twenty days. 'What have I done? What a disgrace. Why are you dissatisfied with me?'

Sultan told her to pull herself together. No one in the family backed him up, not even his own sons. Nevertheless, no one dared speak out against him – he always got his own way.

Sharifa was inconsolable. What really rankled was the fact that the man had picked an illiterate, someone who had not even completed nursery school. She, Sharifa, was a qualified Persian language teacher. 'What has she got that I haven't got?' she sobbed.

Sultan rose above his wife's tears.

No one wanted to attend the engagement party. But Sharifa had to bite the bullet and dress up for the celebrations.

'I want everyone to see that you agree and support me. In the future we will all be living under the same roof and you must show that Sonya is welcome,' he demanded. Sharifa had always humoured her husband, and now too, in this worst circumstance, giving him to someone else, she knuckled under. He even demanded that Sharifa should put the rings on his and Sonya's fingers.

Twenty days after the proposal of marriage the solemn engagement ritual took place. Sharifa pulled herself together and put on a brave face. Her female relatives did their best to unsettle her. 'How awful for you,' they said. 'How badly he has treated you. You must be suffering.'

The wedding took place two months after the engagement, on the day of the Muslim New Year's Eve. This time Sharifa refused to attend.

'I can't,' she told her husband.

The female family members backed her up. No one bought new dresses or applied the normal amount of make-up required at wedding ceremonies. They wore simple coiffures and stiff smiles – in deference to the superannuated wife who would no longer share Sultan Khan's bed. It was now reserved for the young, terrified bride – but they would all be under the same roof, until death did them part.

Burning Books

On a freezing cold afternoon in November 1999, a bon-fire blazed on the roundabout at Charhai-e-Sadarat in Kabul. Street children gathered round the flames that cast dancing shadows across their dirty faces. They played a game of dare – who could get closest to the flames? Grown-ups stole a glance at the fire and hastened by. It was safer that way; it was obvious to all that this fire had not been lit by street watchmen to warm their hands. It was a fire in the service of God.

Queen Soraya's sleeveless dress curled and twisted and turned to ash, as did her shapely white arms and serious face. King Amanullah, her husband, burnt too, and all his medals with him. The whole line of kings spluttered on the fire, together with little girls in Afghan dress, Mujahedeen soldiers on horseback and farmers at a Kandahar bazaar.

The religious police went conscientiously to work in Sultan Khan's bookshop that November afternoon. Any books portraying living things, be they human or animal, were torn from the shelves and tossed on the fire. Yellowed pages, innocent postcards, and dried-out covers from old reference books were sacrificed to the flames.

Amidst the children round the bonfire stood the foot soldiers of the religious police, carrying whips, long sticks and Kalashnikovs. These men considered anyone who loved pictures or books, sculptures or music, dance, film or free thought enemies of society.

Today they were interested only in pictures. Heretical texts, even those on the shelves right in front of their eyes, were overlooked. The soldiers were illiterate and could not distinguish orthodox Taliban doctrine from heresy. But they could distinguish pictures from letters and animate creatures from inanimate things.

Finally only ashes remained, caught by the wind and swirled with the dust and dirt in the streets and sewers of Kabul. The bookseller, bereft of his beloved books, was bundled into a car, a Taliban soldier on either side. The soldiers closed and sealed the shop and Sultan was sent to jail for anti-Islamic behaviour.

Lucky the armed half-wits did not look behind the shelves, Sultan thought on his way to detention. The most prohibited books he had stashed away ingeniously. He only brought them out if someone asked specially for them and if he thought he could trust the person who asked.

Sultan had expected this. He had been selling illegal books, pictures and writings for many years. The soldiers had often menaced him, seized a few books and then left. Threats had been issued from the Taliban's highest authority and he had even been called in to the Minister for Culture, in the Government's attempts to try and convert the enterprising bookseller and recruit him to the Taliban cause.

Sultan Khan willingly sold some Taliban publications. He was a freethinker and of the opinion that everyone had

the right to be heard. But along with their gloomy doc-
trines he also wanted to sell history books, scientific
publications, ideological works on Islam, and not least,
novels and poetry. The Taliban regarded debate as heresy
and doubt as sin. Anything other than Koran-swotting was
unnecessary, even dangerous. When the Taliban came to
power in Kabul in the autumn of 1996 the ministries were
emptied of professionals and replaced by mullahs. From the
central bank to the university – the mullahs controlled
everything. Their goal was to re-create a society like the
one the Prophet Muhammad had lived in on the Arab
peninsula in the seventh century. Even when the Taliban
negotiated with foreign oil companies, ignorant mullahs
sat around the negotiating table, lacking any technical
expertise.

Sultan was convinced that under the Taliban the country
grew increasingly poor, dismal and insular. The authorities
resisted all modernisation; they had no wish to either
understand or adopt ideas of progress or economic devel-
opment. They shunned scientific debate, whether
conducted in the West or in the Muslim world. Their man-
ifesto was above all a few pathetic arguments about how
people should dress or cover themselves, how men should
respect the hour of prayer, and women be separated from
the rest of society. They were not conversant with the history of Islam or of Afghanistan, and had no interest in
either.

Sultan Khan sat in the car squashed between the illiterate Taliban soldiers, cursing his country for being ruled by
either warriors or mullahs. He was a believer, but a mod-
erate Muslim. He prayed to Allah every morning, but
usually ignored the following four calls to prayer unless
the religious police pulled him in to the nearest mosque

with other men they had snatched up from the streets. He reluctantly respected the fast during Ramadan and did not eat between sunup and sundown, at least not when anyone was looking. He was faithful to his two wives, brought up his children with a firm hand and taught them to be good God-fearing Muslims. He had nothing but contempt for the Taliban whom he considered illiterate peasant priests; they originated from the poorest and most conservative part of the country, where literacy was low.

The Department for the Promotion of Virtue and Extermination of Sin, better known as the Ministry of Morality, was behind his arrest. During the interrogation in the prison Sultan Khan stroked his beard. He wore it according to Taliban requirements, the length of a clenched fist. He straightened his *shalwar kameez*; it too conformed to Taliban standards – tunic below the knees, trousers below the ankle. He answered proudly: 'You can burn my books, you can embitter my life, you can even kill me, but you cannot wipe out Afghanistan's history.'

Books were Sultan's life. Ever since he was given his first book at school, books and stories had captivated him. He was born to a poor family, and grew up during the fifties in the village of Deh Khudaidad outside Kabul. Neither his mother nor his father could read, but they scraped together enough money to send him to school. As the oldest son any savings were spent on him. His sister, who was born before him, never set foot inside a school and never learnt to read or write. Today she can barely tell the right time. After all, her only future was to be married off.

But Sultan, he was destined for greatness. The first hurdle was the road to school. Little Sultan refused to walk it because he had no shoes. His mother sent him packing.

'Oh yes, you can, you just see,' she said and gave him a blow over the head. Soon he had earned enough money to buy shoes. He worked throughout his schooling. In the mornings before class and every afternoon until dark, he fired bricks to make money for the family. Later he got a job in a shop. He told his parents that the salary was half of what it actually was. He saved the rest and bought books.

He started selling books when he was a teenager. He had been accepted as an engineering student but could not find the appropriate textbooks. During a journey with his uncle to Teheran he happened upon all the required titles in one of the town's many book markets. He bought several sets, which he sold on to fellow students in Kabul for double the price. And so the bookseller was born; he was thrown a lifeline.

Sultan participated in the construction of only two buildings in Kabul before book mania tore him away from the world of engineering. Once again it was the book markets in Teheran that seduced him. The boy from the country wandered around among books in the Persian metropolis, surrounded by old and new, antique and modern, and came across books he had never dreamt even existed. He bought crate upon crate of Persian poetry, art books, history books, and – for the sake of his business – textbooks for engineers.

Back home in Kabul he opened his first little bookshop, amongst the spice merchants and kebab stalls in the centre of town. This was the seventies and society teetered between the modern and the traditional. Zahir Shah, the liberal and rather lazy king, ruled, and his half-hearted attempts at modernising the country provoked sharp censure from religious quarters. When a number of mullahs protested against women of the royal family exposing themselves in public without the veil, they were thrown into prison.

The number of universities and establishments of learning increased, followed closely by student demonstrations. These were brutally put down by the authorities and many students were killed. A profusion of parties and political groups mushroomed — although free elections were never held — from radical left wing to religious fundamentalism. The groups fought amongst themselves and the unstable atmosphere in the country spread. The economy stagnated following three years of drought, and during a catastrophic famine in 1973, while Zahir Shah was consulting a doctor in Italy, his cousin Daoud seized power in a coup and abolished the monarchy.

President Daoud's regime was more oppressive than that of his cousin. But Sultan's bookshop flourished. He sold books and periodicals published by the various political groups, from Marxist to fundamentalist. He lived at home in the village with his parents and cycled in to the stall in Kabul every morning and back every evening. His only problem was his mother's constant nagging about finding a wife. She constantly introduced new candidates — a cousin or the girl next door. Sultan was not ready to start a family. He had several irons in the fire and was in no hurry. He wanted freedom to travel and often visited Teheran, Tashkent and Moscow. In Moscow he had a Russian sweetheart — Ludmila.

A few months before the Soviet Union invaded the country in December 1979, he made his first mistake. The unyielding Communist Nur Mohammad Taraki ruled the country. The entire presidential family, from Daoud down to the youngest baby, had been killed in a coup. The prisons were overflowing, and tens of thousands of political opponents were arrested, tortured and executed.

The Communists wanted to consolidate their control of the whole country and tried to suppress Islamic groups. The holy warriors, the Mujahedeen, took up arms against the regime, a conflict that later turned into a merciless guerrilla war against the Soviet Union.

The Mujahedeen represented a profusion of ideologies and trends. The various groups published periodicals supporting *jihad* – the fight against the heathen regime – and the Islamification of the country. On its part the regime tightened its grip on everyone who was suspected of being in league with the Mujahedeen, and it was strictly forbidden to print or distribute their ideological publications.

Sultan sold periodicals published by Mujahedeen and Communist alike. Moreover, he suffered from collecting mania and could not resist buying a few copies of each and every book or periodical he came across, in order to sell them on for a profit. Sultan was of the opinion that he was obliged to procure whatever anyone wanted. The banned publications he hid under the counter.

It did not take long for someone to inform on him. A customer was arrested in possession of books he had bought from Sultan. During a raid the police uncovered several illegal publications. The first book pyre was lit. Sultan was taken in, beaten up and condemned to a year in prison. He spent the time in the political prisoners' section, where writing materials and books were forbidden. Months on end Sultan stared at the wall. But he managed to bribe one of the guards with his mother's food parcels and books were smuggled in every week. Within the damp stone walls Sultan's interest in Afghan culture and literature grew. He lost himself in Persian poetry and the dramatic past of his country. When he was let out he was absolutely sure of his ground: he would fight to promote knowledge of Afghan culture and history. He continued to sell illegal publications, by the Islamic guerrillas and the pro-China Communist opposition, but he was more cautious than before.

The authorities kept an eye on him and five years later he was arrested again. Once more he was given the opportunity to meditate on Persian philosophy behind prison walls, but now a new accusation was added to the old one; he was labelled petit bourgeois, middle-class, according to Communism one of the worst terms of abuse. The charge was that he made money after the capitalist model.

This all happened during the period when Afghanistan's Communist regime, in the heat of suffering caused by war, tried to wind up tribal society and introduce 'joyful' Communism. Attempts to collectivise farming led to severe hardship amongst the population. Many poor farmers refused to accept land that had been compulsorily purchased from rich landowners, as it was contrary to Islam to sow in stolen soil. The countryside rose in protest and as a consequence the Communist schemes were seldom successful. In time the authorities gave up. War sapped everyone's strength; after ten years it had claimed 1.5 million Afghan lives.

When the petit bourgeois was let out of prison, he was thirty-five years old. The war against the Soviet Union was, on the whole, being fought in the countryside and Kabul was left more or less intact. The grind of daily life occupied people. This time his mother managed to persuade him to marry. She produced Sharifa, a general's daughter, a beautiful and bright woman. They married and had three sons and a daughter, one baby every other year.

The Soviet Union withdrew from Afghanistan in 1989

and the inhabitants looked forward to peace at last. But because the regime in Kabul continued to be propped up by the Soviets the Mujahedeen did not lay down arms. They took Kabul in May 1992 and civil war broke out. The apartment that the family had bought in a Soviet-built block of flats was situated right on the front line, between the warring factions. Rockets hit the walls, bullets shattered the windows and tanks rolled over the courtyard. After they had cowered on the floor for a week, the hail of shells quietened down for a few hours and Sultan took himself and his family off to Pakistan.

While he was in Pakistan his bookstall was robbed, as was the public library. Valuable books went to collectors for a song – or were exchanged for tanks, bullets and grenades. Sultan himself bought up some of the books stolen from the national library when he returned from Pakistan to see to his shop. He got some real bargains. For a handful of dollars he bought works hundreds of years old, amongst them a 500-year-old manuscript from Uzbekistan for which the Uzbek government later offered him $25,000. He found Zahir Shah's personal copy of his own favourite, the epic poet Ferdusi's great work *Shah Nama*, and bought several books dirt cheap from the thieves, who were unable even to read the titles.

After nearly five years of intense fighting between the mujahedeen warlords, half of Kabul had been reduced to a pile of rubble and had lost 50,000 citizens. When Kabul's inhabitants woke on the morning of 27 September 1996, the city was totally quiet. The previous evening Ahmed Shah Massoud and his army had escaped up towards the Panshir valley.

Two bodies hung from a pole outside the presidential

palace. The larger was soaked through with blood from head to foot. It had been castrated, the fingers were crushed, the torso and face battered and there was a bullet hole through the forehead. The other had merely been shot and hanged, the pockets stuffed full of Afghani, the local currency, as a sign of contempt. The bodies were those of former president Muhammad Najibullah and his brother. Najibullah was a hated man. He had been head of the secret police at the time of the Soviet invasion and was said to have ordered the execution of 80,000 so-called enemies of society. He was the country's president from 1986 to 1992, supported by the Russians. After the mujahedeen coup Massoud became defence minister, with Sibghatullah Mujadidi as president for the first three months followed by Burhanuddin Rabbani. Najibullah sought refuge with the UN after an attempt to flee from Kabul airport was thwarted, and he remained thereafter in confinement in a UN compound in Kabul.

When the Taliban made their way through the eastern districts of Kabul and the Mujahedeen government decided to flee, Massoud invited the prominent prisoner to accompany them. Najibullah feared for his life outside the capital and chose to stay behind with the security guards in the UN building. Besides, as a Pashtoon he reasoned that he could negotiate with Taliban Pashtoons. Early the next morning all the guards had disappeared. White flags – Taliban's holy colour – flew over the mosques.

Kabul's inhabitants gathered in disbelief round the pole in Ariana Square. They gazed at the men who hung there and returned quietly home. The war was over. A new war would start – a war that would trample all joy under foot.

The Taliban established law and order, but simultaneously dealt Afghan art and culture the final blow. The regime burnt Sultan's books and turned up at Kabul Museum carrying axes, towing along with them, as a witness, their own Minister for Culture.

Not much remained in the museum when they arrived. All loose items had been looted during the civil war: potsherds from the time Alexander the Great conquered the country, swords that could have been used in the battles against Genghis Khan and his Mongol hordes, Persian miniatures and gold coins. Anonymous collectors from all over the world bought most of it. Very few artefacts were saved before the looting started in earnest.

A few enormous sculptures of Afghan kings and princes were left standing, and thousand-year-old Buddha statues and murals. The foot soldiers went to work, exhibiting the same spirit as when they had devastated Sultan's bookshop. The museum guards cried when the Taliban started chopping away at what remained of the art. They hacked at the sculptures till only the plinth remained, in a heap of dust amidst lumps of clay. It took them half a day to annihilate a thousand years of history. All that remained after the vandals had done was an ornamental tablet, a quotation from the Koran, which the Minister for Culture had thought best left alone.

When the Taliban's art executioners left the bombed-out museum building — it had also been a frontline target during the civil war — the guards were left standing amongst the debris. Laboriously they gathered up the bits and swept up the dust. They put the bits in boxes and labelled them. Some of the pieces were still identifiable: a hand off one statue, a wavy lock of hair from another. The boxes were put in the basement in the hope that sometime in the future the statues could be restored.

Six months before the Taliban fell the enormous Buddha

statues in Bamiyan were blown up. They were close to two thousand years old and Afghanistan's greatest cultural heritage. The dynamite was so powerful that there were no bits left to gather up.

It was against the backdrop of this regime that Sultan Khan tried to save parts of Afghanistan's culture. Following the book pyre at the roundabout he bribed someone to get out of prison, and the same day he broke open the seal on the shop. Standing amongst the remnants of his treasures, he cried. He painted big black lines and squiggles over the living creatures in the books the soldiers had overlooked. That was preferable to them being burnt. Then he thought of a better idea – he pasted his business cards over the pictures. Thus he covered the pictures but could just as easily uncover them. At the same time he put his own stamp on the works. It might one day be possible to remove the cards.

But the regime turned relentlessly more ruthless. As the years passed it adhered more and more rigorously to the puritanical line and its goal of living ever more closely by the rules from the era of Muhammad. Once again the Minister for Culture called Sultan in. 'Someone is out to get you,' he said, 'and I cannot protect you.'

That was when, in the summer of 2001, he decided to leave the country. He applied for a visa for himself, his two wives, sons and daughter to settle in Canada. His wives and children lived at that time in Pakistan and loathed the refugee existence. But Sultan knew he could not give up his books. He now owned three bookshops in Kabul. One shop was run by his younger brother, another by his sixteen-year-old son Mansur, and the third he ran himself.

Only a fraction of his books were displayed on the shelves. The majority, about ten thousand, were hidden away in attics all over Kabul. He could not allow this collection, which he had built up over a period of thirty years, to be lost. He could not allow the Taliban, or other aggressors, to destroy even more of the Afghan soul. Anyhow, he had a secret plan, a dream, for his collection. When the Taliban had gone and a reliable government returned to Afghanistan, he promised himself that he would donate the complete book collection to the looted public library in town, where once hundreds of thousands of books had adorned the shelves.

Owing to the death-threat Sultan Khan and his family were granted a visa to Canada. But he never went. While his wives packed and prepared for the journey, he invented all sorts of excuses to delay. He was expecting some books, the bookshop was threatened, or a relative had died. Something always got in the way.

Then came September 11. When the bombs started to rain down over Afghanistan, Sultan left for Pakistan. He commanded Yunus, one of his younger, unmarried brothers, to stay behind in Kabul and look after the shops.

When the Taliban fell, two months after the terrorist attac on the USA, Sultan was one of the first to arrive back in Kabul. At last he could stock up his shelves with all the books he wanted. The history books with black lines and squiggles he could now sell to foreigners as curiosities, and he could remove the business cards that had been glued over pictures of living creatures. He could once more show off Queen Soraya's white arms and King Amanullah's chest, plastered with decorations.

One morning he was in his shop, drinking a cup of steaming tea, watching Kabul wake up. He laid plans for how to realise his dream and thought of a quotation by his favourite poet Ferdusi. 'To succeed you must sometimes be a wolf and sometimes a lamb.' The time has come to be a wolf, thought Sultan.

Crime and Punishment

From all sides stones whizzed towards the stake, and most struck. The woman refused to cry out, but a cheer soon rose from the crowd. One powerful man had found an especially good stone, large and jagged, and he threw this with force, aiming it carefully at her body, and it struck so violently in her abdomen that soon the first blood of the afternoon showed through the chaderi. It was this that brought the cheer. Another stone of equal size struck the woman's shoulder. It brought both blood and cheers.

James A. Michener, *Caravans*

Sharifa, the pensioned-off wife, is waiting in Peshawar. She has no peace. She knows that Sultan will turn up one of these days, but he can never be bothered to tell her exactly when he is leaving Kabul, so Sharifa expects him home every hour for days on end.

Every meal is prepared in case her husband shows up: a plump chicken, the spinach he loves, the green homemade chilli sauce. On the bed are clean, freshly ironed clothes; letters lie orderly in a box.

The hours pass. The chicken is wrapped up, the spinach can be reheated and the chilli sauce is put back in the cupboard. Sharifa sweeps the floors, washes curtains, busies herself with the perpetual dusting, sits down, sighs, sheds a few tears. It's not that she misses him. But she misses the life she once had as the wife of an enterprising bookseller, respected and esteemed, the mother of his sons and daughters; the anointed.

Sometimes she hates him for having ruined her life, taken away her children, shamed her in the eyes of the world.

Eighteen years have passed since Sultan and Sharifa got married and two years since he got himself wife number two. Sharifa lives like a divorced woman, but without the freedom granted divorced women. Sultan is still her master. He has decided that she must live in Pakistan in order to look after the house where he keeps his most precious books. Here is the computer, a telephone. From this address he can send off book parcels to clients, receive emails – everything which is impossible in Kabul where post, telephone and computers won't function. She lives in Pakistan because it suits Sultan.

Divorce is not an alternative. If a woman demands divorce she loses virtually all her rights and privileges. The husband is awarded the children and can even refuse the wife access to them. She is a disgrace to her family, often ostracised, and all property falls to the husband. Sharifa would have to move to the home of one of her brothers.

*

During the civil war early in the nineties, and for some years under the Taliban, the whole family lived in Peshawar, in the district called Hayatabad, where nine out of ten inhabitants are Afghans. But one by one they moved back to Kabul, the brothers, sisters, Sultan, Sonya, the sons; first sixteen-year-old Mansur, then twelve-year-old Aimal and lastly Eqbal who was fourteen. Only Sharifa and her youngest daughter Shabnam stay behind. They keep hoping that Sultan will take them back to Kabul, to family and friends, and he keeps promising, but something always gets in the way. The tumbledown house in Peshawar, which was meant as a temporary shelter against the bullets and grenades of Kabul, has now become her prison. She cannot move without permission from her husband.

The first year following Sultan's second marriage, Sharifa lived together with him and the new wife. In Sharifa's eyes, Sonya was not only stupid but lazy too. Maybe she wasn't lazy, but Sultan never let her lift a finger. Sharifa cooked, served, washed and made the beds. At first Sultan would lock himself and Sonya into the bedroom for days on end, only occasionally demanding tea or water. Sharifa heard whispering and laughter commingling with sounds that cut her to the heart.

She swallowed her pride and appeared the model wife. Her relatives and girl friends recommended her for first prize in the wife contest. No one ever heard her complain, quarrel with Sonya or show her up.

When the honeymoon was over, and Sultan left the bedroom to attend to his business, the two women were thrown into each other's company. Sonya powdered her face and tried on new dresses. Sharifa tried to chirp like a fussing mother hen. She took on the heaviest chores and little by little taught Sonya how to make Sultan's favourite dish, showed her how he liked his clothes organised, the temperature of the water he washed in and other details that a wife should know about her husband.

But oh, the shame! Although it is not unusual for a man to take a second wife, and sometimes even a third, nevertheless, it is humiliating. The slighted wife will always be labelled inadequate. Anyway, that is how Sharifa felt, because Sultan so obviously preferred his younger wife.

It was necessary for Sharifa to justify this new wife of Sultan's. She had to make up an excuse to show it was not her, Sharifa, who was at fault, but external circumstances that had ousted her.

To anyone who was willing to listen she divulged that a polyp had developed in her womb. It had been removed and the doctor had warned her that if she wanted to survive she could no longer lie with her husband. It was she, Sharifa, who had asked her husband to find a new wife and it was she who had chosen Sonya. After all, he was a man, she said.

In Sharifa's eyes this imaginary ailment was less shaming than the fact that she, the mother of his children, was no longer up to the mark. After all, he had only followed the doctor's advice.

When Sharifa really wanted to lay it on thick, she would recount, with sparkling eyes, how she loved Sonya like a sister, and Latifa, her child, like her own daughter.

In contrast to Sultan, men with more than one wife usually keep a balance in the relationships, spending one night with one wife, the next night with the other, for decades. The wives give birth to children who grow up as siblings. The mothers keep an eagle eye on the children's treatment; no one is favoured in front of the other. They also make sure that they themselves receive the same amount of clothes and gifts as the other wife. Many of these co-wives hate each other intensely and never speak. Others accept that it is the husband's right to have several wives, and become good friends. After all, the rival will most likely have been married in a put-up job, arranged by the parents and often against her own will. Few young girls' pipe dream is to be the second wife of an old man. Whereas the first wife gets his youth, she gets old age. In some cases none of the wives really want him in their bed every night and are delighted to be let off the hook.

Sharifa's beautiful brown eyes, the ones Sultan once said were the most lovely in Kabul, stare into space. They have lost their radiance and are encircled by heavy lids and soft lines. She discreetly covers her light, blotchy skin with make-up. Her white skin has always compensated for her short legs. Height and fair skin are the most important Afghan status symbols. It has always been a fight to keep up her youthful appearance – she conceals the fact that she is a few years older than her husband. Grey hair is kept at bay by home colouring, but the sad facial features she can do nothing about.

She crosses the floor heavily. There is little to do since her husband took her three sons back to Kabul. The carpets have been swept, the food is ready. She turns on TV and watches an American thriller, a fantasy film. Good-looking heroes fight dragons, monsters and skeletons and conquer evil creatures. Sharifa watches intently, in spite of not understanding the language, English. When the film is over she phones her sister-in-law. Then she gets up and walks over to the window. From the second floor she can see everything that goes on in the backyards below. Head-high brick walls surround the yards. Like Sharifa's they are all full of clothes hanging out to dry.

But in Hayatabad it is not necessary to see in order to know. In your own living room, with closed eyes, you know that the neighbour is playing loud, piercing Pakistani pop music, that children are yelling or playing, that a mother is bawling, that a woman is banging her carpets and another washing up in the sun, that a neighbour is burning food and yet another cutting up garlic.

What the sounds and smells do not divulge, gossip supplies. It spreads like wildfire in the neighbourhood, where everyone is watching one another's morals.

Sharifa shares the old, tumbledown brick house and the minute concrete backyard with three families. When it looks as if Sultan will not turn up, she pops down to the neighbours. The women of the house and a few assorted women from the surrounding backyards are gathered. Every Thursday afternoon they congregate for *nazar*, a religious feast – to gossip and pray.

They tie their shawls tightly round their heads, place individual prayer mats facing the direction of Mecca and bow, pray, rise up, pray, bow again, four times in all. The invocation is done in silence, only the lips move. As the prayer mats become free others take over.

In the Name of Allah, the Beneficent, the Merciful
Praise be to Allah, Lord of the Worlds,
The Beneficent, the Merciful,
Owner of the Day of Judgement
Thee alone we worship; Thee alone we ask for help.
Show us the straight path,
The path of those whom Thou hast favoured;
Not the path of those who earn Thine anger nor of those who
*   go astray.*

Barely has it finished than the whispered prayer is succeeded by loud, chattering voices. The women seat themselves on cushions along the wall. The oilcloth on the floor is laid with cups and saucers. Freshly brewed cardamom tea and a dry sweetmeat made of biscuit-crumbs and sugar is put out. Everyone puts their hands to their face and prays again, joining in the whispering chorus round the food: 'La Elaha Ellallahu Muhammad-u-Rasoollullah' – There is no other god but God and Muhammad is His prophet.

When the prayer is over they pass their hands over their face, from nose up to forehead, out and down the cheeks to the chin until the hands stop at the lips, as though they were eating the prayer. From mother to daughter, they have all been taught that if they pray in this manner at *nazar*, their prayers will be heard, if they deserve it. These prayers go straight to Allah, who will decide whether to answer them or not.

Sharifa prays that Sultan will fetch her and Shabnam back to Kabul. Then she will be surrounded by all her children.

When everyone has asked Allah to answer their prayer, the actual Thursday ritual can begin: eat sweetmeats, drink cardamom tea and exchange the latest news. Sharifa mumbles a few words about expecting Sultan any moment, but no one takes any notice. Her *ménage à trois* is no longer the hot topic in street 103 in Hayatabad. Sixteen-year-old Saliqa is the current star of gossip. The object herself is shut up in the back room following an unpardonable crime a few days earlier. She lies on her mattress, bruised and battered, with a bleeding face and a back full of red swollen streaks.

Those who do not know the story's details listen rapturously.

Saliqa's crime began six months earlier. One afternoon, Sharifa's daughter Shabnam passed Saliqa a slip of paper.

'I promised not to say who it is from, but it's from a boy,' she said, tiptoeing with excitement and delight at the thought of the important mission. 'He doesn't dare show himself. But I know who it is.'

Shabnam kept appearing with notes from the boy, scraps of paper full of hearts pierced with arrows and the words 'I love you' written in clumsy letters, notes telling her how beautiful she is. Saliqa saw the unknown letter-writer in every boy she encountered. She took care how she dressed, that her hair was glossy and shining, and cursed her uncle for making her wear the long veil.

One day he wrote that he would be standing by the lamppost a few houses past hers and that he would be wearing a red sweater. Saliqa quivered with excitement when she left home. She had dressed up in a pale blue velvet costume and was using the jewels she loved, gold-coloured bracelets and heavy chains. She was with a friend and barely dared walk past the tall, slender boy in the red sweater. His face was turned away and he never moved.

Now *she* took the letter-writing initiative. 'Tomorrow you must turn round,' she wrote and pushed the note to Shabnam, the ever-obliging and eager go-between. But again he did not move. Then, on the third day, he turned towards her. Saliqa felt her heart hit her stomach, but she kept on walking. The suspense had been replaced by obsessive love. He wasn't especially good-looking, but it was him, the letter-writer. For many months they exchanged notes and stolen glances.

New crimes were added to this first one – that she had even accepted notes from a boy and, God forbid, had answered. Now she had fallen in love with someone not chosen by her parents. She knew they would dislike him. He was uneducated, had no money and was from an inferior family. In Hayatabad it is the parents' wishes that count. Saliqa's sister married after a five-year fight with her father. She had fallen in love with someone other than the one her parents had chosen and she refused to give him up. The battle ended when the two lovers each emptied a bottle full of pills and were sent in great haste to hospital to be pumped. Only then did the parents consent.

One day circumstances brought Saliqa and Nadim together. Her mother was spending the weekend with relatives in Islamabad and the uncle was away all day. Only his wife was at home. Saliqa told her she was visiting friends.

'Have you got permission?' her uncle's wife asked. Her uncle was head of the family as long as Saliqa's father was living in a refugee reception centre in Belgium. He was waiting for a resident's permit to enable him to get employment and send money home – or better still, send for his whole family.

'Mummy said I could go as soon as I had finished my chores,' Saliqa lied.

She didn't go to her girl friend; she went to meet Nadim, face to face.

'We can't talk here,' she says quickly when they seemingly meet by chance on the street corner. He hails a taxi and pushes her in. Saliqa has never sat in a taxi with a strange boy and her heart is in her throat. They stop by a park, a park in Peshawar where men and women can walk together.

They sit on a bench in the park and talk for a short half-hour. Nadim is making grand plans for the future, he wants to buy a shop or sell carpets. Saliqa is first and foremost terrified someone is going to spot them. Less than half an hour after leaving home she is back. But all hell has already broken loose. Shabnam saw her and Nadim in the taxi and went and told Sharifa who informed the uncle's wife.

The aunt hits Saliqa hard on the mouth when she returns, locks her into a room and phones the mother in Islamabad. When the uncle comes home the whole family enters the room and demands to know what she has done. The uncle shakes with anger when he hears about the taxi, the park, and the bench. He grabs a piece of broken wire and beats her repeatedly over the back while her aunt holds on to her. He hits her face until she bleeds from mouth and nose.

'What have you done, what have you done? You're a whore,' the uncle screams. 'You are a disgrace to the family. A stain on our honour. A rotten branch.'

His voice reverberates throughout the house, in through the neighbours' open windows. Before long everyone knew of Saliqa's crime. The crime that caused her to lie locked in her room, praying to Allah that Nadim will propose to her, that her parents will allow her to marry, that Nadim will get work in a carpet shop and that they can move away.

'If she can sit alone in a taxi with a boy, I'm sure she is capable of other things,' says Nasrin, a friend of the aunt, and looks haughtily over at Saliqa's mother. Nasrin shovels sweetmeats into her mouth with a big spoon, and waits for answers to her pronouncement.

'She was only in the park, there is no need to beat her within an inch of her life,' says Shirin, who is a doctor.

'If we hadn't stopped him we would have had to take her to the hospital,' says Sharifa. 'She was out in the courtyard all night praying,' she continues. In her sleepless state she had caught sight of the wretched girl. 'She was there until the call for prayer early this morning,' she added.

The women sigh, one mutters a prayer. They all agree that Saliqa made a big mistake by meeting Nadim in the park, but they cannot agree whether she was merely disobedient or had committed a serious crime.

'What a disgrace, what a disgrace,' Saliqa's mother wails. 'How could a daughter of mine do something like that?'

The women discuss the way forward. If he proposes to her the disgrace can be forgotten. But Saliqa's mother is not keen on the idea of Nadim as son-in-law. His family is poor, he is uneducated, and for the most part he just roams the streets. The only job he ever had, but subsequently lost, was in a carpet factory. If Saliqa married him she would have to move in with his family. They could never afford their own house.

'His mother is not a good housewife,' one of the women claims. 'Their house is shabby and dirty. She's lazy and doesn't stay at home.'

One of the older women recalls Nadim's grandmother. 'When they lived in Kabul they entertained anybody,' she says and adds slyly: 'Men even came to her apartment when she was alone, and they weren't relatives.'

'With all due respect,' one of the women says, turning towards Saliqa's mother, 'I must admit I always thought Saliqa was a bit of a show-off, always made up, dressed up to the nines. You should have realised that she had dirty thoughts.'

For a while no one says anything, as though they all agree, without actually saying so, in sympathy for Saliqa's mother. One woman wipes her mouth; it is time to think of supper. The others get up, one by one. Sharifa mounts the stairs to her three rooms. She passes the back room where Saliqa is shut up. She will stay there until the family have decided what to do with her.

Sharifa sighs. She thinks of the punishment that befell her neighbour Jamila.

Jamila came from a superior family, she was rich, immaculate, and beautiful as a flower. A relative had put aside money earned abroad and thus could afford the eighteen-year-old beauty. The wedding was exceptional, five hundred guests, the food sumptuous, the bride radiantly beautiful. Jamila did not meet the man she was to marry prior to the wedding; the parents had arranged everything. The groom, a tall, thin man of forty-something, travelled from overseas to get married the Afghan way. He and Jamila spent two weeks together as newlyweds before he returned to arrange for a visa in order that she could join him. In the meantime Jamila lived with his two brothers and their wives.

They got her after three months. The police had ratted on her. They had spied a man crawling in through her window.

They never got the man, but the husband's two brothers found some of his belongings in Jamila's room, proof of the relationship. The family immediately dissolved the marriage and sent her packing home. She was locked up for two days while a family council was held.

Three days later Jamila's brother told their neighbours that his sister had died as the result of an accident with a fan which short-circuited.

The funeral was held the next day; lots of flowers, lots of serious faces. The mother and sisters were inconsolable. All mourned the short life allotted Jamila.

'Like the wedding,' they said, 'a wonderful funeral.'

The family's honour had been salvaged.

Sharifa had a video from the wedding, but Jamila's brother came to borrow it. She never got it back. Nothing would remain to suggest that a wedding had ever taken place. But Sharifa keeps a few photos. The bridal couple look formal and serious as they cut the cake. Jamila's face betrays nothing and she looks lovely in the innocent white dress and veil, black hair and red mouth.

Sharifa sighs. Jamila committed a serious crime, but more from ignorance than a wicked heart.

'She did not deserve to die. But Allah rules,' she mumbles and breathes a prayer.

However, one thing bothers her: the two days of family council when Jamila's mother, her own mother, agreed to kill her. She, the mother, it was, who in the end dispatched her three sons to kill her daughter. The brothers entered the room together. Together they put a pillow over her face; together they pushed it down, harder, harder, until life was extinguished.

Then they returned to the mother.

Suicide and Song

In Afghanistan a woman's longing for love is taboo. It is forbidden by the tribes' notion of honour and by the mullahs. Young people have no right to meet, to love or to choose. Love has little to do with romance; on the contrary, love can be interpreted as committing a serious crime, punishable by death. The undisciplined are cruelly killed. Should only one guilty party be executed it is invariably the woman.

Young women are above all objects to be bartered or sold. Marriage is a contract between families or within families. Decisions are made according to the advantages the marriage brings to the tribe – feelings are rarely taken into consideration. Throughout the centuries Afghan women have had to put up with injustices committed in their name. But in song and poem women have testified about their lives. The songs are not meant for publication, but the echo lingers on in the mountains and the desert.

'They protest with suicide and song', writes the Afghan poet Sayd Bahodine Majrouh in a book of poems by

Pashtoon women.* He collected the poems with the aid of his sister-in-law. Majrouh was himself murdered by fundamentalists in Peshawar in 1988.

The poems or rhymes live on in popular sayings and are swapped by the well, on the way to the fields, by the baking oven. They talk of forbidden love, and without exception the beloved is someone other than the one the woman is married to; they talk of loathing the (often much older) husband. But they also express pride and courage. The poems are called *landay*, which means 'short'. They are of few lines, short and rhythmical, 'like a scream or a knife stab', writes Majrouh.

> *Cruel people, you can see the old man*
> *On his way to my bed*
> *And you ask me why I cry and tear my hair.*

> *Oh, my God, yet again you have bestowed on me a dark night*
> *And yet again I tremble from head to foot*
> *I have to step into the bed I hate.*

But the women in the poems are also rebellious; they risk their lives for love – in a society where passion is prohibited and punishment merciless.

> *Give me your hand, my loved one, and we will hide in the*
> *   meadow*
> *To love or fall down beneath the knife stabs.*

> *I jump in the river, but the current does not carry me away.*
> *My husband is fortunate; I am always thrown back on to the*
> *   bank.*

Le suicide et le chant. Poésie populaire des femmes pashtounes, by Sayd Bahodine Majrouh, Gallimard 1994.

> *Tomorrow morning I will be killed because of you.*
> *Do not say that you did not love me.*

Nearly all the 'screams' deal with disappointments and life unlived. One woman asks God to make her a stone in the next life, rather than a woman. None of the poems are about hope – on the contrary, hopelessness reigns. The women have not lived enough, never tasted the fruits of their beauty, their youth, or the pleasures of love.

> *I was beautiful like a rose.*
> *Beneath you I have turned yellow like an orange.*
>
> *I never knew suffering.*
> *Therefore I grew straight, like a fir-tree.*

The poems are also full of sweetness. The woman glorifies her body with brutal sincerity, sensuous love and forbidden fruit – as though she wants to shock, provoke men's virility.

> *Lay thy mouth over mine,*
> *But let my tongue be free so it can talk of love.*
>
> *Take me first in your arms!*
> *Afterwards you can bind yourself to my velvet thighs.*
>
> *My mouth is yours, eat it up, do not be frightened!*
> *It is not made of sugar, dissolvable.*
>
> *My mouth, you can have it.*
> *But why stir me up – I am already wet.*
>
> *I will turn you into ash*
> *If I only for one moment turn my gaze towards you.*

The Business Trip

It is still cool. The sun's first rays have touched the steep, stony mountain cliffs. The landscape is dust-coloured, brown turning to grey. The mountainsides are all stone; boulders threaten to trigger crushing avalanches, and gravel and bits of clay crunch below the horses' hooves. Thistles growing between the stones scratch the legs of smugglers, refugees and fleeing warriors. A confusion of paths cross and disappear behind rocks and mounds.

This is the route used by smugglers of weapons and opium, cigarettes and Coca-Cola cans between Afghanistan and Pakistan. The paths have been trodden throughout the centuries. These are the paths the Taliban and the Arab al-Qaida warriors crept along when they realised the battle for Afghanistan was lost and they fled into the tribal areas of Pakistan. These are the paths they will use when they return to defeat American soldiers – the infidel who has occupied holy, Muslim soil. Neither Afghan nor Pakistani authorities control the area around the border. Pashtoon tribes command their particular districts on each side of the state boundaries. The lawlessness, preposterously, has found its way into Pakistani law. On the Pakistani side the authorities have the right to operate on tarmacked roads, and up to 20 metres beyond on both sides. Outside the 20 metres tribal law reigns.

On this morning the bookseller Sultan Khan makes his way past the Pakistani border guards. Less than 100 metres away are the Pakistani police. As long as humans, horses and laden donkeys keep their distance, there is nothing they can do.

But if the authorities cannot control the stream, never-theless, many of the travellers are stopped and 'taxed' by armed men, sometimes just ordinary villagers. Sultan has made his provisions; Sonya has sewn the money into the sleeves of his shirt and he carries his possessions in a dirty sugar bag. He is wearing his oldest *shalwar kameez*.

As for most Afghans, the border to Pakistan is closed to Sultan. It matters not that he has family, a house and busi-ness in the country, nor that his daughter goes to school there – he is not welcome. Following pressure from the international community, Pakistan has closed its borders to prevent terrorists and the Taliban from hiding away in the country. A fruitless gesture. After all terrorists and soldiers do not turn up at the borders passport in hand. They use the same paths as Sultan when he travels on busi-ness. Many thousands enter Pakistan daily in this way.

The horses struggle up the steep slope. Sultan, broad and solid, sits astride the saddleless horse. Even in his oldest clothes he looks well dressed. As always his beard is newly trimmed, his small fez fits perfectly on his head. He looks like a distinguished gentleman who has taken a trip to the mountains to admire the view – even when, terrified, he grabs the reins tightly. He feels shaky. One false step and they'll be at the bottom of the abyss. But the horse trundles calmly up the well-trodden paths, effortlessly, unaffected by the man it is carrying. The valuable sugar bag is tightly wound round Sultan's hand. It contains books he wants to print for his shop and the draft of what he hopes will become his life's work.

He is surrounded by Afghans on foot, all wanting to cross to the forbidden country. Women wearing burkas ride sidesaddle en route to visit relatives. Amongst them are students returning to the university in Peshawar having celebrated *eid*, a religious festival, with their families. There might be some smugglers in the company, maybe some businessmen. Sultan does not ask. He is concentrating on his contract and the reins, and curses the Pakistani authorities. First one day by car from Kabul to the border, then an overnight stay in a hideous border station, followed by a whole day in the saddle, on foot and in a pick-up. The journey by main road from the border to Peshawar is barely an hour. Sultan finds it degrading being smuggled in to Pakistan; he feels he is being treated like a pariah dog. Pakistan supported the Taliban regime politically, with money and weapons, and he thinks they are now being two-faced, suddenly sucking up to the Americans and closing the border to Afghans.

Pakistan was the only country, besides Saudi Arabia and the United Arab Emirates, to officially recognise the Taliban regime. The Pakistani authorities wanted the Pashtoon to control Afghanistan. The Pashtoon live on both sides of the border and are to a certain extent influenced by Pakistan. Virtually all the Taliban were Pashtoon. They are Afghanistan's largest ethnic group and make up approximately forty per cent of the population. The Tajiks are the largest ethnic group in the north. About one quarter of Afghans are Tajiks. The Northern Alliance, which after September 11 was supported by the Americans, was on the whole made up of Tajiks. Pakistanis look upon them with a certain amount of scepticism. Since the Taliban fell and the Tajiks became a force to be reckoned with in the Government, many Pakistanis now feel that they are surrounded by enemies: India to the east, Afghanistan to the west.

But on the whole there is little tribal hatred between the various Afghan groups. The conflicts are due rather to power struggles between various warlords who have encouraged their own ethnic groups to war against each other. The Tajiks are fearful that if the Pashtoon become too powerful they would be massacred in the event of another war. The Pashtoon fear the Tajiks for the same reason. The same can be said about the Uzbeks and Hazars in the northwest of the country. War has also been waged between tribal chiefs within the same ethnic group.

Sultan couldn't care less what sort of blood flows in his veins, or in the veins of anyone else for that matter. Like many Afghans he is a mixture: his mother is Pashtoon, his father Tajiki. His first wife is a Pashtoon, his second a Tajik. Formally he is a Tajik, because ethnicity is inherited from the father's side. He speaks both languages, Pashtoo and Dari – a Persian dialect spoken by the Tajiks. Sultan is of the opinion that it is high time for the Afghans to put war behind them and start rebuilding the country. The dream is that they one day might make up for what they have lost in relation to their neighbours. But it doesn't look good. Sultan is disappointed by his compatriots. While he works away at a steady pace, trying to expand his business, he grieves over those who fritter away their earnings, and go to Mecca.

Immediately before travelling to Pakistan he had a discussion with his cousin Wahid, who just about manages to keep his head above water running a small spare-parts shop for cars. When Wahid popped into Sultan's shop he told him that at last he had saved up enough money to fly to Mecca. 'Do you think praying will help you?' Sultan asked contemptuously. 'The Koran tells us that we must work, solve our own problems, sweat and toil. But us Afghans, we're too lazy. We ask for help instead, either from the West or from Allah.'

'But the Koran also tells us to worship God,' argued Wahid.

'The Prophet Muhammad would cry if he heard all the shouts, screams and prayers in his name,' continued Sultan. 'It won't help this country however much we bang our heads on the ground. All we know is how to scream, pray and fight. But the prayers are worth nothing if we don't work. We can't just sit and wait for God's mercy.' Sultan was shouting now, egged on by his own torrent of words. 'We search blindly for a holy man, and find a lot of hot air.'

He knew he had provoked his cousin. For Sultan work is the most important thing in life. He tries to teach his sons as much and to live up to it himself. For that reason he has taken his sons out of school to work in the shop, in order that they might help him build his empire of books.

'But to travel to Mecca is one of the five pillars of Islam,' the cousin objected. 'To be a good Muslim you must acknowledge God, fast, pray, give alms and go to Mecca.'

'We might all go to Mecca,' Sultan said at last. 'But only when we deserve it, and then we go to give thanks, not to pray.'

*

I suppose Wahid is on his way to Mecca, in his white flowing pilgrim robes, Sultan thinks now. He snorts and wipes the sweat off his forehead. The sun is at its zenith. At last the pathway descends. On a cart track in a small valley several pick-ups are waiting. These are Khyber Pass taxis, and the owners make a killing transporting unwelcome visitors into the country.

This was once part of the Silk Road, the trade route between the great civilisations of antiquity – China and Rome. Silk was carried west, traded for gold, silver and wool.

The Khyber Pass has been traversed by the uninvited for more than two millennia. Persians, Greeks, Moguls, Mongols, Afghans and the British have tried to conquer India by approaching the country via this route. In the sixth century BC the Persian King Darius conquered large parts of Afghanistan and marched on through the Khyber Pass to India. Two hundred years later, the generals of Alexander the Great marched their troops through the pass. At its narrowest point only one fully-loaded camel or two horses side by side can pass at any one time. Genghis Khan laid waste parts of the Silk Road, while more peaceful travellers, like Marco Polo, merely followed the caravan tracks to the East.

Ever since the time of King Darius and right up to the British invasion of the Khyber Pass in the 1800s, the Pashtoon tribes from the surrounding mountains invariably fiercely resisted the invading armies. Ever since the British withdrew in 1947 the tribes have once more held sway over the pass and all the land to Peshawar. The mightiest of these is the Afridi tribe, feared for its fierce warriors.

Weapons are still the first thing to catch the eye after

crossing the border. Along the Pakistani side of the highway, at regular intervals, dug into the mountainside or painted on dirty signs in the barren landscape, is the name Khyber Rifles. Khyber Rifles is a rifle company and also the name of the local militia who are in charge of security in the area. The militia protect a considerable fortune. The village immediately over the border is famous for its bazaar full of contraband; hashish and weapons go for a song. No one asks for licences, whereas anyone carrying weapons on Pakistani territory risks a long prison sentence. Amongst the clay huts are large, glitzy palaces, paid for with black money. Small stone fortresses and traditional Pashtoon houses, surrounded by tall walls, lie dotted over the mountainside. Now and again walls of concrete loom up in the landscape; they are the so-called dragon's teeth, erected by the British who feared a German Panzer invasion during the Second World War. On several occasions foreigners have been kidnapped in these remote tribal regions, and the authorities have introduced strict measures. Not even on the main road to Peshawar, patrolled by Pakistani troops, are foreigners allowed to drive without guards. Nor can they leave Peshawar for the Afghan border without the correct papers and an armed guard.

After having ridden for two hours along narrow roads, the mountain on one side, the precipice on the other, some hours on horseback remain until Sultan at last descends to the plain and can look towards Peshawar. He takes a taxi into town, to street 103 in the district called Hayatabad.

It has started to get dark when Sharifa hears blows on the gate. He has come after all. She runs down the stairs to open the door. There he is, tired and dirty. He hands her the sugar bag, which she carries up the stairs before him.

'Was the journey OK?'

'Beautiful scenery,' answers Sultan. 'Wonderful sunset.'

While he washes she prepares supper and lays the table-cloth on the floor, between the soft cushions. Sultan emerges from the bathroom clean and wearing freshly ironed clothes. He gives a disgruntled look at the glass plates Sharifa has put out.

'I don't like glass plates, they look cheap,' he says. 'Like something you bought in a dirty bazaar.'

Sharifa exchanges them for porcelain plates.

'That's better. The food tastes better now,' he says.

Sultan recounts the latest news from Kabul, Sharifa the news from Hayatabad. They have not seen each other for many months. They talk about the children, about relatives and plan the next few days. Every time Sultan visits Pakistan he has to endure courtesy visits to those relatives who have not yet returned to Afghanistan. First priority is those in whose families there has been a death. Next come the closest relatives, and so on, as much as he can manage, depending on how many days he has at his disposal.

Sultan dreads having to visit Sharifa's sisters, brothers, in-laws, sisters' in-laws and cousins. It is not possible to keep his visit a secret; everyone knows everything in this town. Besides, these courtesy visits are all that remain of Sharifa's married life. All she can demand of him now is that he is friendly towards her relatives and treats her as his wife during the visits.

When the duty calls have been planned, all that remains is Sharifa's rendering of the latest news from the bottom floor – Saliqa's escapades.

'What a tart,' says Sultan, reclining on a pillow like a Roman emperor. 'That's what she is, a tart.'

Sharifa protests. Saliqa wasn't even alone with the boy.

'Her attitude, her attitude,' says Sultan. 'If she's not a prostitute now, she could easily become one. Having chosen this useless boy, who'll never get a job, how will she ever have enough money for the things she wants, like jewellery and pretty clothes? When a kettle boils without a lid, anything can fall into it. Rubbish, soil, dust, insects, old leaves,' he continues. 'That's how Saliqa's family have lived. Without a lid. All sorts of muck has fallen on them. The father is absent, and even when he lived there he was never at home. Now he's been living as a refugee in Belgium for three years and still hasn't been able to organise the papers to get them over.' Sultan snorts. 'He's a loser, he is. Ever since Saliqa could walk she's been looking for someone to marry. By chance it was poverty-stricken, useless Nadim. First she tried Mansur, d'you remember?' Sultan asks. The bookseller has succumbed to the power of gossip.

'Her mother had a hand in it all,' Sharifa recollects. 'She kept on asking whether it wasn't time to find him a wife. I always answered that it was too soon; the boy was going to study. Least of all I wanted a conceited and pathetic wife like Saliqa for Mansur. When your brother Yunus came to Peshawar, he was bombarded with the same questions, but he would never have entertained the idea of taking such a cheap girl as Saliqa.'

Saliqa's crime is turned over and over until not a grain of dust remains. But the married couple have plenty more relatives they can pick holes in.

'How is your cousin?' laughs Sultan.

One of Sharifa's cousins had spent her life looking after her parents. When they died her brothers married her off to an old man who needed a mother for his children. Sultan is never tired of hearing the story.

'She completely changed after the wedding. At last she was a woman,' he laughs. 'But she never had any children so obviously she must have had her change of life before the wedding. No rest for the wicked, he'd be at it every night,' he laughs again.

'Maybe,' ventures Sharifa. 'Do you remember how thin and wizened she looked before the wedding? She's completely changed now. I suppose she's feeling randy all the time,' she cackles. Sharifa holds her mouth and chuckles as she blurts out the reckless accusations. It is as if the intimacy between the couple has returned, as they lie about on the cushions round the leftovers on the floor.

One story follows another. Sultan and Sharifa lie on the floor, like two little children, roaring with laughter.

To all appearances there is no sex-life in Afghanistan. Women hide behind the burka, and under the burka they wear large, loose clothes. Under the skirts they wear long trousers and even within the four walls of the house low-necked garments are a rarity. Men and women who do not belong to the same family must not sit together in the same room. They must not talk to each other or eat together. In the countryside even the weddings are segregated; the women dance and make merry and so do the men, in different rooms. But under the surface all is seething. In spite of running the risk of the death penalty, in Afghanistan too people have lovers and mistresses. There are prostitutes in the towns to whom young boys and men can resort while they wait for a bride.

Sexuality has its place in Afghan myths and fables. Sultan loves the stories in the masterpiece *Masnavi*, written by the poet Rumi eight hundred years ago. He uses sexuality as a warning against blindly following in the footsteps of others.

A widow had a donkey which she loved dearly. It carried her where she wanted and always obeyed orders. The donkey was well fed and well looked after. But then the animal sickened and lost all its energy. It lost its appetite too. The widow wondered what was wrong and one night she went to the barn to see if it was sleeping. In the barn she found her maid lying in the hay with the donkey on top of her. This repeated itself every night and the widow got nosy and thought to herself she would like to have a go too. She dismissed her maid and lay down in the hay with the donkey on top of her. When the maid returned she found the widow dead. To her horror she saw that the widow had not done as she did – thread a pumpkin over the donkey's organ to shorten it before she indulged herself. For her, the maid, the end bit had sufficed.

After having chortled away, Sultan rises from the cushions, smooths his tunic and goes to read his emails. American universities want periodicals from the seventies, researchers ask for old manuscripts and the printers in Lahore send an estimate of what the cost will be to print his postcards at the new paper prices. Sultan's best source of income is the postcards. It costs him one dollar to print sixty cards and he sells three for a dollar. Everything is going his way, now that the Taliban have gone and he can do as he likes.

The next day he reads his post, visits bookshops, goes to the post office, sends and receives parcels and starts on the endless courtesy visits. First a condolence visit to a cousin whose husband has died of cancer, then a more enjoyable visit to another cousin who is back from pizza-delivering in Germany. Sultan's cousin Said was at one time flight engineer for Ariana Air, Afghanistan's once-proud airline. Said is now thinking of returning to Kabul with the family and applying for his old job. But he needs to save a bit more money. Delivering pizzas in Germany is far more lucrative than working as a flight engineer. And he has not yet found a solution to the problem that awaits him at home. In Peshawar are wife and children. In Germany he is living with wife number two. If he returns to Kabul they will all have to live under one roof. He dreads the thought. The first wife doesn't want to know about number two. They never meet and he sends money home like a dutiful husband. But if they all move in together? It doesn't bear thinking of.

The days in Peshawar are taxing. One relative has been thrown out of his rented accommodation, another wants help to start up a business, a third asks for a loan. Sultan rarely gives money to relatives. Because he himself has done so well he is always asked to help when he goes courtesy visiting. On the whole he declines. He thinks they are mostly lazy and should help themselves. In any case they need to prove themselves before he dishes out the dough and in his eyes few of them come up to scratch.

When the couple are out visiting, Sharifa is the one who keeps the conversation flowing. She tells stories, spreads laughter and smiles. Sultan prefers to sit and listen. Now and again he chips in with comments about work ethics or about his business. But when Sultan with a single word says it's time to leave, the couple go home, daughter Shabnam in tow. They walk peacefully through the dark of Hayatabad's dirty-black streets and step over rubbish as lungs fill with the rank smell from back alleyways.

One evening Sharifa dolls herself up to visit some distant relatives. Normally they would not qualify for courtesy visits even though they live only a few blocks away. Sharifa totters along in sky-high pumps, followed by Sultan and Shabnam sauntering behind, hand in hand.

They are welcomed with open arms. The host puts out dried fruit and nuts, sweets and tea. They start off with formalities and the latest news. The children listen to the parents' prattle. Shabnam cracks pistachios and is bored.

One of the children is missing, thirteen-year-old Belqisa. She knows to stay away; the visit is about her.

Sharifa has been here before, on the same mission. This time Sultan has reluctantly agreed to accompany her, to add gravity to the situation. They are there on behalf of Yunus – Sultan's younger brother. He fell for Belqisa when he lived as a refugee in Pakistan a few years ago, when she was only a child. He has asked Sharifa to propose for him. He has never himself spoken to the girl.

The answer has always been the same: she is too young. On the other hand, if they wanted the older daughter, Shirin, who was twenty, that would be another matter. But Yunus did not want her, she was not nearly as beautiful as Belqisa, and anyhow, she was a bit too eager, he thought. When he visited she was always around him. In addition she had let him hold her hand when the others were not looking, and that, Yunus thought, was a bad sign. She was obviously not a virtuous girl.

But the parents held out for the older daughter, because Yunus was a good proposition. When Shirin had other proposals they approached Sultan and offered her to Yunus for the last time. But Yunus did not want Shirin. His eyes were on Belqisa and there they stayed.

In spite of being rejected, Sharifa has returned continually to ask for Belqisa. It was not seen as rudeness; on the contrary, it indicated the seriousness of the proposal.

Tradition says the mother of a suitor must wear out the soles of her shoes until they are as thin as garlic skin. As Yunus's mother, Bibi Gul, was in Kabul, Sharifa, his sister-in-law, had taken on the role of go-between. She enlarged on Yunus's excellence, how he spoke fluent English, how he worked in the bookshop with Sultan and how their daughter would lack for nothing. But Yunus was nearly thirty. Too old for Belqisa, the parents thought.

Belqisa's mother had her eye on one of the other young boys in the Khan family: Mansur, Sultan's sixteen-year-old son. 'If you offer us Mansur we'll accept on the spot,' she said.

But now it was Sultan's turn to dig his heels in. Mansur was only a few years older than Belqisa, and he had never even cast a glance in her direction. Sharifa thought it was too early to think of marriage. He was going to study, see the world.

'Anyhow, she's not thirteen,' Sharifa said to her girl-friends a bit later. 'I'm sure she's at least fifteen.'

Belqisa walks into the room for a few moments so Sultan can give her the once-over. She is tall and thin and looks older than thirteen. She is wearing a dark-blue velvet costume, and sits down beside her mother – awkward and shy. Belqisa knows exactly what this is all about and feels uncomfortable.

'She's crying, she doesn't want to,' her two older sisters tell Sultan and Sharifa in front of Belqisa. Belqisa looks down.

But Sharifa laughs. It's a good sign when the bride is unwilling. That indicates a pure heart.

Belqisa gets up after a few minutes and disappears. Her mother excuses her and says she has a maths test the next day. But the chosen one is not supposed to be present during the bargaining. First the opposing sides test the water before they get down to actual sums. How much the parents will get, how much will be spent on the wedding, the dress and the flowers. The groom's family pays all expenses. The fact that Sultan is present gives the discussion gravitas; he has the money.

When the visit is over and nothing has been decided, they walk out into the cool March evening. The streets are quiet. 'I don't like the family,' Sultan says. 'They are greedy.'

It is especially Belqisa's mother he is not keen on. She is her husband's second wife. When his first wife never conceived he married again, and the new wife tormented the first one to such a degree that she could stand it no longer and moved in with her brother. Nasty stories circulate about Belqisa's mother. She is grasping, jealous and avaricious. Her oldest daughter married one of Sultan's relatives who said that she was a nightmare during the wedding ceremony, complaining constantly that there was too little food, too few decorations. 'As mother so daughter. Belqisa's a chip off the old block,' states Sultan.

But he adds grudgingly that if she's the one Yunus wants, he'll do his best. 'Unfortunately they'll end up saying yes. Our family is too good to turn down.'

Having done his duty by the family, Sultan can at last start doing what he came to Pakistan for: print books. Early one morning he starts the next stage of the journey, to Lahore, the town of printing, bookbinding and publishing.

He packs a small suitcase with six books, a calendar and a change of clothes. As always when he travels, his money is sewn into his shirtsleeves. The day looks like being warm. The bus depot in Peshawar is seething with people and the bus companies struggle to make themselves heard over the din. 'Islamabad, Karachi, Lahore!' By each bus a man stands and screams. There is no timetable; the buses depart when they are full. Before departure men selling nuts, small cornets full of sunflower seeds, biscuits and crisps, newspapers and magazines board the bus. Beggars content themselves with reaching hands through open windows.

Sultan ignores them. He follows the Prophet Muhammad's advice with regard to alms which he interprets thus: First take care of yourself, then your closest family, then other relatives, then neighbours, and last the unknown poor. He might slip a few Afghani to a beggar in Kabul, but Pakistani beggars are at the bottom of the list. Pakistan will have to see to its own poor.

He sits in the back row of the bus, squashed between other travellers, his suitcase under his feet. In it is his life's undertaking, written on a scrap of paper. He wants to print Afghanistan's new schoolbooks. When the schools open this spring there will hardly be any textbooks. Books printed by the Mujahedeen government and the Taliban are useless. This is how first-year schoolchildren learn the alphabet: 'J is for Jihad, our aim in life, I is for Israel, our enemy, K is for Kalashnikov, we will overcome, M is for Mujahedeen, our heroes, T is for Taliban . . .'

War was the central theme in maths books too. Schoolboys — because the Taliban printed books solely for boys — did not calculate in apples and cakes, but in bullets and Kalashnikovs. Something like this: 'Little Omar has a Kalashnikov with three magazines. There are twenty bullets in each magazine. He uses two thirds of the bullets and kills sixty infidels. How many infidels does he kill with each bullet?'

Books from the Communist period cannot be used either.

Their arithmetic problems deal with land distribution and egalitarian ideals. Red banners and happy collective farmers would guide children towards Communism.

Sultan wanted to return to the books from the time of Zahir Shah, the king who ruled for forty comparatively peaceful years before he was deposed in 1973. He has found old books he can reprint: stories and myths for Persian lessons, maths books where one plus one equals two, and history books cleansed of ideological content other than a bit of innocent nationalism.

UNESCO has promised to finance the country's new schoolbooks. As one of the largest publishers in Kabul, Sultan has had meetings with them and will give them an offer once he has been to Lahore. On the scrap of paper in his waistcoat he has scribbled down page numbers and formats of 113 schoolbooks. The budget is calculated at two million dollars. In Lahore he will investigate which printers come up with the best deals. Thereafter he will return to Kabul and compete for the gilt-edged contract. Sultan contemplates contentedly how large a cut he can demand of the two million. He decides not to be too greedy. If he wins the contract he is assured work for many years to come – from reprints and new books. He reflects as fields and plains whizz past along the road, which is the main thoroughfare between Kabul and Calcutta. The closer they get to Lahore the warmer it gets. Sultan sweats in his homespun clothes from the Afghan highlands. He strokes his hair, where only a few strands remain, and wipes his face with a handkerchief.

In addition to the scrap of paper where the 113 schoolbooks are scribbled down, Sultan also has books he wants to print on his own account. Following the stream of journalists, aid workers and foreign diplomats into Afghanistan, came the demand for English-language books about the country. Sultan does not import books from foreign publishers, he prints them himself.

Pakistan is the piracy printers' paradise. No control exists and few respect royalties and copyrights. Sultan pays one dollar to print a book he can resell for twenty or thirty. The bestseller *Taliban*, by Ahmed Rashid, Sultan has reprinted in several editions. The favourite amongst the foreign soldiers is *My Hidden War*, a book written by a Russian reporter about the disastrous occupation of Afghanistan between 1979 and 1989. It was a reality diametrically opposite to the one experienced by today's international peace-keepers patrolling Kabul, who from time to time drop in and buy postcards and old war books in Sultan's bookshop.

The bus trundles into Lahore bus depot. The heat hits him. The place is heaving with people. Lahore is Pakistan's cultural and artistic stronghold, a busy, polluted and confusing city. Lying in a plain, lacking all natural defences, the town has been conquered, destroyed, rebuilt, conquered, destroyed and rebuilt. But in between conquests and destruction many of the rulers entertained leading poets and writers and Lahore thus became the town of artists and books, in spite of the fact that the palaces the artists visited were constantly being levelled to the ground.

Sultan loves the Lahore book markets; he has pulled off several coups here. Few things warm the cockles of Sultan's heart more than finding a valuable book in a dusty market place and buying it for next to nothing. Sultan is of the opinion that he owns the world's largest book collection on Afghanistan, a collection of about eight or nine thousand volumes. Everything interests him: old myths and stories, old poetry, novels, biographies, recent political literature as well as dictionaries and encyclopaedias. His face lights up when he happens upon a book he hasn't got or doesn't know.

But now he has no time to trawl the book markets. He gets up at dawn, puts on his clean change of clothes, arranges his beard and places the fez on his head. He stands before a holy responsibility – to print new textbooks for Afghanistan's children. He goes straight to the printers he uses most. There he meets Talha. The young man is a third-generation printer and only mildly interested in Sultan's project. It is, quite simply, too big.

Talha invites Sultan to a cup of tea with thick milk, strokes his mouth and looks worried.

'I don't mind taking a few, but a hundred and thirteen titles! That will take us a year.'

Sultan has a two-month deadline. While the sound of the printing presses reverberates through the thin walls in the little office, he tries to convince Talha to put all other jobs aside.

'Impossible,' says Talha. Sultan might well be an important client and printing schoolbooks for Afghan children might well be a holy undertaking, but he has other commissions to take care of. Nevertheless, he makes a quick calculation and reckons the books can be printed for as little as 3 pence per copy. The price will depend on paper quality, colour quality and binding. Talha calculates all combinations of quality and size and makes a long list. Sultan's eyes narrow. He does mental calculations in rupees, dollars, days and weeks. He lied about the deadline to get Talha to speed up and put aside other assignments.

'Don't forget, two months,' he says. 'If you cannot make the time limit, you'll ruin my business, do you understand?'

When they finish talking about the schoolbooks they

negotiate the new books for Sultan's bookshop. Once again they discuss prices, numbers and dates. The books Sultan has brought with him are reproduced straight from the original. The pages are taken apart and copied. The printers stamp them on large metal plates. When they print coloured front-covers a zinc solution is poured over the plates. They are then laid out in the sun, which brings out the right colour. If a page has several colours the plates must be exposed one at a time. Thereafter the plate is put on the press and run. Everything is done on old, semi-automatic machinery. One worker feeds the press with paper; another squats at the opposite end and sorts what emerges. The wireless drones in the background; a cricket match between Sri Lanka and Pakistan. On the wall hangs the mandatory picture of Mecca and a lamp swings from the ceiling, full of dead flies. Streams of yellow acid run on to the floor and down the drains.

After the inspection-round Talha and Sultan sit down on the floor and consider book covers. Sultan has chosen motifs from his postcards. He has some strips of border which he likes and he makes up the pages. After five minutes they have designed six book covers.

In a corner some men sit and drink tea. They are Pakistani publishers and printers who all operate in the same shadowy piracy market as Sultan. They greet each other and get talking about the latest news from Afghanistan, where Hamid Karzai walks a tightrope between the various warlords, while groups of al-Qaida soldiers have launched an attack in the east of the country. American Special Forces have come to the rescue and are bombing caves by the Pakistani border. One of the men sitting on the rug says what a pity the Taliban were driven out of Afghanistan.

'We need a few Taliban here in Pakistan too, to clean up a bit,' he says.

'That's what you say. You have no experience of the Taliban. Pakistan would collapse if the Taliban came to power, don't believe anything else,' Sultan thunders. 'Just imagine: all the advertising posters will come down, and there are at least one thousand in this street alone. All books containing pictures will be burnt, and the same will happen to the whole of Pakistan's film archive, music archive, all instruments will be destroyed. You'll never again hear music, never dance again. All the Internet cafés will be closed, TV is prohibited and confiscated, and all you'll get on the wireless will be religious programmes. Girls are taken out of school, all women are sent home from work. What will happen to Pakistan? The country will lose hundreds of thousands of workplaces and sink into deep depression. And what will happen to all the superfluous people who lose their jobs when Pakistan is no longer a modern country? Maybe they'll become warriors?' Sultan was working himself into a frenzy.

The man shrugged his shoulders. 'Well, maybe not all the Taliban, just a few of them.'

Talha supported the Taliban by duplicating their pamphlets. For a few years he even printed some of their Islamic textbooks. Eventually he helped them set up their own printing works in Kabul. He got hold of a secondhand press from Italy, which he let them have cheaply. In addition he provided paper and other technical equipment. Like most Pakistanis he found it reassuring to have a Pashtoon regime next door.

'You are unscrupulous,' Sultan teases him goodnaturedly, now that he has vented his spleen on his loathing of the Taliban.

Talha squirms, but sticks to his guns. 'Taliban is not in conflict with our culture. They respect the Koran, the Prophet and our traditions. I would never have printed anything that went against Islam.'

'Like what?' Sultan laughs.

After having thought about it Talha says, 'Like *The Satanic Verses*, for instance, or anything else by Salman Rushdie. May Allah lead us to his hideout.

'He should have been killed. But he always gets away. Anyone who prints his books or helps him should also be put down,' says Talha. 'I wouldn't print his stuff if I was offered all the tea in China. He has trampled on Islam.'

'He has hurt and humiliated us, stabbed us. They'll get him one day,' one of the men continues, although neither man has read the book.

Sultan agrees. 'He is trying to destroy our soul and he must be stopped before he corrupts others too. Not even the Communists went as far as that; they behaved with a certain amount of respect and did not try to rubbish our religion. Then you have this smut from someone calling themselves a Muslim.'

They sit silently, as though unable to shrug off the darkness the traitor Rushdie has cast over them. 'They'll get him, you'll see, Inshallah, God willing,' says Talha.

In the following days Sultan stamps around Lahore to all sorts of printers, in backyards, cellars and alleyways. To manage the sheer numbers he must spread his order over a dozen or so print shops. He explains his errand, gets quotations, jots down notes and estimates. His eyes blink when a quote is especially good, and his lips quiver slightly. He runs his tongue over his lips, does a quick mental calculation and assesses the profit margin. After two weeks he has placed orders for all the textbooks and promises to report back to the print shops.

At last he can return to Kabul. This time he doesn't have to struggle across the border on horseback. Afghans are not allowed into Pakistan, but there is no passport control on the return journey and the bookseller can leave the country openly.

Sultan jolts along in an old bus round the tortuous bends from Jalalabad to Kabul. On one side of the road massive boulders threaten to roll off the mountain. Once he sees two overturned buses and a trailer, which have driven off the road. Several dead people are being carried away, amongst them two young boys. He prays for their souls and for himself.

Not only avalanches threaten this road. It is known as the most lawless in Afghanistan. Here foreign journalists, aid workers and local Afghans paid with their lives when, by accident, they stumbled upon outlaws. Soon after the Taliban fell four journalists were murdered. Their driver survived because he recited the Islamic creed. Just after that a busload of Afghans was stopped. All those with shaven beards had their ears and noses cut off – a demonstration by the bandits of how they wished their country to be ruled.

Sultan prays by the spot where the journalists were killed. To be on the safe side he has kept his beard and wears traditional clothes. Only the turban has been exchanged for a small fez.

He is nearing Kabul. Sonya is no doubt angry, he thinks to himself and smiles. He had promised to return within a week. He had tried to explain that he could not possibly do Peshawar and Lahore in one week. But she did not want to understand. 'Then I won't drink my milk,' she'd said. Sultan laughs. He is looking forward to seeing her. Sonya does not like milk, but because she is still breastfeeding Latifa, Sultan has forced her to drink a glass every morning. This glass of milk has become her bargaining chip.

She misses Sultan terribly when he is away. The other members of the family do not treat her so well when he is not there. Then she is no longer mistress of the house, just someone who has dropped in by chance. Suddenly others are in charge and they do what they like when Sultan is absent. 'Peasant-girl', they call her. 'Stupid as an ass!' But they dare not tease her too much because she will complain to Sultan and no one wants him for an enemy.

Sultan misses Sonya too, in a way he never missed Sharifa. Sometimes he feels she is too young for him, that she is like a child, that he must look after her, trick her into drinking milk, surprise her with little presents.

He ponders on the difference between the two wives. When he is with Sharifa she looks after everything, remembers appointments, organises, arranges. Sharifa puts Sultan first, his needs and wants. Sonya does what she is told, but never takes the initiative.

There is only one thing he cannot reconcile himself to, the different hours they keep. Sultan always gets up at five to pray *fajr*, the only hour of prayer he observes. Whereas Sharifa always got up with him, boiled water, made tea, put out his clean clothes, Sonya is like a child, impossible to wake.

Sometimes Sultan thinks he is too old for her; he is not the right one. But then he reminds himself that she could never find anyone better than him. Had she married someone her own age she would never have had the standard of living she now enjoys. It would have been a poverty-stricken boy, for all the boys in her village are poor. We've got ten to twenty happy years ahead, Sultan thinks and his face assumes a contented expression. He feels lucky and happy.

Sultan laughs. He twitches a bit. He is nearing Mikrorayon and the delicious child-woman.

Do You Want My Unhappiness?

The feast is over. Mutton bones and chicken legs lie scattered about on the floor. Lumps of rice have been rubbed into the tablecloth, stained dark red from chilli sauce mixed with puddles of thin, white yoghurt. Bits of bread and orange peel litter the room, as if they had been thrown around during the final moments of the meal.

On the cushions against the walls sit three men and a woman. In the corner by the door two women squat together. They have had no part in the meal, but stare straight ahead beneath the shawls, and make eye contact with no one.

The four round the wall enjoy the tea and drink slowly and thoughtfully – wearily. The important points have been decided and settled. Wakil will get Shakila and Rasul will get Bulbula. Only the price and the wedding date remain to be fixed.

Over tea and glazed almonds the price for Shakila is set at one hundred dollars; Bulbula is free of charge. Wakil has the money ready; he pulls a banknote out of his pocket and hands it to Sultan. Sultan accepts the money for his sister with an arrogant, slightly uninterested expression; not much of a price he got for her. On the other hand, Rasul draws a sigh of relief. It would have taken him at least a year longer to scrape together enough money to buy a bride and pay for the wedding.

Sultan is disgruntled on behalf of his sisters and thinks that their grumpiness cost them many dashing suitors. Fifteen years ago they could have had young, rich men.

'They were too fussy.'

However, it was not Sultan who sealed their fate, but his mother, Bibi Gul, enthroned on the seat of honour. She sits cross-legged, satisfied, rocking from side to side. The kerosene lamp throws a peaceful glow over her wrinkled face. Her hands lie heavily in her lap and she smiles blissfully. She no longer appears to be listening to the conversation. She herself was married off at eleven to a man twenty years older. She was given away as part of a marriage contract between two families. Her parents had asked for one of the neighbouring family's daughters for their son, and they accepted on condition that Bibi Gul was thrown in for good measure for their oldest unmarried son. He had spotted her in the backyard.

After a long marriage, three wars, five coups d'état and thirteen children, the widow has finally given away her third and second last daughters; one remains. She has held on to them for a long time; they are both over thirty and consequently not very attractive with regard to the marriage market. But then their husbands are well worn too. The one who this evening walks out of the door as Shakila's fiancé is a fifty-something widower with ten children. Bulbula's intended husband is also a widower, but he is childless.

Bibi Gul has had her own reasons for holding on to her daughters for so long, although many think she has done them an injustice. She describes Bulbula as not very clever and pretty useless. Bibi Gul voices this loudly, without shame, even when her daughter is present. One of Bulbula's hands is lame and not very strong, and she walks with a limp. 'She would never manage a big family,' her mother says.

Bulbula suddenly fell ill when she was six, and when she recovered she had difficulty moving around. Her brother says it was polio, the doctors do not know, and Bibi Gul thinks she suffers from sorrow. All she knows is that Bulbula became ill, pining for her father in prison. He was arrested and accused of stealing money from the warehouse where he worked. Bibi Gul proclaims his innocence. He was released after a few months but Bulbula never recovered. 'She took on her father's punishment,' says her mother.

Bulbula never went to school. The illness went to her head so she was unable to think clearly, her parents maintained. Bulbula hovered around her mother throughout her childhood. She never did much owing to the mysterious illness. But consequently life dropped her. No one had anything to do with Bulbula; no one played with her or asked her to help.

Few people have anything to say to Bulbula. The thirty-year-old woman has a kind of lassitude hanging over her, as though she drags herself through life, or out of it. She has large empty eyes, and on the whole sits with her mouth half open, the lower lip hanging down, as if about to fall asleep. At best Bulbula pays attention to the conversations of others, other lives, but without much enthusiasm. Bibi Gul was content to have Bulbula slopping around the apartment and sleeping on the mat beside her for the rest of her life. But then something happened that made her change her mind.

One day Bibi Gul wanted to visit her sister in the village. She pulled on her burka, dragged Bulbula with her and hailed a taxi. Normally she would go on foot, but she had grown large the last couple of years, her knees were starting to give out and she did not have the energy to walk. Having experienced starvation in her youth and poverty and toil as a young wife, Bibi Gul developed an obsession with food – she was unable to stop eating until all the dishes were empty.

The taxi-driver who halted by the fat burka and her daughter was their distant relative Rasul. He had lost his wife a few years earlier; she died during confinement.

'Have you found a new wife?' Bibi Gul asked him in the taxi.

'No,' he said.

'Sad. Inshallah – God willing – you will soon find a new one,' said Bibi Gul, before relating the latest news from her own family, the sons, daughters and grandchildren.

Rasul took the hint. A few weeks later his sister came to ask for Bulbula's hand. 'Surely she can manage him as a husband,' thought Bibi Gul.

She agreed without hesitation, which is most unusual. To give away a daughter immediately means she is worthless, that one is pleased to get rid of her. Holding back and hesitating increases the girl's value; the boy's family must come several times, plead, persuade and bring gifts. Not many steps were taken for Bulbula, nor any gifts proffered.

While Bulbula stares into space, as though the conversation does not concern her, her sister Shakila listens attentively. The two are like chalk and cheese. Shakila is quick and loud and the family's centre of attention. Her appetite for life is well developed and she is nice and plump, as behoves an Afghan woman.

Shakila has had several suitors over the last fifteen years; from the time she was a slender teenager, to the present voluptuous woman, sitting in the corner behind the stove, listening speechless to her mother and brother haggling.

Shakila has been choosy. When the suitors' mothers approached Bibi Gul to bid for her, she never asked, as is usual, whether he was rich or not.

'Would you allow her to continue her studies?' was the first question.

The answer was always 'No', and so marriage never came up for discussion. Many of the suitors were themselves illiterate. Shakila completed her studies and became a maths and biology teacher. When yet more mothers came to bid for the dashing Shakila on behalf of their sons, Bibi Gul asked: 'Would you allow her to continue to work?'

No, they would not and so Shakila remained a spinster.

Shakila got her first teaching job while the war against the Soviet Union raged. Every morning she tottered on high heels in knee-length skirts, as dictated by eighties fashion, to the village of Deh Khudaidad, outside Kabul. Neither bullets nor grenades came near. The only thing that exploded was Shakila: she fell in love.

Unfortunately Mahmoud was already married. It was an arranged and loveless marriage. He was a few years older than her and the father of three little children. It was love at first sight when the two colleagues met. No one knew of their feelings for each other, they hid away out of view or phoned and whispered sweet nothings down the receiver. They never met except at school. During one of their clandestine meetings they laid plans for a future together; Mahmoud would take Shakila as his second wife.

But Mahmoud could not simply go to Shakila's parents and ask for her hand. He was dependent on his mother or sisters.

'They'll never do it,' he said. 'And my parents will never say yes,' sighed Shakila.

Mahmoud was of the opinion that only she, Shakila, could get his mother to ask her parents for her. He suggested that she act crazily, desperate; threaten suicide if she could not have Mahmoud; throw herself down in front of her parents; say she was being consumed by love. The parents might give in. To save their lives.

But Shakila had not the courage to scream and shout, and Mahmoud had not the courage to ask the women in his family to go to Shakila's house. He could never mention Shakila to his wife. In vain did Shakila try to approach her mother. But Bibi Gul thought it was a joke; she anyhow chose to interpret it as a joke every time Shakila said she wanted to marry a colleague with three children.

Mahmoud and Shakila walked around each other in the village school for four years. Then Mahmoud was promoted and changed school. He could not refuse the promotion and now the only contact between them was by phone. Shakila was deeply unhappy and longed for her beloved, but no one was supposed to notice. It is a disgrace to be in love with a man one cannot have.

Then civil war broke out, the school was closed and Shakila fled to Pakistan. After four years the Taliban arrived and although the rockets stopped and peace returned to Kabul, her old school never reopened. Girls' schools stayed closed, and, like all women in Kabul, Shakila lost the chance overnight of finding another job. Two thirds of

Kabul's teachers disappeared with her. Several boys' schools were obliged to close too, as many of the teachers had been women. Not enough qualified male teachers could be found.

The years passed by. Her secret liaison with Mahmoud had already been severed when the telephone lines were cut during the civil war. Shakila sat at home with the women of the house. She could not work, she could not go out alone, she had to cover herself up. Life had lost all colour. When she reached thirty the suitors stopped coming.

One day, having been grounded by the Taliban for nearly five years, the sister of her distant relative Wakil came to Bibi Gul to ask for her hand.

'The wife died suddenly. The children need a mother. He is kind. He has some money. He has never been a soldier, he has never acted unlawfully, he is honest and healthy,' said the sister. 'She suddenly went mad and died,' she whispered. 'She was delirious, didn't know any of us. Awful for the children.'

This father of ten needs a wife urgently. At the moment the oldest looks after the youngest, while the house falls apart. Bibi Gul said she would think about it and inquired about the man from friends and relatives. She concluded that he was hardworking and honest.

At any rate, it is an urgent matter if Shakila is going to have children of her own.

'It is written on her forehead that it is time for her to leave this house,' said Bibi Gul to anyone who wanted to listen. As the Taliban did not allow women to work at all she hadn't even bothered to ask whether Wakil would allow it.

She asked Wakil to come in person. Usually a marriage is arranged through the parents, but as this husband was nearing fifty, she wanted to see him with her own eyes. Wakil drove an articulated lorry and was away for days at a time. He dispatched his sister once again, then the brother, once again the sister, and the engagement dragged out.

Then came September 11 and Sultan moved sisters and children once more to Pakistan, to shelter from the bombs he knew would drop. That was when Wakil arrived.

'We'll have to talk about it when things return to normal,' said Sultan.

When the Taliban were driven out of Kabul two months later, Wakil returned. The schools had not yet opened so Bibi Gul never thought of asking whether he would allow Shakila to work.

From the corner behind the stove Shakila follows closely the progress of her destiny and the date of her wedding. The four on the cushions decide everything before the two newly engaged have even had time to give each other the once-over.

Wakil peeps at Shakila. She looks straight ahead, at the wall, into nothing.

'I am glad I found her,' he says addressing himself to Sultan, but looking at his fiancée.

The curfew is about to start, and the two men hasten out into the dark. They leave behind two married-off women. They continue to stare into space. Not even when the men bid farewell did they look up. Bulbula heaves herself up and sighs; it's not her turn yet. It will take years before Rasul scrapes together enough money to pay for the wedding. She appears not to care. She puts a few more sticks of firewood in the oven. No one pesters her with questions; she's just a presence, as always, until she shuffles out of the room to see to her duties, the washing up and the swill bucket.

Shakila blushes when all the sisters throw themselves over her.

'Three weeks! You'll have to hurry.'

'I'll never make it,' she moans. The bridal dress material has already been chosen and is awaiting delivery to the dressmaker. But what about the outfit, the linen, the crockery? Wakil is a widower, so most of it he'll already have, but regardless, the bride must bring something to the marriage.

Shakila is slightly disgruntled. 'He's short, I like tall men,' she tells her sisters. 'He's bald, and he might be a few years younger,' she says and pouts. 'What if he's a bully, what if he's unkind, what if he won't let me go out?' she wonders. Her sisters say nothing and think the same gloomy thoughts. 'What if he won't let me visit you, what if he beats me?'

Shakila and the sisters view the marriage in an increasingly dismal light, until Bibi Gul tells them to shut up. 'He's a good husband for you,' she insists.

Two days after the agreement has been signed, Shakila's sister Mariam arranges a party for the engaged couple. Mariam is twenty-nine and has been married twice. Her first husband was killed during the civil war. Her fifth child is due any moment.

Mariam has laid a long cloth on the floor in the sitting room. Shakila and Wakil sit at one end. Neither Bibi Gul nor Sultan is present. As long as the older members of the family can see them there must be no physical contact. But now, surrounded by younger siblings, they talk together in low voices, hardly aware of the others, who are desperately trying to snatch a few fragments of the conversation.

It is not an especially loving conversation. On the whole

Shakila talks to the air. According to custom she must not make eye contact with her fiancé before the wedding; he on the other hand looks at her all the time.

'I miss you. I can hardly wait two weeks, before you are mine,' he says. Shakila blushes but keeps on staring into space.

'I can't sleep at night, I think of you,' he continues. No reaction from Shakila. 'What do you say to that?' he asks.

Shakila goes on eating.

'Imagine, when we're married, and you've made my supper when I come home. You'll always be there, waiting for me,' Wakil dreams on. 'I'll never be alone again.'

Shakila holds her tongue, but then conjures up enough courage to ask if he will allow her to continue to work when they are married. Wakil says yes, but Shakila does not trust him. He might change his mind as soon as they are married. But he assures her that if working makes her happy, that's OK by him. In addition, of course, to looking after the children and the house.

He takes off his hat, the brown *pakol*, which adherents of the murdered Northern Alliance leader Ahmed Shah Massoud wear.

'That makes you look ugly,' Shakila says cheekily. 'You're bald.'

Now it's Wakil's turn to feel embarrassed. He does not answer his fiancée's insults, but leads the conversation on to safer ground. Shakila has spent the day in the Kabul markets buying things she needs for the wedding and presents for all the relations, hers and her husband's. Wakil will dole out the presents, as a gesture to her family who have given her away. He pays and she buys: pots and pans, cutlery, linen, towels, and fabric for tunics for him and Rasul. She has promised Rasul, Bulbula's fiancé, that he can choose his own colour. She talks about her shopping, and he asks the colour of the material.

'One blue and one brown,' answers Shakila.

'Which one is for me?' he asks.

'I don't know, Rasul can choose first.'

'What?' exclaims Wakil. 'Why? I should choose first, I'm your husband.'

'OK, you choose first,' answers Shakila. 'But they are both nice,' she says and stares ahead.

Wakil lights a cigarette. 'I don't like smoke,' says Shakila. 'I don't like people who smoke. If you smoke I don't like you either.'

Shakila has raised her voice and everyone hears her insult.

'It's difficult to stop, now that I've started,' Wakil says sheepishly.

'It smells,' Shakila continues.

'You should be more polite,' says Wakil. Shakila says nothing.

'And you must cover yourself. It is a woman's duty to wear the burka. Do as you like but if you don't wear the burka you'll make me very unhappy. And do you want to make me unhappy?' Wakil asks, threateningly.

'But if Kabul has changed and women start wearing modern clothes, then I will too,' says Shakila.

'You will not wear modern clothes. Do you want to make me unhappy?'

Shakila does not answer.

Wakil takes a few passport photos out of his wallet, looks at them and gives one to Shakila. 'This one is for you and I want you to wear it next to your heart,' he says. Shakila keeps a straight face, and reluctantly accepts the photo.

Wakil has to leave. It is just before curfew. He asks her how much money she will need to complete her purchases. She answers. He counts, estimates, gives her some notes and replaces some in his wallet.

'Is that enough?'

Shakila nods. They say goodbye. Wakil leaves, Shakila lies down on the red cushions. She heaves a sigh of relief and helps herself to a few pieces of mutton. She made it – she is *supposed* to appear cold and distant until they are married. That shows plain good manners to her family who are losing her.

'Do you like him?' sister Mariam asks.

'Well, yes and no.'

'Are you in love?'

'Hm.'

'What does hm mean?'

'It means hm,' says Shakila. 'Neither yes nor no. He might have been younger and better looking,' she says and turns up her nose. She looks like a disappointed child who did not get the walking, talking doll she wanted but just a rag-doll instead.

'I'm just sad,' she says. 'I regret it. I'm sad because I'll be leaving my family. What if he won't let me visit you? What if he won't let me work, now that it is permitted? What if he locks me up?'

The kerosene lamp on the floor sputters. The sisters are overwhelmed by sinister thoughts. One might as well contemplate them in advance.

No Admission to Heaven

When the Taliban rolled into Kabul in September 1996, sixteen decrees were broadcast on Radio Sharia. A new era had begun.

1. *Prohibition against female exposure.*
   It is prohibited for drivers to pick up women not wearing the burka, on pain of arrest. If such women are observed out on the streets, their homes will be visited and their husbands punished. If the women wear inciting or attractive clothes, and they have no close male relative with them, the driver must not let them into the car.

2. *Prohibition against music.*
   Cassettes and music are forbidden in shops, hotels, vehicles and rickshaws. If a music cassette is found in a shop the owner will be imprisoned and the shop closed. If a cassette is found in a vehicle the vehicle will be impounded and the driver imprisoned.

3. *Prohibition against shaving.*
   Anyone who has shaved off or cut his beard will be imprisoned until the beard has grown to the length of a clenched fist.

4. *Mandatory prayer.*
   Prayer will be observed at fixed times in all districts. The exact time will be announced by the Minister for the Promotion of Virtue and the Extermination of Sin. All transport must cease fifteen minutes before the time of prayer. It is obligatory to go to the mosque during the time of prayer. Any young men seen in shops will automatically be imprisoned.

5. *Prohibition against the rearing of pigeons and bird-fighting.*
   This hobby will cease. Pigeons used for the purpose of games or fights will be killed.

6. *Eradication of narcotics and the users thereof.*
   Abusers of narcotics will be imprisoned, and investigations will be instigated to flush out dealer and shop. The shop will be closed and both criminals, user and owner, will be imprisoned and punished.

7. *Prohibition against kite-flying.*
   Kite-flying has wicked consequences, such as gambling, death amongst children and truancy. Shops selling kites will be removed.

8. *Prohibition against reproduction of pictures.*
   In vehicles, shops, houses, hotels and other places, pictures and portraits must be removed. Proprietors

must destroy all pictures in the above-mentioned places. Vehicles with pictures of living creatures will be stopped.

9. *Prohibition against gambling.*
Centres of gambling will be flushed out and the gamblers will be imprisoned for one month.

10. *Prohibition against British and American hairstyles.*
Men with long hair will be arrested and taken to the Ministry for the Promotion of Virtue and the Extermination of Sin to have their hair cut. The criminal will pay the barber.

11. *Prohibition against interest on loans, exchange charges and charges on transactions.*
The above three types of money-changing are forbidden by Islam. If the rules are broken the criminal will be imprisoned for a lengthy period.

12. *Prohibition against the washing of clothes by river embankments.*
Women who break this law will be respectfully picked up in the manner of Islam, taken to their house and their husbands will be severely punished.

13. *Prohibition against music and dancing at weddings.*
If this prohibition is broken the head of the family will be arrested and punished.

14. *Prohibition against playing drums.*
The religious oligarchy will decide the appropriate punishment for anyone caught playing drums.

15. *Prohibition against tailors sewing women's clothes or taking measurements of women.*
    If fashion magazines are found in the shop the tailor will be imprisoned.

16. *Prohibition against witchcraft.*
    All books dealing with the subject will be burnt and the magicians will be imprisoned until they repent.

In addition to the above sixteen decrees, a separate appeal, aimed at Kabul's women, was broadcast:

Women, you must not leave your homes. If you do, you must not be like those women who wore fashionable clothes and make-up and exposed themselves to every man, before Islam came to the country.

Islam is a religion of deliverance and it has decided that a certain dignity belongs to women. Women must not make it possible to attract the attention of evil people who look lustfully upon them. A woman's responsibility is to bring up and gather her family together and attend to food and clothes. If women need to leave the house they must cover themselves up according to the law of Sharia. If women dress fashionably, wear ornamented, tight, seductive clothes to show off, they will be damned by the Islam Sharia and can never expect to go to heaven. They will be threatened, investigated and severely punished by the religious police, as will the head of the family. The religious police have a duty and responsibility to combat these social problems and will continue their efforts until this evil is uprooted.

Allahu akbar – God is great.

Billowing, Fluttering, Winding

She loses sight of her all the time. The billowing burka merges with every other billowing burka. Sky-blue everywhere. She glances at the ground. In the mud she can distinguish the dirty shoes from other dirty shoes. She can see the trimming on the white trousers and catch a glimpse of the edge of the purple dress worn over them. She walks round the bazaar, looking down, following the fluttering burka. A heavily pregnant burka comes panting and puffing by. She is desperately trying to keep up with the energetic pace of the two leading burkas.

The lead burka has stopped near the bed-linen counter. She feels the material and tries to gauge the colour through the grille. She bargains through the grille, whilst dark eyes can only just be seen, dimly behind the lattice. The burka haggles, arms waving in the air. The nose pokes through the folds like a beak. At last she makes up her mind, gropes for her bag and reaches out a hand with some blue banknotes. The bed-linen seller measures up white bed-linen with pale blue flowers. The material disappears into the bag under the burka.

The smell of saffron, garlic, dried pepper and fresh pakora penetrates the stiff material and mingles with sweat, breath and the smell of strong soap. The nylon material is so dense that one can smell one's own breathing.

They float on, to the cheap Russian-made aluminium teapots. Feel, bargain, haggle, and accept. The teapot too disappears under the burka, which is now overflowing with pots and pans, rugs and brushes and is growing ever larger. Behind the first come two less determined burkas. They stop and smell, feel plastic buckles and gold-coloured bracelets, before looking for the lead burka. She has stopped by a cart brimming with bras, all jumbled together. They are white, pale yellow or pink, of a dubious cut. Some hang on a pole and wave shamelessly in the wind. The burka fingers them and measures with her hand. Both hands emerge from the folds, they check the elastic, pull the cups, and with a visual estimate she settles on a powerful corset-like contraption.

They walk on, and weave around with their heads in all directions to see better. Burka-women are like horses with blinkers, they can only look in one direction. Where the eye narrows the grille stops and thick material takes its place; impossible to glance sideways. The whole head must turn; another trick by the burka-inventor: a man must know what his wife is looking at.

After a bit of head rotating the other two find the lead burka in the narrow alleyways of the bazaar's interior. She is assessing lace edging. Thick, synthetic lace, like Soviet-style curtain borders. She spends a long time on the lace. This purchase is so important that she flips the front piece over her head in order to see better and defies her future husband's command about not being seen. It is difficult to assess lace from behind a gauze grille. Only the stall vendor sees her face. Even in Kabul's cool mountain air it is covered in beads of sweat. Shakila rocks her head to and fro, smiles roguishly and laughs, she haggles, yes, she even flirts. Under the sky-blue one can detect her coquettish game. She has been doing it all along, and the vendor can decipher the moods of a waving, nodding, billowing burka with ease. She can flirt with her little finger, with a foot, with the movement of a hand. Shakila swathes her face in lace, which is suddenly transformed from curtain edging to lace for the veil, the remaining item for the wedding dress. Of course the white veil needs lace edging. The bargain is struck, the vendor measures, Shakila smiles and the lace disappears into the bag under the burka, which again drops to the ground, as it should. The sisters wriggle further into the bazaar, the alleyways get narrower and narrower.

There is a buzz of voices, a constant murmur. Very few vendors hawk their wares. Most of them are more occupied in gossiping with their neighbours, or lolling about on a sack of flour or a carpet mountain, keeping up with bazaar life, than bawling out their stock. Customers buy what they want, no matter what.

It is as though time has stood still in Kabul's bazaar. The goods are the same as when Darius of Persia roamed here around 500 BC. On large carpets under the open sky or in cramped stalls the magnificent and the necessary lie side by side, turned and fingered by discerning customers. Pistachio nuts, dried apricots and green raisins are kept in large hessian sacks; small hybrid fruit of lime and lemon lie on ramshackle carts, with skin so thin the peel is eaten too. One vendor has sacks of cackling and wriggling hens; the spice merchant has chilli, paprika, curry and ginger heaped up on his barrow. The spice merchant also acts as medicine man and recommends dried herbs, roots, fruit and tea, which, with the precision of a doctor, he explains will heal all illnesses, from the simple to the more mysterious.

Fresh coriander, garlic, leather and cardamom all mingle with the smell of the drains from the river, the stinking dried-up watercourse, which divides the bazaar in two. On the bridge over the river slippers of thick sheep's hide are on sale, cotton in bulk, material in many patterns and in all the colours of the rainbow, knives, spades and pick-axes.

Now and again one happens upon goods not known in the time of Darius. Contraband like cigarettes with exotic names such as Pleasure, Wave or Pine, and pirate-produced Coke from Pakistan. The routes used by the smugglers have not changed much throughout the centuries: over the Khyber Pass from Pakistan or over the mountains from Iran; some goods on donkeys, some on lorries, along the same trails used for the smuggling of heroin, opium and hashish. Money used is up to date; the moneychangers, in tunics and turbans, stand in a long row clutching large bundles of blue Afghani notes, 35,000 Afghani for one dollar.

One man sells a brand of vacuum cleaners called 'National'; his neighbour sells vacuum cleaners marked 'Nautionl' for the same price. But both the original and the copy are selling badly. Owing to Kabul's precarious supply of electricity most people resort to the broom.

The shoes walk on in the dust. All around are brown sandals, dirty shoes, black shoes, worn shoes, once a pair of nice shoes and pink plastic shoes with bows. Some are even white, a colour forbidden by the Taliban, as their flag was white. The Taliban forbade shoes with solid heels; the sound of women walking could distract men. But times have changed and if it were possible to click-clack in the mud the whole bazaar would resound with an arousing cacophony of click-clack. Now and again one catches a glimpse of painted toenails under the burka, yet another little sign of freedom. The Taliban forbade nail-varnish and introduced an import embargo. A few unlucky women had the tip of a finger or a toe cut off because they had committed an offence against the legal system. The liberation of women during the first spring following the fall of the Taliban has on the whole restricted itself to the shoe and nail-varnish level, and has not yet reached further than the muddy edge of women's burkas.

Not that they haven't tried. Since the fall of the Taliban several women's associations have been formed. Some of them were even active during the Taliban reign, for instance organising schooling for girls, teaching women about hygiene and running literacy courses. The great heroine from the Taliban time is Karzai's health minister, Souhaila Sedique, Afghanistan's only female general. She kept up the instruction of medicine for women and managed to reopen the women's section at the hospital where she worked after the Taliban had closed it. She was one of very few women under the Taliban who refused to wear the burka. In her own words: 'When the religious police came with their canes and raised their arms to hit me, I raised mine to hit them back. Then they lowered their arms and let me go.'

But even Souhaila seldom went out while the Taliban ruled. She was driven to the hospital every morning, wrapped up in a big shawl, and driven back every evening. 'Afghan women have lost their confidence,' she said bitterly after the Taliban fell.

A women's organisation tried to organise a demonstration just one week after the Taliban fled. They gathered in Mikrorayon, in pumps and slippers, to march on the town. Most of them had tossed the burka recklessly over their shoulders, but the authorities stopped the demonstration, arguing that they could not guarantee the women's safety. Each time they tried to gather they were stopped.

Now the girls' schools have reopened and young women flock to the universities; some have even got their old jobs back. A weekly magazine is published, by and for women, and Hamid Karzai never lets an opportunity pass without talking about the rights of women.

Several women were prominent during the legislative assembly Loya Jirga in June 2002. The most outspoken were made fun of by the turbaned men in the assembly, but they never gave up. One of them demanded a female Minister of Defence, to great booing. 'France has that,' she maintained.

But for the masses very little has changed. In the families, tradition is all – the men decide. Only a small number of Kabul women renounced the burka during the first spring after the fall of the Taliban, and very few of them know that their ancestors, Afghan women in the last century, were strangers to the burka. The burka had been used for centuries but not by large numbers of the population. It was reintroduced during the reign of Habibullah, from 1901 to 1919. He decreed that the two hundred women in his harem should wear them, so as not to entice other men with their pretty faces when they were outside the palace doors. Their veils were of silk with intricate embroidery and Habibullah's princesses wore burkas embroidered with gold thread. The burka became a garment of the upper classes, shielding women from the eyes of the masses.

During the fifties the use of the burka was widespread, but only amongst the rich.

The concealment of women had its opponents. In 1959 the prime minister, Prince Daoud, shocked the population when he and his wife appeared on the national day, she without a burka. He had persuaded his brother to make his wife do the same, and he asked ministers to throw away their wives' burkas. Already the next day, in Kabul's streets, women were walking around in long coats, dark glasses and a little hat; women who had previously tramped around completely covered up. As the use of the burka had started amongst the upper classes, so they were the first to throw them off. The garment was now a status symbol amongst the poor, and many maids and servant girls took over the silk burkas of their employers. Initially it was only the ruling Pashtoon who covered their women, but now other ethnic groups took on the custom. But Prince Daoud wanted to rid the country of the burka completely. In 1961 a law was passed which forbade the use of the burka by civil servants. They were encouraged to dress in western clothes. It took many years for the law to be implemented but in the 1970s there was hardly a teacher or secretary in Kabul who did not wear a skirt and blouse; the men wore suits. However, the underdressed women risked being shot in the legs or having acid sprayed in their faces by fundamentalists. When the civil war broke out and Islamic law took over, more and more women covered up. When the Taliban arrived all female faces disappeared from Kabul's streets.

The lead burka's shoes disappear amongst other shoes on one of the narrow footbridges over the dried-up water-course. Further back the sisters' sandals have been caught up in the throng. They can only follow the crowd's movements. To look for each other's shoes is not possible, even less stop or turn. The burkas are hemmed in by other burkas and men carrying goods, on their heads, under their arms or on their backs. They can no longer see the ground.

Over on the other side three burkas are looking for each other. One is wearing black shoes, white lace trousers and the hem of the dress is scarlet; one has brown plastic sandals and a black hem; the last, slimmest burka-silhouette has pink plastic shoes, purple trousers and hem. They find each other and raise their sights to consult. The lead burka leads the way into a shop, a real shop with windows and displays on the outskirts of the bazaar. She wants a blanket and has fallen head over heels for a shiny, quilted, pink thing called 'Paris'. The blanket comes with frilly pillows, hearts and flowers. All is folded together in a handy, see-through plastic suitcase. 'Product of Pakistan' is written on the suitcase, under the word 'Paris' and a picture of the Eiffel Tower.

This is the blanket the burka wants on her future conjugal bed. A bed she has neither seen nor tried, and that she, God forbid, will not see until her wedding night. She haggles. The assistant wants several million Afghani for the blanket and the pillows in the plastic suitcase.

'A preposterous sum!'

She continues to haggle, but the vendor is obstinate. She is about to leave when he gives in. The billowing burka has got the blanket for under one third of the initial price, but as she is about to hand him the money she changes her mind. She does not want the baby pink but the signal red instead. The blanket vendor wraps it up and throws in a red lipstick for good measure. As she is getting married.

She thanks him sweetly and lifts the veil to test the lipstick. After all, Shakila has become quite familiar with the blanket-and-cosmetic vendor. Apart from him there are only women in the shop. Leila and Mariam pluck up courage, lift up the burka, and three pale lips are transformed. They look in the mirror and devour the glamour displayed under the glass counter. Shakila searches for skinbleaching cream. To be pale is an important Afghan beauty feature. A bride must be pale.

The blanket-and-cosmetic seller recommends a cream called Perfact. 'Aloe White Block Cream' is written on the box, the rest is in Chinese. Shakila tries some, and ends up looking as if her skin has been bleached with thick zinc cream. Her skin is paler – for a while. Her real skin colour can be seen through the cream; the result is blotched brown-white.

The wonder cream is stuffed down into the already full bag. The three sisters laugh and promise to return each time one of them gets married.

Shakila is pleased and wants to return home to show off her purchases. They find a bus and push their way in, up the back running board, and down on the seats behind the curtain. The back rows are reserved for burkas, babies and shopping bags. The burkas are pulled in all directions, get caught up and trampled upon. They have to be raised slightly when the sisters sit down so they can look around without the material pulling the head down. They force themselves down on the outside of a seat with their bags on their laps and between their legs. Not many seats are reserved for women and as more get on the bus the burkas are hemmed in by other burkas and bodies and arms and bags and shoes.

The three exhausted sisters and their parcels fall off the

bus when it stops at the bombed-out house. They flap into the cool apartment, pull the burkas over their heads, hang them up on nails and heave a sigh of relief. Their faces have been restored. The faces the burkas stole.

A Third-rate Wedding

The evening before the big day. The room is heaving. All available floor space is occupied by some woman's body, eating, dancing or chatting. It is the henna-night. Tonight the bride and groom will be painted with henna on their palms and the soles of their feet. The orange pattern on their hands will, allegedly, guarantee a happy marriage.

But the bride and groom are not together. The men feast by themselves, likewise the women. Left alone the women display a fierce, almost frightening power. They hit each other's bottoms, pinch each other's breasts, and dance for each other, arms flailing like snakes, hips like Arab belly dancers. Little girls dance as though they were born to seduce and wriggle across the floor with challenging looks and raised eyebrows. Even the old grannies test the water, but give up halfway, before the dance is over. The old magic is still there, but they haven't got the stamina to see the dance out.

Shakila is sitting on the only piece of furniture in the room, a sofa which has been brought in for the occasion.

She watches from a distance and is forbidden to either smile or dance. Happiness would hurt the mother she is leaving, sorrow irritate the future mother-in-law. A bride's face must be non-committal, she is not supposed to turn her head or look around, but must stare fixedly straight ahead. Shakila passes with flying colours, as though she has rehearsed this night all her life. She sits upright like a queen and converses quietly with whoever is sitting beside her on the sofa – an honour taken in turns. Only her lips move when she answers the questions of the guest on the sofa.

Her costume is red, green, black and gold. It looks as though the Afghan flag, strewn with gold dust, has been draped over her. Her breasts stand out like mountain peaks. The bra she bought, measured by eye, obviously fits. The waistline is drawn in tightly, under the dress. She has applied a thick layer of Perfact on her face, the eyes have been outlined with kohl and she is wearing the new, red lipstick. Her appearance, too, is perfect. A bride must look artificial, like a doll. The word for doll and bride is the same – *arus*.

During the evening a procession of tambourines, drums and lanterns enters the gate. It is the women from Wakil's house – his sisters, in-laws and daughters. They sing out in the pitch-black night, while they clap and dance:

> *We are taking this girl from her home and leading her to our*
> > *home*
> *Bride, do not bow your head and cry bitter tears*
> *This is God's wish, thank God.*
> *Oh, Muhammad, God's messenger, solve her problems*
> *Make difficult things easy!*

Wakil's women dance a sensual dance, framing their bodies and faces in shawls and scarves. The room is damp and smells of sweet sweat. All the windows are flung open and the curtains flutter in the breeze, but the fresh spring air cannot cool down these women.

It is not until there is a pause in the dancing that brimming plates of pilau are carried in. Everyone drops down on to the floor at the spot where they were standing or dancing. Only the oldest sit on cushions along the wall. Shakila's little sister Leila and the younger cousins carry the food in, cooked in huge pots in the courtyard outside. Pots with rice, large hunks of mutton, aubergine in yoghurt sauce, noodles stuffed with spinach and garlic and potatoes in paprika sauce are laid out on the floor. The women collect around the pots. With the right hand they squeeze the rice into balls and stuff them into their mouths. Meat and gravy is mopped up with pieces torn off large chunks of bread, always using the right hand. The left hand, the dirty hand, must remain still. The sound of women eating is all that can be heard. The meal is consumed in peace. The silence is broken only when they urge each other to eat more. It is good manners to push the juiciest morsels over to your neighbour.

When everyone is replete the henna ceremony can begin. The night is far spent, no one is dancing. Some sleep, others lie or sit around Shakila and watch while Wakil's sister rubs the moss-green paste over Shakila's hands and feet and sings the henna-song. Once Shakila's hands have been covered she must close them. Her future sister-in-law binds reams of material round each fist to ensure a pattern is formed, and then rolls them in some soft cloth to avoid dirtying clothes and bed-linen. She undresses her down to her underwear, long white cotton trousers and a long tunic, and lies her down on a mat in the middle of the floor with a pillow for her head. She is then fed with large pieces of meat, fried liver and uncooked onion sections, specially prepared by the sisters of the one who is about to leave the family.

Bibi Gul follows everything closely. She watches each piece the sisters put into Shakila's mouth. She starts to cry. Then everyone follows suit; but they assure each other that Shakila will be well treated.

After Shakila has been fed, she lies down close against Bibi Gul, curled-up in the foetal position. She has never in her life slept in a room without her mother. This is the last night in the bosom of her family. The following night belongs to her husband.

A few hours later she is woken and the sisters unwrap the cloth around her hands. They scrape off the henna, and an orange pattern has formed on the palms of her hands and on the soles of her feet. Shakila washes off last night's doll-face and eats a good breakfast, as usual: fried meat, bread, a sweet pudding and tea.

At nine she is ready to be made up, have her hair dressed and be titivated. Shakila, little sister Leila, Sultan's second wife Sonya and a cousin troop into a flat in Mikrorayon. This is the beauty salon – a salon that also existed under the Taliban. Then too, in spite of it being illegal, brides desired glamour. They wanted to be dolled up to the nines. Here a Taliban decree was an actual help. They arrived in a burka and left in a burka, but with a new face underneath.

The beautician has a mirror, a stool, and a shelf full of bottles and tubes, which, from appearance and design, look to be several decades old. On the wall she has put up posters of Indian Bollywood stars. The beauties in low-necked costumes smile ingratiatingly at Shakila, who sits silent and broad on the stool.

Few would say that Shakila is beautiful. Her skin is coarse and the eyelids swollen. The face is wide and the jaw powerful. But she has the loveliest teeth, shining hair and a cheeky look, and has been the most sought after of Bibi Gul's daughters.

'I don't understand why I like you so much,' Wakil said to her during the dinner in Mariam's house. 'You're not even beautiful.' But he had said it lovingly and Shakila took it as a compliment.

Now she is nervous about not being beautiful enough and the playful look has disappeared. A wedding is deadly serious.

First the dark mop of hair is rolled round little wooden curlers. Next the bushy eyebrows, which are so strong they have met in the middle, are plucked. This is the most important sign of her intended marriage, as unmarried women cannot pluck their eyebrows. Shakila screams, the beautician plucks. The brows are turned into beautiful arches and Shakila admires herself in the mirror. Somehow her face is lifted up.

'If you had come earlier, I would have bleached the hairs on your upper lip,' says the woman. She shows her something mysterious. On the peeling tube are the words: 'Cream bleach for unwanted hair'. 'But we won't have time now.'

Then she rubs Perfact over Shakila's face. She applies a heavy shimmering red and gold eye shadow on the eyelids. She outlines the eyes with a thick kohl pencil and selects a dark, brown-red lipstick.

'Whatever I do I'll never be as beautiful as you,' Shakila

says to her youngest sister-in-law Sonya, Sultan's second wife. Sonya smiles and mumbles under her breath. She is pulling a pale-blue tulle dress over her head.

Once Shakila has been made up it is Sonya's turn to be beautified. Shakila is being helped into her dress. Leila has lent her a tummy belt, a broad elasticated band that will give Shakila a waist. The dress is of a penetrating, shining, mint-green material, with synthetic lace, ruche and gold borders. The dress must be green – the colour of happiness and Islam.

When the dress has been fitted and her feet have been forced into sky-high, white, gold-buckled pumps, the hairdresser unrolls the curlers. The hair is now frizzy and is fixed on top of the head with a tight comb, whilst the fringe, aided by copious amounts of hair spray, is forced into a wave and fixed to one side of the face. Now it's the turn of the mint-green veil, and the icing on the cake, right at the end, are little stickers strewn over the hair, sky-blue with golden borders. Shakila's cheeks are given the same treatment, three little silver stars on each side. She is beginning to look like the Bollywood stars on the wall.

'Oh no, the cloth, the piece of cloth,' sister Leila suddenly cries. 'Oh no.'

'Oh no,' exclaims Sonya and looks at Shakila, who does not bat an eyelid.

Leila gets up and rushes out. Luckily home is not far. What if she had forgotten about the piece of cloth, the most important item of all?

The others remain behind, unaffected by Leila's panic. They all apply stickers to hair and cheek and then on with the burkas. Shakila tries to get into hers without ruining the bridal hairdo. She refrains from pulling it tight over her head, but lets it rest lightly on top of the frizz. That means that the grille is not in the right place, in front of the eyes, but rather on top of her head. Sonya and the cousin have to lead her, like a blind person, down the stairs. Shakila would rather fall over than be seen without a burka.

The burka is removed only when – the frizz slightly crushed – she is in Mariam's backyard, where the wedding is being held. The guests fling themselves on her when she enters. Wakil is yet to arrive. The backyard is teeming with people in full swing, stuffing themselves with pilau, kebabs and meatballs. Hundreds of relatives have been invited. A chef and his son have been chopping, cutting and cooking since dawn. 150 kilos of rice have been bought in for the wedding meal, 56 kilos of mutton, 14 kilos of veal, 42 kilos of potatoes, 30 kilos of onions, 50 kilos of spinach, 35 kilos of carrots, 1 kilo of garlic, 8 kilos of raisins, 2 kilos of nuts, 32 kilos of oil, 14 kilos of sugar, 2 kilos of flour, 20 eggs, several varieties of spice, 2 kilos of green tea, 2 kilos of black tea, 14 kilos of sweets and 3 kilos of caramels.

After the meal some of the menfolk disappear into the house next door where Wakil is sitting. The last negotiations are about to take place. Detailed discussions about money and pledges for the future follow. Wakil is obliged to guarantee a certain sum should he divorce Shakila without reason, and he must promise to keep her in clothes, food and shelter. Big brother Sultan negotiates on Shakila's behalf, and men from both families sign the contract.

When they have come to an agreement they leave the house next door. Shakila sits in Mariam's house with her sisters, observing it all from behind curtains. While the men negotiate she changes into the white dress. The Russian lace curtain is drawn down over her face. She is waiting for Wakil to be led in to her so they can walk out together. He enters rather shyly; they greet each other, eyes on the floor, as demanded, and walk out, shoulder to shoulder, without looking at each other. When they stop they must each try to put one foot over the other's. The winner is declared the boss in the marriage. Wakil wins, or Shakila lets him win, as she should. It looks bad to appropriate power which is not hers by right.

Two chairs have been put out in the yard. They must sit down at the same time. If the groom sits down first, the bride will dominate all decisions. Neither wants to sit down, and in the end Sultan walks up behind them and pushes them down on to the chairs, exactly at the same time. Applause all around.

Shakila's older sister Feroza drapes a blanket over the newly married couple and holds up a mirror in front of them. They must both look into it. According to tradition, this moment is the first time their eyes meet. Wakil and Shakila stare hard into the mirror, as they should, and as though they have never seen each other before. Feroza holds the Koran over their heads and a mullah reads a blessing. With bowed heads they accept the word of God.

Then a dish containing a pudding made of cake crumbs, sugar and oil, seasoned with cardamom, is put in front of them. They feed each other with a spoon while everyone applauds. They also pour drink into each other, signifying that they desire a happy life for their spouse.

But not everyone is equally enthralled with the slurping of lemonade.

'Once upon a time we toasted in champagne,' an aunt whispers. She remembers more liberal times, when both wine and champagne were served at weddings. 'But those times will never return,' she sighs. The era of nylon stockings, western dress, bare arms and – not least – the era before burkas, are faint memories.

'A third-rate wedding,' Sultan's oldest son Mansur whispers back. 'Bad food, cheap clothes, meatballs and rice, tunics and veils. When I get married I'm going to hire the ballroom at the Intercontinental. Everyone will have to wear modern clothes and we'll serve only the best. Imported food,' he emphasises. 'Anyhow, I'm going to get married abroad,' he adds.

Shakila and Wakil's wedding feast takes place in Mariam's mud house, in the backyard where nothing grows. The walls are peppered with bullet holes and the evidence of shell splinters. The couple pose for the photographers staring fixedly ahead. The lack of smiles and the bullet holes in the background give a tragic atmosphere to the picture.

They have arrived at the cake. They hold the knife and concentrate on cutting. They feed each other through half-open mouths, as though they shrink from opening them completely, and spill crumbs all over each other.

After the cake there is music and dancing. For many of the guests this is the first wedding they have celebrated since the Taliban left Kabul, in other words the first wedding with music and dancing. The Taliban deprived people of half the joy of wedding feasts when they took the music away. Everyone throws themselves into the dance, except the newlyweds, who sit and watch. It is late afternoon. Owing to the curfew, wedding feasts have been moved from evening to daytime; everyone must be home by ten.

When dusk arrives the newly married couple disappear from the party, accompanied by hooting and howls. They drive to Wakil's house in a car decorated with ribbons and flowers. Anyone who can bag a seat in a car joins the cortège. Eight people cram into Wakil and Shakila's car, even more in other cars. They take a turn through the streets of Kabul. As this is the time of *eid* the roads are empty and the cars tackle the roundabouts at sixty miles an hour, battling to lead the procession. Two cars crash, which puts a small damper on the celebrations, but no one is seriously hurt. The cars, lights broken and chassis dented, drive off to Wakil's house. The trip is a symbolic surrender. Shakila leaves her family and is adopted by her husband's family.

The closest relatives are allowed into Wakil's house where his sisters await with tea. These are the women with whom Shakila will share the backyard. Here they will meet at the water pump, here they will wash clothes and feed the chickens. Snotty-nosed kids look inquisitively at the woman who is to be their new mother. They hide behind their aunts' skirts and look reverently up at the shimmering bride. The music is far off, the jubilant shouts have subsided. Shakila steps into her new home with dignity. It is reasonably large with high ceilings. Like all other houses in the village it is made of clay and has heavy rafters. The windows are covered in plastic. Not even Wakil dares hope that the bombs have stopped dropping, so he will wait to change the plastic sheeting.

Everyone takes off their shoes and walks quietly through the house. Shakila's feet are red and swollen after a day in the tight, white high heels. The remaining guests, the closest family, walk into the bedroom. A huge double bed takes up virtually all the space. Shakila admires the shining, smooth, red bed cover and cushions she bought, and the new, red curtains that she made herself. Her sister Mariam fixed the room the day before, hung up the curtains, made the bed, arranged the wedding decorations. Shakila herself has never been in this house; from now on and for the rest of her life, it will be her domain.

During the entire wedding ceremony no one has seen the newlyweds exchange a single smile. Now, in her new home, Shakila can't help smiling. 'What a wonderful job you've done,' she says to Mariam. For the first time in her life she will have her own bedroom. For the first time in her life she will sleep in a bed. She sits down beside Wakil on the soft bedspread.

The final ceremony remains. One of Wakil's sisters hands Shakila a large nail and a hammer. She knows what to do and walks quietly over to the bedroom door. Over the door she drives in the nail. When it is right in everyone applauds. Bibi Gul sniffles. The implication is that she has nailed her destiny to the house.

The next day, before breakfast, Wakil's aunt comes over to Bibi Gul, Shakila's mother. In her bag she has the piece of cloth that Leila nearly forgot, the most important item of all. The old woman takes it reverently out of the bag and hands it to Shakila's mother. It is covered in blood. Bibi Gul thanks her and smiles while tears run down her cheek. Quickly she recites a prayer of thanks. All the women of the house rush up to have a look and Bibi Gul shows anyone who wants to see. Even Mariam's little daughters are shown the bloody piece of cloth.

Without the blood, it would have been Shakila, not the piece of cloth, that was returned to the family.

The Matriarch

A wedding is like a small death. The bride's family mourns in the days following the wedding, as though it were a funeral. A daughter is lost, sold or given away. The mothers especially grieve. They have had complete control over their daughters, where they go, who they meet, what they wear, what they eat. They have spent most of the day together, got up together, swept the house together, and cooked together. After the wedding the daughter disappears, completely; she goes from one family to the other. She cannot visit when she wants, only when her husband allows her. Her family cannot drop in on her without an invitation.

In an apartment in block no. 37 in Mikrorayon a mother laments her daughter, who now lives an hour's walk away. But it makes no difference whether Shakila is in the village Deh Khudaidad immediately outside Kabul, or in a foreign country thousands of miles away across the sea. As long as she is not on the mat by her mother's side, drinking tea and eating sugared almonds, the loss is just as hard to bear.

Bibi Gul cracks another almond; she had hidden it under the mattress so her youngest daughter Leila would not find it. Leila makes sure that her mother does not eat herself to death. Like a nurse at a health-spa, she has forbidden sugar and fat and snatches the food out of Bibi Gul's hand if she helps herself to something banned. When she can afford the time she cooks special fat-free food for her mother. But Bibi Gul pours fat from the family's plates over her food when Leila is not watching. She loves the taste of cooking-oil, warm mutton fat and deep-fried pakora, or sucking marrow from bones at the end of a meal. Food is her comfort. If she feels peckish after supper she often gets up at night to lick pots and scrape pans. Bibi Gul never loses weight, in spite of Leila's efforts; on the contrary, her girth increases every year. And anyhow, she has her little stashes everywhere, in old chests, under carpets, behind a crate. Or in her bag. That's where she carries cream toffees: discoloured, mealy, grainy cream toffees from Pakistan, cloyingly sweet and sometimes even rancid. But they are cream toffees, there is a picture of cows on the wrapper and no one can hear her sucking them.

The almonds, on the other hand, she must crack in silence. Bibi Gul feels sorry for herself. She is alone in the room. She sits on the mat and rocks backwards and forwards, while hiding the almonds in her hand. She stares into space. The sound of pots and pans banging in the kitchen reaches her. Soon all the daughters will have left. Shakila has gone, Bulbula is on her way out. When Leila goes she won't know what to do. No one will be left to look after her.

'No one is going to get Leila before I die,' she says about her nineteen-year-old. Many have asked for her but Bibi Gul's answer has always been no. No one else will look after her the way Leila does.

Bibi Gul doesn't do a stroke of work any more. She sits in the corner, drinks tea and broods. Her working life is over. When a woman has grown-up daughters, she becomes a sort of warden who bestows advice, guards the family's morals – in practice, the morals of the daughters. She makes sure they do not go out alone, that they cover up appropriately, that they do not meet men outside the family, that they are obedient and polite. Politeness is, according to Bibi Gul, the greatest virtue. After Sultan, she is second in command.

Her thoughts drift to Shakila who now lives behind tall mud walls; unfamiliar walls. She pictures her heaving heavy buckets full of water from the well in the backyard, sur-rounded by chickens and ten motherless children. Bibi Gul worries that she might have made a mistake. What if he is unkind? Anyhow, the flat is so empty without Shakila.

In truth, the little flat is only a tiny bit emptier without the daughter. Instead of twelve, eleven people now live in the four rooms. Sultan, Sonya and their year-old daughter sleep in one room. Sultan's brother Yunus and the oldest son Mansur sleep in a second. In the third room, the remainder: Bibi Gul, her two unmarried daughters Bulbula and Leila, Sultan's two younger sons Eqbal and Aimal, and Mariam's son Fazil – their cousin and Bibi Gul's grandson.

The fourth room is a storage room for books and post-cards, rice and bread, winter clothes in the summer and summer clothes in the winter. The family's clothes are stored in big boxes, as none of the rooms has cupboards. Every day a lot of time is taken up searching. Standing or sitting amongst the boxes the women of the family exam-ine garments, shoes, a lopsided bag, a broken container, a ribbon, a pair of scissors or a tablecloth. The items are either deemed worthy of wearing, or are just studied and put back into the box again. Only rarely is anything thrown away, and the number of boxes grows. Every day a little reshuffling takes place in the storage room; everything has to be moved if someone is looking for something at the bottom of a box.

In addition to the huge boxes containing family clothes and rubbish, every member of the family has a small chest with a lock. The women wear the key fastened to their dress. The chest is the only private item they possess and every day one can see them sitting on the floor bent over it. They take up a piece of jewellery, look at it, maybe try it on, put it back, apply some cream they forgot they had, or sniff some perfume someone gave them once. Maybe they pore over a photograph of a cousin and get lost in a dream, or, like Bibi Gul, take out some cream toffees or a biscuit squirrelled away.

Sultan has a glass-fronted bookcase through which the covers can be read and which he can lock. The bookcase contains collections of poetry by Hafez and Rumi, and hundred-year-old travelogues and frayed old atlases. In secret places between the pages he also hides his money. Afghanistan's banking system cannot be trusted. In this book-cupboard Sultan has his most precious works, books that have been dedicated, books that he wants to read sometime in the future. But for now he is in his bookshop all day and has no time. He leaves home before eight and returns at eight in the evening. There is only time left to play with baby Latifa, eat supper and lay down the law should anything have happened in the family while he was away. Usually it has not; life for the housebound women is quiet and it is beneath Sultan's dignity to resolve their squabbles.

In the bottom of the cupboard Sonya keeps her personal things. Some pretty shawls, some money, toys that the mother, from her simple background, thinks are too good for Latifa to play with. The Barbie doll copy, which Latifa was given on her first birthday, still sits on top of the cupboard, wrapped in wrinkled cellophane.

The bookcase is the only furniture in the house; there is neither TV nor radio. The only ornaments are threadbare mats along the walls and large, uncomfortable cushions. The mats are used for sleeping on at night, sitting on in the daytime. The cushions are pillows at night and prop up backs during the day. For meals a waxed cloth is put out on the floor. Everyone sits around, cross-legged, and eats with their fingers. When the meal is over the cloth is washed and rolled up.

The floors are cold stone covered with large rugs. The walls are cracked. The doors are lopsided and some cannot be closed and have to remain open. Some of the rooms are separated by just a bed-sheet. The holes in the windows are stopped with old towels.

In the kitchen there is a sink, a gas primus and a hot plate on the floor. On the windowsills lie vegetables and bits and pieces from the previous day. The shelves have curtains to protect the crockery from dirt and smoke from the primus. But however hard they try to keep it clean, there is always a layer of grease, to which a sprinkling of Kabul's perpetual dust clings, over benches, shelves and sills.

The bathroom is a cubicle in the kitchen, divided off by a wall with an open hatch; it is not much more than a hole in the concrete floor and a tap. In one corner is a wood-burning stove where water can be boiled for washing up. There is also a large water-tank, which can be filled when there is water in the pipes. Over the tank is a small shelf with a shampoo bottle, a bar of soap, which is always black, some toothbrushes and a Chinese toothpaste tube containing a grainy substance with an unidentifiable chemical taste.

'This was once a nice flat,' Sultan reminisces. 'We had water, electricity, paintings on the walls, everything.'

But during the civil war the flat was pillaged and burnt. When the family returned the flat had virtually been demolished and they had to make do as well as they could. The oldest part of Mikrorayon, where the Khan family lived, lay on the front line between the forces of Mujahedeen hero Massoud and those of the hated Gulbuddin Hekmatyar. Massoud was in control of large parts of Kabul, while Hekmatyar's power was concentrated on a height outside Kabul. They shot at each other with rockets, many of which landed on Mikrorayon. On yet another height the Uzbek Abdul Rashid Dostum had established himself, on a third the fundamentalist Abdul Rasul Sayyaf. Their rockets landed on other parts of the town. The fronts moved from street to street. The warlords fought for four years until at last the Taliban rolled into Kabul and the warlords fled to make way for the priestlings.

The battles ceased six years ago but Mikrorayon still resembles a battlefield. The building is peppered with bullets and shell holes. Many windows are covered in plastic rather than glass. There are cracks in the ceilings and the top flats are burnt out; gaping wounds where rockets once exploded. Some of the fiercest battles of the civil war took place in Mikrorayon and most of the inhabitants fled. On the heights of Maranjan, above Mikrorayon, where Hekmatyar's forces were assembled, nothing has been done to clear up after the civil war. Rocket-launchers, destroyed vehicles and tanks lie scattered around, a mere fifteen-minute walk from the Khan family home. This was once a popular picnic spot. Here too is the grave of Nadir Shah, Zahir Shah's father, who was assassinated in 1933. Now the tomb is a ruin, the cupola full of holes and the pillar broken. The less impressive tomb of his wife, next to his, is in an even worse condition. It looms up like a skeleton on a projection overlooking the town, all in bits. Someone has tried to fit the pieces together, so the quotations from the Koran can be read.

The whole hillside is mined, but amongst the broken rocket-casings and metal rubbish can be seen something that bears witness to peace. Inside a circle of round stones orange marigolds grow. They alone have survived civil war, drought and the Taliban.

From the heights, at a good distance, Mikrorayon looks like any place one might chance upon in the former Soviet Union. The buildings were a gift from the Russians. In the fifties and sixties Soviet engineers were sent to Afghanistan to build the so-called Khrushchev blocks which eventually filled the Soviet Union, and which were exactly the same wherever they were built, in Kabul, Kaliningrad or Kiev: five-storey apartment blocks with two, three or four rooms.

When one gets closer to it is clear that the shabby impression is due not to customary Soviet decay, but bullets and war. Even the concrete benches by the front doors are smashed and lie like overturned wrecks on the pitted earth that was once asphalt.

In Russia babushkas sit on these benches, old women with walking sticks, moustaches and headscarves, watching everything that goes on around them. In Mikrorayon it is only old men who sit outside the houses and gossip, while the prayer beads slide between their fingers. Barely a hand-ful of trees are left standing to give them meagre shade. The women hurry past carrying shopping bags under the burkas. One rarely sees women stop to have a chat with a neighbour. In Mikrorayon women go visiting if they want to chat, and make sure no men outside their own family see them.

The apartments were designed on Soviet principles of equality, but there is certainly no equality inside the four walls. While the idea behind the building of the apart-ments might have been to create classless dwellings in a classless society, in practice the Mikrorayon flats were seen as residences for the middle classes. At the time they were built, it was a sign of status to move from the mud huts in the villages around Kabul to the apartments with running water. Engineers and teachers, shop-owners and truck-drivers moved here. But the word middle-class now means little in a country where so many have lost all they had, and where everything has regressed. The once so-enviable running water has been a joke for the last ten years. On the first floor there is cold water in the pipes for a few hours each morning. Then nothing. Water reaches the second floor now and again, but no water ever reaches the third floor, the pressure is too weak. Wells have been dug outside the flats and every day children stream up and down the staircase carrying buckets, bottles and kettles.

Likewise, the electricity supply used to be the pride of the apartments. Now, on the whole the inhabitants live in darkness. Owing to the drought electricity is rationed. Every other day there is power for four hours, between six and ten in the evening. When there is power in one part of town, another part is blacked out. Sometimes everyone is blacked out. The only solution is to get out the oil lamps and sit around in semi-darkness while the acid smoke stings the eyes and makes them water.

The Khan family live in one of the older apartment blocks, by the dried-out Kabul River. Bibi Gul looks on the gloomy side of things, as she sits confined within the cracked concrete desert, far from the village where she grew up. Bibi Gul has not been happy since her husband died. According to his relatives he was hard-working, deeply religious, strict but fair.

When his father died Sultan took over the throne. His word is law. Anyone who does not obey him will be punished. Not only does he lord it over the household, but he also tries to rule over the siblings who have moved away. The brother only two years younger than him kisses his hand when they meet and God help him if he dares contradict Sultan, or even worse, lights up a cigarette in front of him. Respect must be shown to the older brother in every way. Sultan has his reasons for such strict behaviour. He believes that if families are not disciplined and hard-working, there will never be a new, prosperous Afghanistan.

If neither scolding nor hitting has any effect, the next punishment is rejection. Sultan never talks with or about his younger brother Farid. Farid refused to work for Sultan in his bookshop and started up his own bookshop and bindery; Sultan has never spoken to him since. Nor is anyone else in the family allowed to talk to him. Farid's name is never mentioned. He is no longer Sultan's brother.

Farid also lives in one of the devastated apartments in Mikrorayon, only a few minutes away from the Khans. When Sultan is in his bookshop Bibi Gul visits Farid and his family, without Sultan's knowledge. So do his siblings. In spite of the prohibition Shakila accepted her brother's

invitation before her wedding and spent a whole evening
with him, telling Sultan that she was with an aunt. Before
a girl gets married all the family must each invite her to a
farewell dinner. Sultan is invited to family celebrations
but not his brother. None of the cousins or uncles or
aunts wants to fall out with Sultan; that would be
unpleasant and unprofitable. But Farid is the one they
love.

No one really remembers any longer what happened
between Sultan and Farid, just that Farid left his big brother
in a rage while Sultan shouted after him that the bond
between them was broken for ever. Bib Gul asks them both
to be reconciled, but the two brothers just shrug their
shoulders. Sultan, because it is the duty of the younger to
ask for forgiveness, Farid because he feels it is Sultan's
fault.

Bibi Gul has given birth to thirteen children. When she was
fourteen she had her first daughter, Feroza. At last life was
worth living. She had cried throughout the first years as a
child bride; now life was better. As the oldest Feroza never
got any education. The family was poor and Feroza carried
water, swept and looked after her younger siblings. When
she was fifteen she was married to a man of forty. He was
rich and Bibi Gul thought the wealth would bring happiness. Feroza was pretty and they got 20,000 Afghani for
her.

The two following children died in infancy. A quarter of
Afghanistan's children die before they reach five. The country has the world's highest infant mortality rate. Children
die of measles, mumps, colds, but first and foremost of
diarrhoea. Many parents mistakenly think they must not
give the children anything when they suffer from diarrhoea,

it will all come out anyway. They think they can dry up the illness, a misunderstanding that has cost thousands of young lives. Bibi Gul can no longer remember what her two died of. 'They just died,' says Bibi Gul.

Then Sultan arrived, beloved Sultan, revered Sultan. When Bibi Gul's son reached maturity, her position amongst her in-laws strengthened considerably. The value of a bride is her maidenhead, the value of a wife the number of sons she bears.

As the oldest son he was always given the best, in spite of the family's poverty. The money they received for Feroza was used to pay for Sultan's education. From the time he was small he was given a position of authority and was the one his father trusted with responsible assignments. When he was seven he was already in full-time work, besides his schooling.

A few years after Sultan, Farid arrived. He was a madcap who always got caught up in fights and came home with torn clothes and a bloody nose. He drank and smoked, of course without his parents' knowledge, but was good as gold when he was not angry. Bibi Gul found him a wife and now he is married with two daughters and a son. But he has been excommunicated from the apartment in block no. 37 in Mikrorayon. Bibi Gul sighs. Her heart is torn apart by the enmity between the two oldest sons. Why can they not behave reasonably?

After Farid came Shakila. Cheerful, tough, strong Shakila. Bibi Gul sheds a tear. She visualises her daughter, dragging heavy water buckets.

Next was Nesar Ahmad. When Bibi Gul thinks of him the tears start to flow. Nesar Ahmad was quiet, kind and scholarly. He attended high school in Kabul and wanted to be an engineer like Sultan. But one day he never returned.

His classmates said that the military police had grabbed the strongest boys in the class and forced them to enlist in the army. This was during the Soviet occupation and Afghan Government forces functioned as Soviet ground troops. They were put in the front line against the Mujahedeen. The Mujahedeen had better troops, knew the terrain and entrenched themselves in the mountains. There they waited for the Russians and their allied Afghans to roll into the mountain passes. Nesar Ahmad disappeared in such a mountain pass. Bibi Gul thinks he is still alive. Maybe he was taken captive. Maybe he lost his memory and lives happily somewhere. She prays to Allah every day that he will return.

After Nesar Ahmad came Bulbula who sickened with sorrow when her father was imprisoned, and who generally sits at home all day, staring into space.

There was more life in Mariam, who was born a few years later. She was clever, keen and a wizard at school. She grew up to be beautiful and had lots of suitors. When she was eighteen she was married to a boy from the same village. He owned a shop and Bibi Gul thought he was a good match. Mariam moved into his home, where his brother and mother also lived. There was a lot to do; his mother's hands were useless, she had burnt them badly in a baking oven. Some fingers are lost, some melted together. Both thumbs are stumps, but she can feed herself, look after little children and carry certain things if she holds them against her body.

Mariam was happy in her new home. Then the civil war came. When one of Mariam's cousins got married in Jalalabad the family took the chance, in spite of the uncertain roads, to travel there. Her husband, Karimullah, stayed behind to look after the shop in Kabul.

One morning, when he arrived to open it, he was caught in crossfire. A bullet pierced his heart and he died on the spot.

Mariam cried for three years. In the end Bibi Gul and Karimullah's mother decided that she must marry the deceased husband's brother, Hazim. She had a new family and pulled herself together for the sake of the two children. Now she is pregnant with her fifth child. Her oldest son, from her marriage to Karimullah – Fazil – is ten and already in full-time employment. He carries cases and sells books in one of Sultan's shops and lives with Sultan, to relieve Mariam.

Then Yunus arrived, Bibi Gul's favourite. He is the one who mollycoddles her, buys her little presents, asks what she needs and ends up with his head in her lap in the evening, after supper, when the family sits or lies around on the mats dozing. Yunus's date of birth is the only one the mother knows with certainty. He was born the day Zahir Shah lost power in a coup, 17 July 1973.

The other children have neither birthday nor birth date. Sultan's year of birth ranges from 1947 to 1955, depending on which document you are reading. When Sultan adds up years as a child, years in school, years at university, the first war, the second war and the third war, he arrives at fifty-something. This is the way everyone works out their age. And because no one knows, you can be the age you want to be. In this way Shakila can be thirty, but she could easily be five or six years older.

After Yunus came Basir. He lives in Canada after his mother arranged a marriage for him there with a relative. She has never seen him or spoken to him since he moved away two years ago. Bibi Gul sheds another tear. She hates being far away from her children. They are all she has in life, apart from the glazed almonds at the bottom of the chest.

The last-born son was the cause of Bibi Gul's eating habits. A few days after the birth she had to give him away to a childless relative. The milk kept seeping out and Bibi Gul cried. A woman gains stature by being a mother, especially of sons. A sterile woman is not appreciated. Bibi Gul's relative had been childless for fifteen years, had prayed to God, despaired, tried every conceivable medicine and remedy, and when Bibi Gul was expecting her twelfth child, she asked to have it.

Bibi Gul refused. 'I cannot give my child away.'

The relative continued to beg, whimper, threaten. 'Have mercy on me, you already have a large family, I have none. Just give me this one,' she cried. 'I cannot live without children,' she sniffled.

In the end Bibi Gul gave in and promised her the child. When her son was born she kept him for twenty days. She nursed him, cuddled him and cried over having to give him away. Bibi Gul was an important woman by virtue of her children. She wanted as many as possible. But she kept her promise and after the agreed twenty days she gave him to the relative, and though the milk flowed she could not nurse him again. All ties to the mother had to be severed and from then on he was only a relative. Bibi Gul knows that he is well cared for, but still mourns the loss of her son. When she meets him she feigns indifference, as she promised when she gave him away.

Bibi Gul's youngest daughter is Leila. Clever, industrious Leila who does most of the family housework. She is the afterthought at nineteen and at the bottom of the pecking order: youngest, unmarried and a girl.

When Bibi Gul was her age she had already given birth

to four children, two who died and two who lived. But she doesn't think of that now. Her tea is cold and she is cold. She hides the almonds under the mattress and wants someone to fetch her woollen shawl.

'Leila,' she calls. Leila gets up from the pots.

Temptations

She arrives with the sunshine. A billowing bundle of charm steps into the darkened room. Mansur wakes up from his doze with a start and adjusts his sleepy gaze as he beholds the apparition stealing along the shelves.

'Can I help you?'

He knows immediately that here is a beautiful, young woman. He sees it in her bearing, her hands, her feet, how she carries her handbag. She has long, white fingers.

'Have you got *Advanced Chemistry*?'

Mansur puts on his most professional bookseller's look. He knows he does not have the book but he asks her to accompany him to the back of the premises to look for it. He stands close to her and looks through the shelves while her perfume tickles his nose. He stretches and bends, pretending to hunt for the book. In between he turns to her and searches the shadows of her eyes. He has never heard of the book.

'Unfortunately we are sold out, but I have a few copies at home. Could you come back tomorrow and I will bring one in for you?'

He waits for the goddess all the next day, armed not with a chemistry book, but a plan. While he waits he spins ever more fantasies. Then night closes in and he shuts up shop. The shop has metal gratings, which protect the cracked windows at night. Frustrated, he slams them closed.

The next day he is in a bad mood and sits sulking behind the counter. The room is in semi-darkness, there is no electricity. Where the sun's rays enter the dust dances and makes the room appear even drearier. When customers arrive and ask for books Mansur answers surlily that he has not got them, despite the fact that the book is sitting on the shelf right opposite him. He curses the fact that he is tied to his father's bookshop, that not even Fridays are free, and that his father will not allow him to study, won't allow him to buy a bicycle, won't allow him to see friends. He hates the dusty tomes on the shelves. He really hates books, and has always hated them and hasn't finished a single one since he was taken out of school.

The sound of light footsteps and the rustling of heavy material wake him out of his sombre mood. She stands, like the first time, in the middle of a ray of sun that makes the dust from the books frolic around her. Mansur takes care not to leap up with joy and puts on his bookseller's look.

'I was expecting you yesterday,' he says, professionally friendly. 'I have the book at home, but did not know which edition, binding or what price you wanted to pay. The book has been published in so many editions that I could not bring them all. So if you would like to come with me and choose the one you want?'

The burka looks surprised. She twiddles her bag with an air of uncertainty.

'Home with you?'

They are quiet for a moment. Silence is the best persuasion, Mansur thinks, quivering with nerves. He has issued a daring invitation.

'You need the book, don't you?' he asks in the end.

Wonder of wonders, she agrees. The girl settles in the back seat, positioned so she can look at him in the mirror. Mansur tries to hold what he thinks is her gaze while they talk.

'Nice car,' she says. 'Is it yours?'

'Yes, but it's not much,' Mansur answers casually. This makes the car even more wonderful and him even richer.

He drives aimlessly round the streets of Kabul with a burka in the back seat. He has no book, and anyhow at home are his grandmother and all his aunts. It makes him nervous and excited to be so close to someone unknown. In a moment of boldness he asks to see her face. She sits for a few seconds, absolutely stiff, then lifts up the front piece of the burka and holds his gaze in the mirror. He knew it; she is very beautiful, with beautiful, big, dark, made-up eyes, a few years older than him. With the aid of the most exceptional capers, insistent charm and the art of persuasion he makes her forget the chemistry book and invites her to lunch in a restaurant. He stops the car, she creeps out and up the steps to Marco Polo restaurant, where Mansur orders the entire menu: grilled chicken, kebab, mantu – Afghan noodles filled with meat and pilau – rice with large pieces of mutton and, for dessert, pistachio pudding.

During lunch he tries to make her laugh, to feel special, to eat more. She sits with the burka over her head, with her back to the other tables, in a corner of the restaurant. Like most Afghans she ignores the knife and fork and eats with her fingers. She talks about her life, her family, her studies, but Mansur can hardly follow, he is too worked up. His first date. His absolutely illegal date. He tips the waiters exorbitantly when they leave, the student makes big eyes. He sees by her dress that she is not rich, but not poor either. Mansur must hurry back to the shop, the burka jumps into a taxi. During the Taliban that could have led to a whipping and imprisonment for both her and the driver. The meeting at the restaurant would have been an impossibility; unrelated men and women could not walk on the streets together, and far less could she have taken off the burka in public. Things have changed, luckily for Mansur. He promises to bring the book next day.

All the next day he tries to think of what to say when she turns up. Tactics will have to be changed from bookseller to seducer. Mansur's only experience of the language of love is from Indian and Pakistani films, where each dramatic statement exceeds the one before. The films start off with an encounter, flirt with hatred, betrayal and disappointment, and finish off with rose-red words of everlasting love – useful preparation for a young lover. Behind the counter, by a stack of books and papers, Mansur dreams of how the conversation with the student will unfold.

'I have thought of you every moment since you left me yesterday. I knew there was something special about you; you are made for me. You are my destiny!' She would no doubt love to hear that, and then he would stare into her eyes, maybe grab her wrists. 'I must be alone with you. I want to feast my eyes on all of you, I want to drown in your eyes,' he will say. Or he might be slightly less presuming: 'I don't ask for much, if only you might drop by when you have nothing else to do, I would understand if you don't want to, but maybe just once a week?'

Maybe he could make a few promises: 'When I'm eighteen we'll get married.'

He must be Mansur with the expensive car, Mansur with the posh shop, Mansur with the tips, Mansur with the western clothes. He must entice her with the life she would lead together with him. 'You'll have a big house with a garden and masses of servants, and we will go on holidays abroad.' And he must make her feel special, handpicked, and aware of how much she means to him. 'I love only you. I suffer every second I do not see you.'

If she does not agree to his wishes, he must become more dramatic. 'If you leave me, kill me first! Or I will set fire to the whole world!'

But the student does not return the day after the visit to the restaurant, nor the next day, or the next. Mansur continues to practise his speech, but is becoming increasingly more dispirited. Did she not like him? Did her parents discover what she had done? Is she grounded? Did someone see them and spill the beans? A neighbour, a relative? Did he say something stupid?

An elderly man with a walking stick and a large turban interrupts his churning thoughts. He greets Mansur with a growl and asks for a religious work. Mansur finds the book and throws it angrily on the counter. He is no longer Mansur the seducer. Just Mansur, the bookseller's son with the rose-red dreams.

He waits for her every day. Every day he locks the grating over the door without her having visited. The hours in the shop are increasingly dreary.

In the street where Sultan has his bookshop there are several other bookshops and shops that sell writing materials, bind books or copy documents for people. Rahimullah works in one of these stalls. He sometimes drops in on Mansur to drink tea and gossip. This time Mansur slips over to him to pour out his troubles. Rahimullah just laughs.

'You mustn't try it on with a student. They are too virtuous. Try someone who needs money. Beggars are the easiest. Some of them are not too bad. Or go to where the UN doles out flour and oil. There are lots of young widows there.'

Mansur gapes. He knows the corner where they distribute food to the most needy, primarily war widows and little children. They get a ration every month and some of them stay standing on the corner trying to exchange part of the ration for money.

'Go there and find someone who looks young. Buy a bottle of oil and ask her to come here. "If you come to my shop I will help you in the future," I usually say. When they come I offer them some money and take them into the back room. They arrive in a burka, they leave in a burka – no one is suspicious. I get what I want and they get money for the children.'

Mansur looks at Rahimullah with disbelief. Rahimullah opens the door to the back room, barely a metre square. On the floor lie several cardboard boxes, dirty and trodden down. Dark blotches stain the cardboard.

'I take off the veil, the dress, the sandals, trousers. Having got there it is too late for regret. It would be useless to scream, because if anyone came to the rescue, the fault would lie with her, no matter what. The scandal would ruin her for life. It's easy with the widows. But if they are young girls, virgins, I do it between their legs. I just ask them to press their legs together. Or I do it from, well, you know, from behind,' says the merchant.

Mansur looks at the salesman in disbelief. How could he talk about things like that in such an easy and casual way?

When he stops by the mass of blue burkas that same afternoon, he realises it is not as easy as all that. He buys a bottle of oil. But the hands selling it are rough and worn. He looks around and sees only poverty. He throws the bottle on to the back seat and drives off.

He has given up swotting words from Bollywood. But one day he thinks he might need them after all. A young girl enters the shop and asks for an English dictionary. Mansur puts on his most charming manner. He finds out that she has enrolled in English classes for beginners. The gallant bookseller's son offers his help.

'Very few people come in here, so I can examine your homework, now and again.' But the girl never returns.

'My heart is dirty,' he confides to his younger brother. He knows he should not think about girls.

A little girl comes into the shop. Maybe she is twelve, maybe fourteen. She reaches out a dirty hand and looks pleadingly up at them. Over her head is a dirty-white shawl with red flowers. She is too young to wear the burka. That is only donned once the girl has reached puberty.

Beggars often come into the shops. Mansur usually sends them packing. But Rahimullah remains standing and watches the childish heart-shaped face and takes ten notes out of his pocket. The beggar girl looks at them wide-eyed and grabs them greedily. But just as she is about to get them Rahimullah's hand slips away. He makes a large circle in the air with his hand and holds her gaze.

'Nothing is free in life,' he says.

The girl's hand freezes. Rahimullah gives her two notes.

'Go to a hammam, wash and come back, and I'll give you the rest.'

She quickly puts the money in the pocket of her dress and hides her face behind the dirty shawl with the red flowers. She looks at him through one eye. One cheek has smallpox scars from old sores. Sandflies have left their mark on her forehead. She turns and leaves; the slim body disappears down Kabul's streets.

A few hours later she returns, clean.

'What the hell,' says Rahimullah, in spite of her wearing the same dirty clothes. 'Come with me to the back room and I'll give you the rest of the money.' He smiles at her and they go into the room.

Mansur is uncomfortable, left on his own in the shop – he doesn't know if he should leave. Suddenly the salesman comes back out.

'She is yours,' he says to Mansur.

Mansur is frozen to the spot. He stares at Rahimullah. He glances at the door to the back room, then tears out of the shop.

The Call from Ali

He feels sick for days. Unforgivable, he thinks. Unforgivable. He tries to wash, but nothing helps. He tries to pray, but to no avail. He searches the Koran, he visits the mosque, but he feels dirty, dirty. The unclean thoughts he has been harbouring of late make him a bad Muslim. God will punish him. Everything you do comes back to you, he thinks. A child. I have sinned against a child. I let him abuse her. I did nothing.

The nausea turns to world-weariness when, after a time, the memory of the beggar girl recedes. He is tired of life, the routine, the hassle. He is bad-tempered and grumpy towards everyone. He is angry with his father who chains him to the shop while life goes on without him.

I am seventeen, he thinks. Life is over before it has even started.

He sits moping behind the counter, elbows on the tabletop, forehead in his hands. He lifts his head and looks around: at books about Islam, the Prophet Muhammad, famous interpretations of the Koran. He sees books on

Afghan fairytales, biographies of Afghan kings and sovereigns, large tomes about the wars against the British, magnificent books about Afghan precious stones, textbooks on Afghan embroidery, and thin 'pancakes' from photocopied books about Afghan custom and traditions. He scowls at them and bangs his fist on the table.

Why was I born an Afghan? I hate being an Afghan. All these pig-headed customs and traditions are slowly killing me. Respect this and respect that; I have no freedom, I can't decide anything. Sultan is only interested in counting money from sales, he thinks. 'He can take his books and stuff them,' he says under his breath. He hopes no one heard him. Next to Allah and the prophets, 'father' is the single most important person within the Afghan social order. To oppose him is impossible, even for an operator like Mansur. Mansur quarrels with and walks all over everyone else – his aunts, his sisters, his mother, his brothers – but never, never his father. I'm a slave, he thinks. I am worked to the bone for board and lodging and clean clothes. Most of all Mansur wants to study. He misses his friends and the life he led in Pakistan. Here he has no time for friends, and the one friend he had, Rahimullah, he does not want to see again.

It is just before the Afghan New Year – *nauroz*. Big feasts are planned all over the country. For the last five years the Taliban forbade feasting. They considered *nauroz* a heathen celebration, a worship of the sun, because its roots were in the Zoroastrian religion – the worship of fire – which originated in Persia in the sixth century BC. And so they also forbade the traditional New Year's pilgrimage to Ali's tomb in Mazar-i-Sharif. For centuries pilgrims had flocked to Ali's grave, to purge themselves from sin, ask forgiveness, be healed and greet the new year, which according to the Afghan calendar starts on 21 March, the spring equinox, when night and day are of equal length.

Ali was the Prophet Muhammad's cousin and son-in-law and he was the fourth caliph. He is the cause of the polemic between Shia Muslims and Sunni Muslims. To Shia Muslims Ali is second in the order of succession after Muhammad, to Sunni Muslims he is fourth. But even for Sunni Muslims, like Mansur and most Afghans, he is one of Islam's great heroes. A brave warrior, sword in hand, says history. Ali was murdered in Kufa in 661, and, according to most historians, buried in Najaf in Iraq. But Afghans maintain that his followers, who feared that enemies would take revenge on his body and mutilate it, exhumed him. They lashed his body to the back of a white she-camel and made it run as far as it could. Where it collapsed they would bury him. That was, according to legend, the place that came to be known as Mazar-i-Sharif, 'the tomb of the exalted'. For five hundred years only a small stone marked the grave, but in the twelfth century a small tomb was built after a local mullah was visited by Ali in a dream. Then Genghis Khan arrived on the scene and desecrated the tomb, and once again the grave lay unmarked for several hundred years. At the beginning of the fifteenth century a new mausoleum was built above what Afghans believe are the remains of Ali. It is this burial chamber – and the mosque that was later built beside it – that draws the pilgrims.

Mansur is determined to make the pilgrimage. He has been thinking about it for some time. He needs only to get Sultan's permission, as the journey will entail being away from the shop for several days. If there is anything Sultan hates, it is Mansur being away.

He has even got hold of a travelling companion, in the

shape of an Iranian journalist who often buys books from him. They got into a conversation about New Year's Eve celebrations and the Iranian said he had room in his car. I am saved, Mansur thought. Ali calls me. He wants to forgive me.

But then Sultan says no. His father will not do without him for the short time the trip will take. He says Mansur must catalogue, supervise carpenters putting up new shelves, sell books. He won't trust anyone else. He won't even trust his future brother-in-law Rasul. Mansur seethes with anger. Because he dreaded asking his father he postponed it until the last night before departure. But not on your life. Mansur nagged, his father refused.

'You are my son and you jolly well do what I say,' says Sultan. 'I need you in the shop.'

'Books, books, money, money, all you think of is money,' Mansur shouts. 'I'm supposed to sell books about Afghanistan, without knowing the country. I've hardly ever been outside Kabul,' he says crossly.

The Iranian leaves next morning. Mansur is in revolt. How could his father deny him this? He drives his father to the shop without a word, and gives monosyllabic answers when asked a question. The accumulated hatred against his father rages inside him. Mansur had only finished ten classes when his father took him out of school and put him into the bookshop. He never completed high school. He gets a no to all his demands. The only thing his father has given him is a car, to enable Mansur to drive him around, and the responsibility for a bookshop where he is turning to dust amongst the shelves.

'As you like,' he says suddenly. 'I will do everything you ask me to, but please do not think I am doing it willingly. You never let me do what I want. You're crushing me.'

'You can go next year,' Sultan says.

'No, I'll never go. And I'll never ask you for anything again.'

It is alleged that only those whom Ali calls can go to Mazar. Why does Ali not want him? Were his thoughts so unforgivable? Or does his father not hear that Ali calls him?

Sultan is chilled by Mansur's hostility. He glances over at the repressed, tall teenager and is frightened.

Having driven his father to his shop and the two brothers to theirs, Mansur opens up his own and sits down behind the dusty desk. He sits in his 'think-dark-thoughts' position with elbows on the counter and feels life imprisoning and overwhelming him with dust from the books.

A new consignment of books has arrived. For the sake of appearances he feels he must know what is in them. It is a collection of poems from the mystic Rumi, one of his father's favourite poets and the best-known of the Afghan Sufists, Islamic mystics. Rumi was born in the 1200s in Balkh, near Mazar-i-Sharif. Yet another sign, Mansur thinks. He decides to look for signs that will underpin his decision and show his father up. The poems are about cleansing oneself in order to get closer to God – who is Perfection. They deal with forgetting oneself, one's own ego. Rumi says: 'The Ego is a veil between humans and God.' Mansur reads how he can turn to God and how life should revolve around God and not around oneself. Mansur feels dirty again. The more he reads the more he is determined to go. He keeps returning to one of the simpler poems:

The water said to the dirty one, 'Come here.'
The dirty one said, 'I am too ashamed.'
The water replied: 'How will your shame be washed away
*   without me?'*

The water, God and Rumi all seem to be deserting Mansur. The Iranian is no doubt high up in the snow-clad Hindu Kush mountains by now. Mansur is angry all day. When night falls it is time to lock up, fetch his father and brothers and take them home, to yet another bowl of rice, to yet another evening in the company of his witless family.

As he fastens the shutters over the door with a heavy-duty padlock, Akbar, the Iranian journalist, suddenly appears. Mansur thinks he is seeing ghosts.

'Haven't you gone?' he asks in an astonished voice.

'We did, but the Salang tunnel was closed today, so we'll try tomorrow,' he says. 'I met your father down the road, he asked me to take you with him. We'll leave my place at five tomorrow morning, as soon as the curfew is lifted.'

'Did he really say that?' Mansur is speechless. 'It must be Ali calling – imagine that, he really did call me,' he mumbles.

Mansur spends the night with Akbar to make sure he wakes up and as a guarantee that his father won't change his mind. The next morning, before dawn, they are off. Mansur's only luggage consists of a plastic bag full of Coke and Fanta cans and biscuits with banana and kiwi filling. Akbar has a friend with him and everyone is in high spirits. They play Indian film music and sing at the top of their voices. Mansur has brought his treasure with him, a western cassette, *Pop from the 80s*. 'Is this love? Baby, don't hurt me, don't hurt me no more', resounds out into the cool morning. Before they have driven half an hour Mansur has eaten the first packet of biscuits and drunk two Cokes. He feels free. He wants to scream and shout, and sticks his head out of the window. 'Ouhhhh! Aliiii! Ali! Here I come!'

They pass areas he has never before seen. Immediately north of Kabul is the Shomali Plain, one of the most war-torn areas of Afghanistan. Here bombs from American B52s shook the ground only a few months ago. 'How beautiful,' Mansur shouts. And from a distance the plain is beautiful, against the backdrop of the mighty snow-clad Hindu Kush mountains that proudly rise up to the sky. Hindu Kush means the Hindu killer. Thousands of Indian soldiers have frozen to death in these mountain ranges, during military sorties on Kabul.

When one enters the plateau the landscape of war is apparent. In contrast to the Indian soldiers, the Hindu Kush did not stop the B52s. Many of the Taliban's bombed-out camps have not yet been cleared. Their shelters have been turned into large craters or are strewn over the area, exploding when the bombs hit the ground. A twisted iron bed, where a Taliban might have been shot in his sleep, resembles a skeleton by the roadside. A bullet-ridden mattress lies near by.

But the camps have mostly been looted. Mere hours after the Taliban fled the local population was in there, pilfering soldiers' washbasins, gas lamps, carpets and mattresses. Poverty made the plundering of corpses inevitable. No one cried over dead bodies by the roadside or in the sand. On the contrary, the locals desecrated many of them: eyes gouged out, skin torn off, body parts cut off or chopped into bits. That was revenge for the Taliban having terrorised the Shomali Plain people for years.

For five years the plain was the front line between the Taliban and Massoud's men from the Northern Alliance, and sovereignty of the Plain changed six times. Because the front was continually moving, the local population had to flee, either up towards the Panshir valley or south towards Kabul. The locals were mostly Tajiks and anyone who dragged their feet might suffer the Taliban's ethnic cleansing.

Before the Taliban withdrew they poisoned wells and blew up water pipes and dams, vital to the dry plain, which before the war had been part of Kabul's bread basket.

Mansur stares in silence at the awful villages they pass. Most of them are in ruins and rear up in the landscape like skeletons. The Taliban systematically razed many of the villages to the ground when they tried to subdue the last part of the country, the missing tenth, the Panshir valley, the Hindu Kush mountains and the desert areas bordering Tajikistan. They might have made it had September 11 not happened and the world started to care about Afghanistan.

The remains of twisted tanks, wrecked military vehicles and bits of metal whose purpose Mansur can only guess at, lie thrown around. A lonely man walks behind a plough. In the middle of his patch lies a large tank. He walks laboriously around it – it is too heavy to move.

The car drives fast over the pot-holed road. Mansur tries to spot his mother's village. He has not been there since he was five or six. His finger constantly points to more ruins. There! There! But nothing distinguishes one village from another. The place where he visited his mother's relatives as a little boy could be any one of these heaps of rubble. He remembers how he ran around on paths and fields. Now the plain is the most mined place in the world. Only the roads are safe. Children with bundles of firewood and women with buckets of water walk along the side of the road. They try to avoid the ditches where the mines might be. The car with the pilgrims passes a team of mine-clearers who systematically blow up or render the explosives harmless. A few metres are cleared each day.

Over the death traps the ditches are full of wild, dark-red, short-stemmed tulips. But the flowers must be admired at a distance. Picking them means risking blowing off an arm or a leg.

Akbar is having fun with a book published by the Afghan Tourist Organisation in 1967.

'"Along the roads children sell chains of pink tulips",' he reads. '"In the spring cherries, apricots, almond and pear trees jostle for the attention of the traveller. A flowering spectacle follows the traveller all the way to Kabul".' They laugh. This spring they spot a lone rebellious cherry tree or two that have survived bombs, rockets, a three-year drought and poisoned wells. But it's doubtful whether anyone can find a mine-free path to the cherries. '"The local pottery is amongst the most beautiful in Afghanistan. We recommend you stop and take a look in the workshops along the road, where artisans make plates and vessels following centuries-old tradition",' Akbar reads.

'Those traditions seem to have suffered,' says Said, Akbar's friend, who is driving the car. Not a single pottery workshop can be seen on the road up to the Salang Pass. They start to ascend. Mansur opens the third Coke, empties it and throws it elegantly out of the car. Better to litter a bomb crater than mess the car up. The road crawls up to the world's highest mountain tunnel. It narrows; on one side the sheer mountain cliff, on the other running water, sometimes a waterfall, sometimes a stream. '"The Government has put trout out in the river. In a few years there will be a viable colony",' Akbar reads on. There are no trout in the river now. The Government has had other things on its mind than fish-farming in the years since the guide was written.

Burnt-out tanks lie in the most incredible places: down the valley side, in the river, tottering over a precipice, sideways, upside down or broken into many bits. Mansur quickly arrives at a hundred when he starts counting. The majority originate from the war against the Soviet Union, when the Red Army rolled in from the Central Soviet Republics in the north and thought they had the Afghans under control. The Russians soon fell victim to the Mujahedeen's shrewd warfare. The Mujahedeen moved around the mountainside like goats. From afar, from the lookout posts in the mountains, they could spot the Russian tanks snailing along in the valley bottoms. Even with their homemade weapons the guerrillas were virtually invulnerable when laying an ambush. The soldiers were everywhere, disguised as goatherds, the Kalashnikov hidden under the goat's belly. They could make surprise attacks whenever needed.

'Under the bellies of long-haired goats you could even hide rocket launchers,' Akbar relates, who has read everything available about the war against the Soviet Union.

Alexander the Great also struggled up these mountain roads. Having captured the area around Kabul he walked over the Hindu Kush on his way to central Asia on the other side of the Oxus river. 'Alexander is supposed to have composed odes to the mountains, which "inspired mystic thoughts and eternal rest".' Akbar continues to recite from the Tourist Organisation guidebook.

'The Government made plans for a ski centre here,' he suddenly shouts and looks up at the steep mountainsides. 'In 1967! As soon as the roads have been tarmacked it says!'

The roads were tarmacked, as promised by the Tourist Organisation. But not much is left of the tarmac. Plans for the ski centre remained on the drawing board.

'That would have made for an explosive descent,' Akbar laughs. 'Or maybe the mines can be marked with slalom gates! Adventurous Travels! Or Afghan AdvenTours – for the world-weary.'

They all laugh. The tragic reality sometimes presents the appearance of a cartoon film, or rather a thriller. They visualise colourful snowboarders being blown to smithereens down the mountainside.

Tourism, once an important source of income for Afghanistan, belongs to a bygone era. They drive along what was once called 'the hippie trail'. Here progressive and not so progressive youths came to enjoy beautiful scenery, a wild lifestyle and the cheapest hashish in the world. For the more experienced, opium. In the sixties and seventies several thousand hippies came to the mountain country every year, hired old Ladas and set off. Even women travelled alone around the mountain country. In those days bandits and highwaymen might attack them, but that only added to the thrill of the journey. Even the coup against Zahir Shah in 1973 failed to stem the flow. It was the Communist coup in 1978, and invasion the year after, which eventually put an end to the 'hippie trailers'.

The three boys have been driving for a couple of hours when they catch up with the backlog of pilgrims. The queue is immovable. It has started to snow. Fog rolls in, the car starts to slide. Said is not carrying chains. 'You don't need chains with a four-wheel drive,' he assures them.

An increasing number of cars start spinning in the deep, icy and snow-filled ruts. When one car stops they all stop. The road is too narrow to overtake. Today the traffic is all from south to north, from Kabul to Mazar. Next day it will be the opposite. The mountain road doesn't have the capacity to take cars driving in both directions. The 450-kilometre road from Kabul to Mazar takes at least twelve hours to travel, sometimes twice or even four times as long.

'Many of the cars that have been taken by snowstorms and avalanches are only dug out in the summer. Most of them disappear in the spring,' Akbar teases.

They pass the bus that has caused the queue; it has been pushed right on to the side, while its passengers on their way to Ali's tomb thumb lifts with cars that snail past. Mansur smiles when he sees what is written on the side of the bus: '"Hmbork–Frankfork–Landan–Kabal",' he reads, and shrieks with laughter when he sees the lettering on the windscreen: 'Wellcam! Kaing of Road' is written in fresh red paint. 'What a regal tour,' he screams. They do not pick up any passengers from the Kabal-express. Said, Mansur and Akbar are wrapped up in their own little world.

They drive into the first gallery – solid concrete pillars covered by a roof to protect the road from avalanches. But the galleries too are difficult to negotiate. Because they are open to the elements they are full of snow, which has blown in and turned to ice. Deep frozen ruts are a challenge to a car without chains.

The Salang tunnel, 3,400 metres above sea level, and the galleries, some of them up to 5,000 metres above sea level, were a gift to Afghanistan when the Soviet Union tried to turn the country into a satellite state. Work was started by Soviet engineers in 1956, and completed in 1964. The Russians also started tarmacking the first roads in the country in the fifties. During Zahir Shah's reign Afghanistan was considered a friendly country. The liberal King was forced to turn to the Soviet Union, because neither the US nor Europe were interested in investing in his mountainous country. The King needed money and expertise and chose to ignore the fact that ties with the Communist superpower were becoming increasingly tighter.

The tunnel was strategically important in the resistance against the Taliban. At the end of the nineties it was blown up by the Mujahedeen hero Massoud, in a desperate bid to stop the Taliban's advance to the north. They got so far, but no further.

It is completely dark, or completely grey. The car slides, gets stuck in the snow, wedged in the deep ruts. The wind whistles, nothing can be distinguished in the blizzard and Said can follow only what he thinks are tracks. They are driving on snow and black ice. Without chains only Ali can guarantee a safe outcome. I can't die before I get to his grave, Mansur thinks. Ali has called me.

It brightens slightly. They are at the entrance to the Salang tunnel. A sign outside warns: 'Caution. Danger of poisoning. If you are blocked in, turn the engine off and make for the nearest exit'. Mansur looks questioningly at Akbar.

'Only a month ago fifty people were holed up inside the tunnel because of an avalanche,' the well-informed Akbar tells them. 'It was minus twenty and the driver left the engine running to keep warm. After several hours, when they had managed to shovel all the snow away, ten or twenty people had fallen asleep from the carbon monoxide and died. That happens all the time,' says Akbar as they drive slowly into the tunnel.

The car stops, the queue is at a standstill.

'I'm sure I'm just imagining it,' says Akbar, 'but I feel a headache coming on.'

'I agree,' says Mansur. 'Shall we head for the nearest exit?'

'No, let's hope the queue will move soon,' says Said.

'Imagine if the queue starts moving and we have left the car, then we'll be the ones causing the queue.'

'Is this what it feels like to die of carbon monoxide poisoning?' asks Mansur. They sit behind closed windows. Said lights a cigarette. Mansur screams. 'Are you mad?' shouts Akbar and snatches the cigarette from his mouth and stubs it out. 'Do you want to poison us even more?'

An irritable feeling of panic spreads. They are still not moving. Then something happens. The cars in front crawl forward. The three boys pick their way out of the tunnel and emerge with splitting headaches. When the fresh air hits them the headaches evaporate. They still see nothing; the fog is like a greyish, white, whirling porridge. They follow the ruts and the dim lights ahead. It would be impossible to turn. They drive on in a fellowship of destiny. Every pilgrim is following the same worn, icy ruts. Even Mansur has stopped munching biscuits. It is like driving into oblivion, but oblivion where precipices, mines, avalanches and other dangers might suddenly strike.

At last the fog lifts, but they are still driving along a precipice. It is worse now that they can see. They have started the descent. The car lurches from side to side. Suddenly it slides sideways down the road. Said has lost control and swears. Akbar and Mansur hold on tight, as if that might help if they go over the side. Nervous silence descends once again on the car. The car slides sideways, rights itself, slides sideways again, and then swerves from side to side. They pass a sign which puts the fear of daylight into them: 'Warning! Mines!' Immediately outside – even inside their skid-zone – there are mines. All the snow in the world can't protect them from anti-tank mines. This is madness, thinks Mansur, but he says nothing. He does not want to gain a reputation as a coward. And anyhow, he is the youngest. He looks down on tanks that lie scattered about, snow-covered, together with cars that have not made it either. He prays. Ali can't have called him just to see him plunge over a cliff. Although at times his behaviour has been contrary to Islam, he has come to cleanse himself, put evil thoughts behind him and become a good Muslim. That last part down the mountain he experiences as if in a trance.

They enter the snow-free plains after what seems like an eternity. The last hours of the journey to Mazar-i-Sharif are child's play in comparison.

On the road into town they are overtaken by pick-ups laden with heavily armed men. Bearded soldiers sit in open lorries carrying Kalashnikovs pointing in all directions. They bump along at sixty miles per hour over the rutty roads. The scenery is desert, steppe and stony hills. Now and again they pass little green oases and villages with mud huts. At the entrance to town a road-post stops them. Gruff men wave them through the barrier, which is a piece of rope stretched between two rocket-shells.

They drive into town, tired and stiff. Amazingly they have made the trip in twelve hours. 'So this was an absolutely normal trip through the Salang tunnel,' says Mansur. 'What about those who take several days? Wow, we've made it. Ali, here I come.'

Soldiers with weapons at the ready stand on rooftops. Disturbances have been predicted for New Year's Eve and there are no international peace-keepers here, just two or three opposing warlords. The soldiers on the rooftops belong to the governor, who is a Hazara. The soldiers in the pick-ups are the Tajik Atta Muhammad's men. A particular uniform is the hallmark of the Uzbek Abdul Rashid Dostum. All the weapons are aimed at the ground, where thousands of pilgrims are wandering around, or sit in groups and talk: by the mosque, in the park and on the pavements.

The blue mosque is a revelation, shining in the dark. It is the most beautiful building Mansur has ever seen. The floodlight is a gift from the American Embassy, on the occasion of the ambassador's New Year visit to the town. Red lanterns light up the park around the mosque, which is teeming with pilgrims.

This is where Mansur will ask for forgiveness for his sins. Here he will be cleansed. It makes him faint just looking at the large mosque. And hungry. Coke, and banana-and-kiwi-filled biscuits are scant fare for a traveller.

The restaurants are packed with pilgrims. Mansur, Said and Akbar find the corner of a carpet to sit on in a dark restaurant in Kebab Street. Permeating everything are the fumes of grilled mutton, served with bread and whole onions.

Mansur bites into the onion and feels drunk. He wants to shout for joy. But he sits quietly and stuffs himself with the food, like the others. He is no child, and he tries to keep the same façade as Akbar and Said: cool, relaxed, worldly-wise.

The next morning Mansur is awakened by the prayer call of the mullah. '*Allahu akhbar*' – 'God is great' booms out as if someone had fastened enormous loudspeakers to his ears. He looks out of the window, straight on to the blue mosque, which is sparkling in the morning sunshine. Hundreds of white doves fly over the holy place. They live in two dovecotes by the tomb and it is alleged that if a grey dove joins the flight its colour will change within forty days. Also, every seventh dove is a holy soul.

Together with Akbar and Said Mansur pushes through the enclosure. It is about half-past seven. Aided by Akbar's press card they shove their way up to the podium. Many have spent the night here to get as close as possible when Ali's banner is raised by Hamid Karzai, Afghanistan's new leader. The women sit on one side, some wearing the burka, some only a white veil. The men sit opposite. While the women sit quietly on the ground, amongst the men there is a lot of pushing and shoving. The trees outside are black with people. The police walk around wielding whips, but more and more pass through into the enclosure; they jump over the fence and avoid the whips. Security is tight as all the Government ministers are expected.

The Government enter, Hamid Karzai leading the way, wearing his characteristic blue and green striped silk cloak. He dresses so as to represent all of Afghanistan: lambskin cap from Kandahar in the south, cloak from the north and shirt from the western provinces bordering Iran.

Mansur strains his neck and tries to get closer. He has never seen Karzai before. Karzai, the Pashtoon from Kandahar, had himself for a short period supported the Taliban but later used his position as chief of the Popolzai tribe to win over supporters for the fight against the Taliban. When the Americans started their bombing campaign, he left on a suicidal motorcycle tour of Taliban strongholds to try and convince the oligarchy that the Taliban was finished. It is alleged they were more convinced by his courage than his arguments. Later he was nearly killed by American friendly fire. At the UN conference in Bonn, drawn together to map out Afghanistan's future, he was chosen as the country's new leader.

'They tried to ruin our culture. They tried to crush our traditions. They tried to rob us of Islam,' Karzai shouts to the crowd. 'The Taliban tried to dirty Islam, pull us all down in the mud, fight the whole world. But we know what Islam stands for. Islam is peace. The New Year that starts today, the year 1381, is the year of renewal. That is the year in which it will be safe and secure to live in Afghanistan. We will safeguard peace and develop our society. Today we accept help from the whole world, one day, one day, we will be a country that helps the world,' he cries and the multitude shout for joy.

'Us?' Mansur whispers. 'Help the world?'

That is to him an absurd thought. Mansur has lived out his whole life in war. Afghanistan is a country that receives everything from the outside world, from food to weapons.

Following on from Karzai, ex-president Burhanuddin Rabbani takes to the podium. A man of great weight but little authority. A theologian and professor at Cairo University who formed the Jamiat-i-Islami party, which united a fraction of the Mujahedeen. He persuaded the military strategist Ahmed Shah Massoud to join him. Massoud was to emerge as the great hero in the war against the Soviet Union, the civil war and the resistance against the Taliban. He was a charismatic leader, deeply religious, but also pro-western. He spoke French and wanted to modernise the country. He was assassinated by two Tunisian suicide bombers two days before September 11, and has achieved mythical status. The Tunisians were in possession of Belgian passports and presented themselves as journalists. 'Commander, what will you do with Osama bin Laden once you have conquered all of Afghanistan?' was the last question he was supposed to hear. He managed a laugh before the terrorists triggered the bomb hidden in the camera. Even some Pashtoon now display pictures of Massoud, the lion of Panshir.

Rabbani dedicates his speech to Massoud, but Rabbani's golden age was the holy war against the Soviet Union. 'We forced the Communists out of our country, we can force all invaders out of our holy Afghanistan,' he proclaims.

The Russian troops withdrew in 1989. A few months later the Berlin Wall fell, an event for which Rabbani takes the credit, in addition to the break-up of the Soviet Union.

'Had it not been for *jihad*, the whole world would still be in the Communist grip. The Berlin Wall fell because of the wounds which we inflicted on the Soviet Union, and the inspiration we gave all oppressed people. We broke the Soviet Union up into fifteen parts. We liberated people from Communism. *Jihad* led to a freer world. We saved the world because Communism met its grave here in Afghanistan!'

Mansur is fumbling with his camera. He has pushed his way right up to the podium to get close-ups of those who are speaking. He is keen to get Karzai. He snaps and snaps pictures of the small, slim man. This will be something to show his father.

One after the other the men talk, pray, talk from the podium. A mullah thanks Allah, the Minister for Education portrays an Afghanistan where weapons give way to the Internet.

'Exchange weapons for computers,' he cries. He adds that Afghans must stop discriminating between ethnic groups. 'Look at America, they live in one country, they are all Americans. They co-exist without problems.'

During the speeches the whips are continually in operation on the public. But nothing helps. An increasing number squeeze over the barriers and into the holy interior. The audience scream and shout and it is virtually impossible to hear the speeches. It all seems more like a 'happening' than a religious ceremony. Armed soldiers man the steps and rooftops surrounding the mosque. A dozen American Special Forces soldiers, carrying machine-guns and wearing sunglasses, have positioned themselves on the flat roof of the mosque to protect the pale-pink American ambassador. Others flank him. To many Afghans it is sacrilege that infidels should walk about on the mosque roof. No non-Muslims are allowed into the mosque. Guards make sure that non-believers are weeded out. But there are not many of them; western tourists do not exactly make a pilgrimage to Afghanistan the first spring following the fall of the Taliban. Only a relief worker or two has got lost in the New Year's celebrations.

The town's warring warlords, Atta Muhammad and General Abdul Rashid Dostum, both have a place on the podium. The Tajik Atta Muhammad rules the town; the Uzbek Dostum thinks *he* should. The two bitter enemies stand side by side and listen to the speeches, Atta Muhammad sporting a beard like a Taliban, Dostum with the authority of a has-been boxer. They co-operated grudgingly during the last offensive against the Taliban. Now the cold front between them has once again descended. Dostum is the most infamous member of the new Government, and was included for the simple reason that it might prevent him from sabotaging the others. The man who now squints into the sun, his arms peacefully folded over his large body, has more gruesome stories attached to his name than anyone else in Afghanistan. As punishment for a misdemeanour he would tie soldiers to one of his tanks – and drive until only bloody rags remained. On one occasion thousands of Taliban soldiers were driven out into the desert and put into containers. When the containers were opened several days later the prisoners were dead and their skin burnt to cinders by the heat. Dostum is also known as the master of deceit. He has served many masters and deceived them all in turn. He fought for the Russians when the Soviet Union attacked, was said to be an atheist and heavy vodka drinker. Now he presents a deferential air, praises Allah and preaches pacifism. 'In 1381 no one has the right to distribute weapons that will lead to fighting and new conflicts. This is the year for gathering up weapons, not doling them out!'

Mansur laughs. Dostum is known as a virtual illiterate. He stutters his way through his script, reading it like a pre-schooler. Sometimes he comes to a complete halt, but makes up for it by roaring even louder.

The last mullah urges a campaign against terrorism. In today's Afghanistan everything is a campaign against some pet hate, which varies according to who is speaking. 'Only Islam's holy book speaks out against terrorism. Terrorists have turned their faces towards Afghanistan – it is our duty to oppose them. No other holy book talks the same language. God said to Muhammad: "You must not pray in a mosque built by terrorists." Real Muslims are not terrorists, because Islam is the most tolerant of religions. When Hitler killed Europe's Jews, the Jews were safe in Muslim countries. Terrorists are false Muslims!'

After hours of speeches the flag is to be raised at last, Ali's green flag, *janda*, which has not been raised for five years. The flagpole lies on the ground, the top facing the mosque. To the beating of drums and the rejoicing of the crowds Karzai raises the pole, and the religious flag is run up. It will fly for forty days. Shots are fired and the barriers opened. The ten thousand who have been waiting outside pile in, to the mosque, the tomb and the flag.

Mansur has had enough of crowds and celebrations and wants to shop. Ali will have to wait. He has been thinking about it for a long time. Every family member will get a present. If everyone gets a bite of the journey his father will be better disposed towards him in the future.

He buys prayer rugs, kerchiefs and prayer beads. Then he buys sugar crystals – big crystals which one bites pieces off and crunches in tea. He knows that his grandmother, Bibi Gul, will forgive every sin he has ever committed or is ever likely to commit if he returns home with the heavy sugar crystals that are made only in Mazar. In addition he buys dresses and jewellery for his aunts, and sunglasses for his uncles and brothers. He has never seen sunglasses for sale in Kabul. Loaded down with all this, in large, pink plastic bags advertising 'Pleasure – Special Light Cigarettes', he returns to Kalif Ali's grave. The New Year presents must be blessed.

He carries them into the actual crypt, and goes over to the mullahs who are sitting by the gold-painted wall inside the tomb. He places the gifts in front of one of them, who reads from the Koran and breathes over the gifts. When the prayer has been said, Mansur packs the things back into the plastic bags and hastens on.

By the golden wall one can utter a wish. In keeping with the patriotic speeches he leans his forehead against the wall and prays: That he one day will be proud of being an Afghan. That he one day will be proud of himself and his country and that Afghanistan may become a country that will be respected in the world. Not even Hamid Karzai could have put it better.

Intoxicated by all the sights and sounds, Mansur has forgotten the prayer of purification and forgiveness, the reason for his coming to Mazar. He has forgotten the little beggar girl, her thin little body, the big pale-brown eyes, the matted hair.

He leaves the tomb and goes over to Ali's flag. Here too are mullahs who accept Mansur's plastic bags. But they do not have time to take the gifts out of the bags. The queue of people who want carpets, beads, food and kerchiefs blessed is enormous. The mullahs just grab Mansur's plastic bags, brush them hastily up against the pole, mumble a prayer and give them back. Mansur tosses them some notes; the prayer carpets and sugar lumps have been blessed yet again.

He looks forward to giving them away, to his grand-mother, to Sultan, to his aunts and uncles. Mansur walks around smiling. He is pure happiness. Away from the shop, away from his father's grip. He walks down the pavement outside the mosque with Akbar and Said.

'This is the best day of my life! The best day,' he cries. Akbar and Said look at him in astonishment, rather embar-rassed, but they are touched that he is so happy. 'I love Mazar, I love Ali, I love freedom! I love you!' he cries and jumps along the street. It is the first time he has travelled alone, the first day in his whole life that he has not seen a member of his family.

They decide to watch a *buzkashi* fight. The northern ter-ritories are famous for having the hardest, roughest, fastest *buzkashis*. From afar they see that the fight has already started. Clouds of dust lie over the plain, where two hun-dred mounted men fight over a headless calf's carcass. The horses bite and kick, rear up and jump, while the horse-men, whip between their teeth, try to snatch the carcass on the ground. Possession of the calf changes so rapidly that it looks as if it is thrown from rider to rider. The aim is to move the calf from one end of the plain to the other and place it inside a circle on the ground. Some fights are so violent that the animal is torn to bits.

To an outsider new to the game it might look as though

the horses are just racing after each other across the plain with the riders balancing in the saddle. The riders wear long embroidered coats, high-heeled, thigh-high, decorated leather boots and *buzkashi* hats, a small lambskin hat like a bowler edged in fur.

'Karzai!' cries Mansur when he spots the Afghan leader out on the plain, 'and Dostum!'

The tribal chief and the warlord are fighting each other for possession of the calf. To emerge as a strong leader it is necessary to take part in *buzkashi* fights and not merely ride around in circles outside the chaos, but commit oneself to the heat of the battle. But everything has a price. Sometimes mighty men pay to win.

Karzai rides around on the outskirts of the battle and is not quite able to maintain the other riders' lethal tempo. The tribal chief from the south never quite learnt the *buzkashi*'s brutal rules. This is a Plains battle. It is the great son of the Plains, General Dostum, who wins, or at least whom the *buzkashi* let win. That might be worth their while. Dostum sits like a commander on his horse and accepts the applause.

Sometimes two teams compete, at other times it is everyone for themselves. *Buzkashi* is one of the wildest games in the world, brought to Afghanistan by the Mongols, who devastated the country under Genghis Khan. It is also a game about money; powerful men amongst the public pay out millions of Afghani for each round. The more money the wilder the game. And it is a game with political significance. A local chief is either himself a good *buzkashi* fighter or keeps a stable with good horses and riders. Victory is synonymous with respect.

Ever since the fifties the Afghan authorities have tried to formalise the fights. The participants merely nod their heads; they know the rules would be impossible to uphold anyway. Even after the Soviet invasion the tournaments continued, in spite of chaos in the country; many participants could not turn up for fights, as they had to cross battlefields to get to the venue. The Communists, who tried to get rid of most of Afghanistan's deep-rooted traditions, never dared touch the *buzkashi* fights. On the contrary, they tried to ingratiate themselves with the locals by arranging tournaments; one Communist dictator after another appeared on the stands, as one relieved another following bloody coups. Nevertheless, Communism tore down much of the foundations of *buzkashi* fights. When collectivisation started few could afford to keep a stable of well-trained horses. The *buzkashi* horses were scattered to the four winds and used as farm-horses. When the landowners disappeared so did the fighting horses and the riders.

The Taliban forbade the fights and classified them as un-Islamic. This one now is the first big *buzkashi* fight since the fall of the Taliban.

Mansur has found a place right at the front; sometimes he has to retreat fast to avoid being trampled on by rearing horses. He takes lots of pictures, of the horses' bellies, which appear towering over him; of the whirling dust; the battered calf; of a tiny Karzai at a great distance; and a victorious Dostum. After the fight he takes a picture of himself beside one of the *buzkashis*.

The sun is setting and sends red rays over the dusty plain. The pilgrims too are covered in dust. Outside the arena they find a café. They sit on thin mats opposite each other and eat in silence. Soup, rice, mutton and raw onion. Mansur gobbles the food and orders another round. They silently greet some men who sit in a circle near them, arm-wrestling. When the tea is served, the talk can begin.

'From Kabul?' ask the men.

Mansur nods.

'Pilgrimage?'

The men hesitate. 'We're actually travelling with quail,' an old, toothless man answers. 'From Herat. We've made a big circle, Kandahar, Kabul and then up here. This is where the best quail fights are.'

He carefully takes a small bag out of his pocket. Out of it trips a bird, a dishevelled little quail. 'It has won all the fights we have entered it for,' he says. 'We have won pots of money. Now it's worth several thousand dollars,' he boasts. The old man feeds the quail with worn, crooked fingers, like eagle's claws. The quail shakes its feathers and wakes up. It is so tiny that it fits into the man's large, rough fist. They are labourers who have taken time off. After five years of secret quail-fighting, hidden from the Taliban, they can now live their passion, to watch two birds pecking each other to death. Or rather, shout with joy, when their own little quail pecks another to death.

'Come tomorrow morning, early, at seven. That's when we'll start,' the old man says. As they are leaving he presses a large piece of hashish on them. 'The best in the world,' he says. 'From Herat.'

In the hotel they try out the hashish and roll one joint after another. Then they sleep like stones for twelve hours.

Mansur wakes up with a start at the mullah's call to prayer. It is half-past twelve. Prayer starts in the mosque outside. Friday prayer. He suddenly feels he cannot live on without Friday prayer. He must go and he must be on time. He has forgotten his *shalwar kameez* in Kabul, the tunic and wide-legged trousers. He cannot go to Friday prayer in his western clothes. He is desperate. Where can he buy proper prayer clothes? All shops are closed. He rages and swears.

'Allah won't mind what you are wearing,' grumbles Akbar sleepily, hoping to get rid of him.

'I must wash, and the water has been turned off in the hotel,' Mansur whimpers. But there is no Leila to blame and Akbar sends him packing when he starts moaning. But water. A Muslim cannot pray without washing his face, hands and feet. Mansur moans again, 'I won't make it.'

'There's water by the mosque,' says Akbar and closes his eyes once more.

Mansur runs out in his dirty travel clothes. How could he forget his tunic on a pilgrimage? Or the prayer cap? He curses his forgetfulness and runs out to the blue mosque to make it on time. By the entrance is a beggar with a club foot. The stiff leg is swollen and discoloured and lies across the path, infected. Mansur tears the prayer cap off him.

'You'll get it back,' he calls and runs off with the grey-white cap. It has a thick yellow-brown sweatband round the edge.

He leaves his shoes by the entrance and walks barefoot over the marble flagstones. They have been polished smooth by thousands of naked feet. He washes hands and feet, pushes the cap down on his head and walks over to the row of men who lie facing Mecca. He made it. In many tens of rows with at least one hundred to a row, pilgrims sit, head bowed, in the huge space. Mansur sits down at the back and follows the prayers; after a while he is right in the midst of the crowd – several rows have been added as more people arrive. He is the only one wearing western clothes, but he pays attention, forehead to the ground, bottom in the air, fifteen times. He recites the prayers he knows and listens to Rabbani's Friday prayer, a repetition from the day before.

Prayers take place by a barrier round the mosque behind which the helplessly sick sit and wait for healings. They have been confined behind high fences so as not to infect the healthy. Pale, consumptive old men with sunken cheeks pray that Ali will give them strength. Amongst them are also the mentally retarded. A teenage boy claps his hands frantically, while an older brother tries to calm him down. But the majority of them gaze dully out through the bars. Mansur has never seen so many terminally ill people. The group smells of sickness and death. Only the most ill have been allowed the honour to sit here and ask Ali for healing. Up against the tomb's walls they sit cheek by jowl; the closer to the blue mosaic wall, the closer to healing.

In two weeks they will all be dead, thinks Mansur. He catches the eye of a man with piercing black eyes and deep, red scars. The long bony arms are full of rashes and sores, which have been scratched until they bleed, as are the legs that poke out of his tunic. But he has beautiful, thin, pale pink lips. Lips like petals from spring's apricot flowers.

Mansur shivers and turns away. His gaze sweeps the next compound. There are the sick women and children. Faded blue burkas cradling children. A mother has fallen asleep, while her mongoloid child tries to say something. But it is like talking to a statue under a blue covering. Maybe the mother has been walking for days, barefoot, to get to the mosque and Ali's grave in time for New Year's Eve. Maybe she carried the child in her arms – to heal it. No doctor can help her, maybe Ali can.

Another child hits its head rhythmically with its hands. Some women sit apathetically, others sleep, some are lame or blind. But the majority of them have come with their children. They are waiting for Ali's miracles.

It gives Mansur the creeps. Gripped by the powerful atmosphere he decides to become a new person. He will become a good person and a pious Muslim. He will respect the hour of prayer, give alms, he will fast, go to the mosque, not look at girls before he is married, he will grow a beard, and go to Mecca.

The moment prayers are over and Mansur has made his promises, it starts to rain. The sun is shining and it is raining. The holy building and the slippery flagstones sparkle. The raindrops shine. It pours down. Mansur runs, finds his shoes and the beggar who owns the prayer cap. He throws him some notes and runs over the square in the cooling rain. 'I am blessed,' he cries. 'I have been forgiven! I have been cleansed!'

> *The water said to the dirty one, 'come here.'*
> *The dirty one said, 'I am too ashamed.'*
> *The water replied, 'How will your shame be washed away*
> *without me?'*

The Smell of Dust

Steam rises from damp bodies. Hands move in quick, rhythmic motions. The sun's rays creep in through two peepholes in the roof, bathing bottoms, breasts and thighs in a picturesque light. Initially the bodies in the room can be seen only dimly through the steam, until one gets used to the magical light. The faces show concentration. This is not pleasure, but hard work.

In two large halls women scrub themselves, lying, sitting or standing. They scrub themselves, each other or their children. Some are Rubenesquely fat, others thin as rakes, with protruding ribs. With large homemade hemp gloves they scrub each other's backs, arms, legs. Hard skin under the feet is scraped off with pumice. Mothers scrub their marriageable daughters whilst carefully scrutinising their bodies. There is not much time before young girls with birdlike chests become breast-feeding mothers. Thin teenage girls have broad stretch marks from births their bodies were not yet ready for. Nearly all the women's bellies have cracked skin from giving birth too early and too frequently.

The children shout and squeal, from fear or joy. Those who are scrubbed and rinsed play with the washbowls. Others howl in pain and wriggle about like fish caught in a net. No one is given a rag to protect eyes from soap. Mothers scrub them with the hemp gloves until the dirty, dark-brown bodies are pink. Bathing and washing is a battle children are condemned to lose, in their mothers' firm fists.

Leila rolls dirt and loose skin off her body. Black strips are rubbed off, into the hemp glove or down on to the floor. Several weeks have passed since Leila washed properly and many months since she visited the hammam. There is not often water at home and Leila does not see the need to wash too often – you only get dirty again anyway.

But today she has accompanied her mother and cousins to the hammam. As unmarried women she and her cousins are especially shy, and have kept their bras and pants on. The hemp glove avoids these places. But arms, thighs, legs, back and neck get rough treatment. Drops of perspiration and water blend on their faces, as they scrub, scrape and scour, the harder the cleaner.

Leila's mother Bibi Gul, who must be nearing seventy, sits naked in a pool on the floor. Her long grey hair, which is normally hidden under a pale-blue shawl, flows down her back. She unties it only in the hammam. It is so long that the ends float around in the pool on the floor. She sits as in a trance, eyes closed, enjoying the heat. Now and again she makes a few lazy efforts at washing. She dips a facecloth in the bowl Leila has put out for her. But she soon gives up, she cannot reach round her tummy and her arms feel too heavy to lift. Her breasts rest heavily over her big stomach. She remains sitting in a trance, stock still, like a big, grey statue.

*

Leila looks over at her mother now and then to assure herself that she is OK, while she scrubs and prattles with her cousins. The nineteen-year-old has a childlike body, in between girl and woman. The whole Khan family are on the plump side, certainly compared to Afghan standards. The fat and the cooking-oil they pour over their food are manifested on their bodies. Deep-fried pancakes, pieces of potato dripping in fat, mutton in seasoned cooking-oil gravy. Leila's skin is pale and immaculate, soft as a baby's bottom. The facial colour changes between white, yellow and pale grey. The life she leads is reflected in her childlike skin that never sees the sun, and her hands — rough and worn like an old woman's. For a long time, Leila felt dizzy and weak — when she eventually went to see the doctor, he said she needed sun and vitamin D.

Paradoxically Kabul is one of the sunniest towns in the world. The sun shines nearly every day of the year, 1,800 metres above sea level. The sun makes cracks in the earth, dries up what were once moist gardens, burns the children's skin. But Leila never sees it. It never reaches the first-floor flat in Mikrorayon, nor in behind her burka. Not one single curative ray gets past the grille. Only when she visits big sister Mariam, who has a backyard in her village house, does she allow the sun to warm her body. But she goes there only on rare occasions.

Leila is the first to get up in the morning and goes to bed last. She lights the stove in the living room with thin sticks, while the sleeping bodies of her family are still snoring. Next she lights the wood-burning stove in the bathroom and boils water for cooking, washing and washing up. Whilst it is still dark she fills bottles, pots and pans with water. There is never electricity at this time of the day and Leila has got used to groping around in the dark.

Sometimes she carries a small lamp. Then she makes tea. It must be ready by half-past six, when the men in the house wake, otherwise she is in trouble. As long as there is water she keeps on filling receptacles. You never know when the water might go off, sometimes after an hour, sometimes after two.

Eqbal squeals every morning like a stuck pig. The howls jar everyone's nerves. He lies on his mat, stretched out or bent double, and refuses to get up. The fourteen-year-old invents new illnesses every day to avoid spending twelve hours in the shop. But there is no mercy. Every day he has to get up eventually, but next day the same performance is repeated.

'You bitch! Lazybones! My socks have got holes in them,' he cries and throws them after Leila. He takes it out on anyone he can, while his real wish is to go to school.

'Leila! The water is cold! There's not enough warm water! Where are my clothes, my socks? Get some tea! Breakfast! Polish my shoes! Why did you get up so late?'

Doors are slammed and walls pounded. The rooms, the corridor and the bathroom are like a battleground. Sultan's sons howl, quarrel and cry. Sultan usually sits on his own with Sonya drinking tea and eating breakfast. Sonya looks after him, Leila does the rest: fills up the washbasins, puts out clothes, pours tea, fries eggs, fetches bread, polishes shoes. The five men of the house are off to work.

With great reluctance she helps her three nephews Mansur, Eqbal and Aimal to get away. No one says thank you, no one ever helps. 'Uneducated children,' Leila hisses under her breath, when the three boys, only a few years younger than her, order her around.

'Haven't we got any milk? I told you to buy some!' Mansur taunts her. 'You parasite,' he adds. If she bristles, he always responds with the same cruel answer: 'Shut up, you old bag.' 'This is not your home, it is my home,' he says fiercely. Leila does not feel it is her home either. It is Sultan's home, for Sultan and his sons and second wife. She, Bulbula, Bibi Gul and Yunus all feel unwelcome in the family. But moving is not an alternative. It is a scandal to split up a family. Besides, they are good servants – Leila is anyway.

Sometimes Leila is bitter that she was not, like her older brother, given away at birth. 'Then I would have attended computer courses and English courses from an early age, and I would have been at university now,' she dreams. 'I would have had fine clothes, I wouldn't have had to slave away.' Leila loves her mother, but she feels that no one really cares about *her*. She has always been at the bottom of the pecking order, where she has remained; Bibi Gul had no more children.

After the chaos of the morning, when Sultan and the sons have left, Leila can relax, drink tea and have breakfast. Then she sweeps the rooms, for the first time of the day. She goes through the rooms with a small broom, bent over, sweeping, sweeping, sweeping. Most of the dust whirls into the air, floats around, and settles down again behind her. The smell of dust never leaves the flat. She never gets rid of the dust, it has settled on her movements, her body, her thoughts. But she scoops up bits of bread, paper scraps and rubbish. Several times each day she sweeps her way through the rooms. Everything takes place on the floor and it quickly gets dirty.

This is the grime she now tries to scrub off her body. It rolls off in fat little rolls. It is the dust that sticks to her life.

'If only I had a house that needed washing just once a day, that stayed clean all day, that I would have to sweep only in the morning,' Leila sighs to her cousins. They agree. The youngest girls of their family, their lives are like hers.

Leila has brought some underwear she wants to wash in the hammam. Normally washing is done in the twilight on a stool by the loo hole in the bathroom. She uses several large basins, one with soap, one without soap, one for whites, one for colours. She washes sheets, blankets, towels and the family's clothes. They are scrubbed and wrung before being hung up. It is difficult to dry them, especially in winter. Ropes have been rigged up outside the block of flats, but clothes are often stolen, so she does not want to hang them up there, unless one of the children watches them until they are dry. Otherwise they hang, closely packed, on the little balcony. The balcony is a few square metres in size and full of food and rubbish: a bag of potatoes, a basket of onions, one of garlic, a large sack of rice, cardboard boxes, old shoes, and a few clothes and other things that no one dares throw away as they might come in useful one day.

At home Leila wears old shaggy, frayed sweaters, spotty shirts and skirts that sweep the floor. The skirts collect the dust she cannot get at. She wears down-at-heel plastic san-dals and a scarf on her head. The only glitter comes from large gold-coloured earrings and smooth bracelets.

'Leila!'

A voice calls her weakly, tired, over the screaming chil-dren. It just manages to drown the splashes that crash on the floor when the women throw water-buckets over each other.

'Leilaaa!'

Bibi Gul has woken from her trance. She sits holding a cloth, looking helplessly at Leila. Leila takes the hemp glove, soap, shampoo and the basin over to her large, naked mother.

'Lie on your back,' she says. Bibi Gul manoeuvres her torso down on to the floor. Leila rubs and kneads the wobbling body. Bibi Gul laughs; she too sees the comical side to it. The small, neat daughter and the large, old mother. The age difference is somewhere near fifty years. When they laugh the others can smile too. Suddenly everyone laughs.

'You are so fat, Mummy, you'll die of it one day,' Leila ticks her off, while she washes wherever the mother can't reach. Then she rolls her over on to her stomach, helped by her cousins, who each scrub one of Bibi Gul's enormous body parts. Then her long, soft hair is washed. The pink shampoo from China is poured over her scalp. Leila massages carefully as though she is frightened that what is left of the hair will disappear. The shampoo bottle is nearly empty. It is a leftover from the Taliban era. The lady on the bottle has been scribbled out with a thick, waterproof felt pen. When the religious police mutilated Sultan's books, they also tackled packaging. Every lady's face on a shampoo bottle or baby's face on a piece of soap was removed. Living creatures must not be portrayed.

The water is cooling. Children who have not yet been done howl even louder. Soon only cold water remains in the once steaming hammam. The women leave the baths and as they go the dirt is visible. Eggshells and rotten apples lurk in the corners. Lines of muck are left on the floors – the women use the same plastic sandals in the hammam as they do on the village paths, in the outside loos and in their backyards.

Bibi Gul tumbles out with Leila and the cousins in tow. Then on with the clothes. No one brought a change; they pull on the same clothes as the ones they arrived in. The burkas are pulled over clean heads: the burkas with their own odours. Little air gets in and so the burkas have their own peculiar smell. Bibi Gul's reeks of the indeterminable aroma she surrounds herself with, old breath mixed with sweet flowers and something sour. Leila's smells of young sweat and cooking-fumes. Actually, all the Khan family burkas stink of cooking-fumes, because they hang on nails near the kitchen. The women are now spotlessly clean under the burkas and the clothes, but the soft soap and the pink shampoo desperately fight against heavy odds. The women's own smell is soon restored; the burkas force it down over them. The smell of old slave, young slave.

Bibi Gul walks ahead; for once the three young girls linger at the back. They walk together, giggling. In an empty street they whip off the burkas over their heads. Only little boys and dogs roam around here. The cooling wind feels good on their skin, which is still sweating. But the air is not fresh. The back streets and alleyways of Kabul stink of rubbish and sewage. A dirty ditch follows the mud road between the mud huts. But the girls are not aware of the stink from the ditch, or the dust which sticks to their skin and closes their pores. The sun gets to their skin and they laugh. Suddenly a man on a bicycle turns up.

'Cover up, girls, I'm burning,' he shouts as he whizzes past them. They look at each other and laugh at the funny expression on his face, but when he turns up again, they cover up.

'When the King returns, I will never use my burka again,' Leila says, suddenly serious. 'Then we'll have a peaceful country.'

'He'll surely never come back,' the covered-up cousin objects.

'They say he'll return this spring,' says Leila.

But until then it is safest to cover up, the three girls are anyhow alone.

Leila never walks alone. It is not good for a young girl to walk about without company. Who knows where she might be going? Maybe to meet a man, maybe to commit a sin. Leila does not even walk alone to the greengrocer a few minutes away from the apartment. She usually takes a neighbour's boy along with her, or asks him to run errands for her. Alone is an unknown idea for Leila. She has never, ever, anywhere, at any time, been alone. She has never been alone in the apartment, never gone anywhere alone, and never remained anywhere alone, never slept alone. Every night she sleeps on the mat beside her mother. She quite simply does not know what it is to be alone, nor does she miss it. The only thing she wishes for is a bit more peace and not so much to do.

When she gets home, chaos reigns; cases, bags and suitcases everywhere.

'Sharifa has come back! Sharifa!' Bulbula points, happy that Leila has returned and can take over as hostess. Sultan and Sharifa's youngest child, Shabnam, runs around like a happy filly. She hugs Leila, who hugs Sharifa. In the middle of it all, Sultan's second wife Sonya stands smiling, her daughter Latifa on her arm. Unexpectedly, Sultan has brought Sharifa and Shabnam back from Pakistan.

'For the summer,' says Sultan.

'For always,' whispers Sharifa.

Sultan has gone to the bookshop, only the women remain. They sit down in a circle on the floor. Sharifa doles out presents. A dress for Leila, a shawl for Sonya, a bag for

Bulbula, a cardigan for Bibi Gul and clothes and plastic jewellery for the rest of the family. For her sons she has several outfits, bought at Pakistani markets, clothes not available in Kabul. And she has her own precious things. 'No going back,' she says. 'I hate Pakistan.'

But she knows that all rests in Sultan's hands. If Sultan wants her to return, she will have to.

Sultan's two wives sit and prattle like old friends. They inspect the material, try on blouses and jewellery. Sonya pats the things she was given for herself and her little daughter. Sultan rarely brings presents for his young wife, so Sharifa's homecoming is a welcome interruption in her monotonous existence. She dresses Latifa in the pink tutu dress, which makes her look like a doll.

They exchange news. The women have not seen each other for over a year. There is no phone in the flat so they have not spoken either. The major happening in Kabul is Shakila's wedding, which they recount in detail: the presents she got, the dresses they wore, other relations' children, engagements, marriages or deaths.

Sharifa relates news from refugee life. Who has returned home, who has stayed. 'Saliqa is engaged,' she says. 'It had to turn out like that, even if the family were against it. The boy owns nothing, he's lazy too, useless,' she says. Everyone agrees. They all remember Saliqa, always dressed up to kill, but they feel sorry for her because she has to marry a poverty-stricken layabout.

'After they met in the park she was grounded for a month,' Sharifa says. 'Then one day the boy's mother and aunt came to ask for her. Her parents agreed, they had no choice; the damage had already been done. And the engagement party! A scandal!'

The women listen wide-eyed. Especially Sonya. These

are stories she can relate to with all her senses. Sharifa's stories are her soap operas.

'A scandal,' Sharifa repeats, to underline the fact. It is customary that the groom-to-be's family pay for the feast, the dress and the jewels when a young couple get engaged. When they were planning the party, the boy's father put a few thousand rupees in Saliqa's father's hand. Saliqa's father had returned from Europe to help resolve the family tragedy. When he saw the money he just threw it on the floor. 'Do you think you can make an engagement party out of chicken feed?' he shouted. Sharifa was sitting on the stairs listening to it all, so it is absolutely true. 'No, you take your money and we'll foot the bill,' he said.

Saliqa's father wasn't flush with money either. He was waiting to be granted asylum in Belgium and to fetch his family over. Holland had already rejected him and he was now living on money given to him by the Belgian government. But an engagement party is an important symbolic ceremony, and an engagement is virtually unbreakable. If it dissolves the girl will have big problems marrying again, whatever the reason for the break. The engagement party is also an indication to the world how the family is coping. What sort of decorations? What did they cost? What sort of food? What did it cost? What sort of dress? What did it cost? Orchestra, how much did that cost? The party is supposed to show how the boy's family value the new family member. If the feast is miserly, it means they do not appreciate the bride, nor her whole family. That her father had to run up a debt for an engagement party that no one but Saliqa and her sweetheart was happy about meant nothing compared to the shame of hosting a cheap party.

'She's already regretting it,' Sharifa reveals. 'Because he has no money. She soon saw what a good-for-nothing he is.

But it's too late now. If she breaks the engagement no one will want her. She walks around jingling six bracelets he gave her. She says they are gold, but I know, and she knows, that they are metal bracelets painted in gold colour. She didn't even get a new dress for New Year's Eve celebrations. Have you ever known a girl who didn't get a new dress from her fiancé for New Year's Eve?

'He's in their house all day now. Her mother has no control over what they do. Awful, awful, what a disgrace, I have told her,' Sharifa says, before the three others bombard her with new questions.

About that one, and that one and that one. They still have many relatives in Pakistan, aunts, uncles and cousins who do not yet think the situation safe enough to return. Or they have nothing to return to: bombed house, mined land, burnt-down shop. But they all long for home, like Sharifa. It is nearly a year since she last saw her sons.

Leila goes out to the kitchen to make supper. She is glad Sharifa is back, it's right like that, but she dreads the quarrels that will follow, with her sons, in-laws and Leila's mother. She remembers how Sharifa would ask them all to pack their bags and go.

'Take your daughters and just disappear,' she used to say to her mother-in-law, Bibi Gul. 'There's no room here. We want the place to ourselves,' she shrieked when Sultan was not at home. That was when Sharifa ruled the house and Sultan's heart. Only during the last years, after Sultan got himself another wife, has her tone towards Sultan's relatives become milder.

'But we'll have less room,' Leila sighs; no longer eleven, but thirteen in the small rooms. She peels onions and cries bitter onion tears. She rarely cries real tears; she suppresses yearnings, longings and disappointments. The clean smell of soap from the hammam has long gone. Oil from the pan sprays her hair and gives it a smell of acrid fat. Her rough hands ache from the chilli sauce, which penetrates her thin, worn skin.

She cooks a simple supper, nothing special in spite of Sharifa's return. The Khan family is not in the habit of celebrating women. Anyhow, she has to cook what Sultan likes. Meat, rice, spinach and beans, all in mutton fat.

Every evening Sultan returns home with wads of money from his shops. Every evening he locks it into the cupboard. Often he brings home large bags with juicy pomegranates, sweet bananas, mandarins and apples. But the fruit is also locked in the cupboard. Only Sultan and Sonya may eat it. Only they have the key. Sultan thinks it is a heavy burden to feed his large family, and fruit is expensive, especially out of season.

Leila looks at some small, hard oranges lying on the windowsill. They had started to dry out and Sonya put them out in the kitchen – for general use. Leila would not dream of tasting them. If she is condemned to eat beans, eat beans she will. The oranges can lie there until they rot or dry out. Leila tosses her head and places the heavy rice pot over the primus. She pours the chopped onion into the oily pan, adds tomatoes, spices and potatoes. Leila is a good cook. She is good at most things. That is why she is put to do everything. During meals she usually sits in the corner by the door, and leaps up if anyone needs anything, or fills up the plates. When she has seen to everyone else, she fills her plate with the remains, some fatty rice and cooked beans.

She has been brought up to serve, and she has become a servant, ordered around by everyone. In step with every new order, respect for her diminishes. If anyone is in a bad mood, Leila suffers. A spot that has not come off a sweater, meat that has been badly cooked; there are many things one can think of when one needs someone to vent one's wrath on.

When relatives invite the family to a party, Leila turns up early in the morning, having made breakfast for her own family, to peel potatoes, make stock, chop vegetables. And when the guests arrive, she has barely time to change clothes, before continuing to serve and then spend the remainder of the party in the kitchen with the washing up. She is like Cinderella, except there is no prince in Leila's world.

Sultan returns home with Mansur, Eqbal and Aimal. He kisses Sonya in the hall, and greets Sharifa briefly in the sitting room. They spent a whole day in the car from Peshawar to Kabul and have no need for any more conversation. Sultan and the sons sit down. Leila brings in a pewter washbasin and a can. She places the basin in front of each one in turn, they wash their hands, and she hands them a towel. The plastic cloth has been laid on the floor and the meal can be served.

Yunus, Sultan's younger brother, has come home and greets Sharifa warmly. He asks for latest news from relatives, and then, as usual, says nothing. He rarely talks during meals. He is quiet and sober and seldom joins in the family conversations. It is as though he does not care and keeps his unhappiness to himself. The 28-year-old is deeply discontented with his life.

'A dog's life,' he says. Work from dawn to dusk, and crumbs from his brother's table.

Yunus is the only one Leila dances attendance on. She loves this brother. Sometimes he comes home with little presents, a plastic buckle, a comb.

This evening something is bothering Yunus. But he waits to ask. Sharifa takes the wind out of his sails and blurts out: 'It's a bit of a mess with Belqisa. Her father is keen, but the mother says no. Initially the mother said yes, but then she talked to a relative who had a son, a younger son, who wanted to marry Belqisa. They have offered money and the mother has started to doubt. This relative has spread rumours about our family. That's all I can tell you.'

Yunus blushes and scowls silently. The whole situation is embarrassing. Mansur sneers. 'The granddaughter won't marry grandfather,' he mumbles under his breath, so Yunus hears it but not Sultan. Yunus's last hope is reversed and rejected. He feels tired, tired of waiting, tired of seeking, tired of living in a box.

'Tea!' he commands, in order to interrupt Sharifa's flow of words on why Belqisa's family do not want their daughter to marry him. Leila gets up. She is disappointed that Yunus's marriage seems to be dragging on. She had hoped that when Yunus married he would take her and her mother with him. They could all live together; Leila would be so good, so good. She would instruct Belqisa, she would do all the heavy chores. Belqisa could even continue her education if she wanted to. All would be well. Anything to get out of Sultan's household where no one appreciates her. Sultan complains that her cooking is not according to his likes, that she eats too much and that she does not obey Sonya in everything. Mansur is always over her, pecking at her. Often he tells her to go to hell. 'I care about no one who has no significance for my future,' he says. 'And you, you mean nothing to me. You are a parasite, off with you,' he laughs contemptuously, knowing full well that she has nowhere to go.

Leila brings the tea. Weak green tea. She asks Yunus

whether he would like her to press his trousers for the next day. She has just washed them and Yunus has only two pairs, so she needs to know whether he wants to wear the clean ones. Yunus nods silently.

'My aunt is so stupid,' Mansur keeps on saying. 'Whenever she wants to say something, I know what she's going to say. She is the most boring person I know,' he laughs scornfully and mimics her. He has grown up with his three-years-older aunt, not like a brother, but like a master.

It is true that Leila often repeats herself, because she thinks she is not being heard. On the whole she talks about everyday things, because that is her world. But she can laugh and shine, with her cousins, sisters or nieces. She can surprise everyone with funny stories. Her whole face can transform itself with laughter. But not during family suppers – then she is mostly silent. Sometimes she laughs at her nephews' crude jokes, but as she told her cousins in the hammam: 'I laugh with my mouth, not my heart.'

No one says much during Sharifa's first evening meal, following the disappointing news about Belqisa. Aimal plays with Latifa, Shabnam plays with her dolls, Eqbal talks noisily with Mansur and Sultan flirts with Sonya. The others eat in silence, then the family goes to bed. Sharifa and Shabnam are allocated places in the room where Bibi Gul, Leila, Bulbula, Eqbal, Aimal and Fazil already sleep. Sultan and Sonya keep their room. At midnight everyone is on the mats, all except one.

Leila cooks by the light of a candle. Sultan likes home-made food during the day at work. She cooks a chicken in oil, rice, makes a vegetable sauce. While it is cooking she washes up. The flame from the candle lights up her face. There are big, dark rings round her eyes. When the food is done she takes the pan from the hotplate, winds pieces of cloth round it and knots it tightly to keep the lid from falling off when Sultan and his sons take it with them next morning. She washes the oil off her fingers and goes to bed, in the same clothes she has been using all day. She rolls out her mattress, pulls a blanket over her and falls asleep, until the mullah wakes her a few hours later. A new day begins, to the sound of 'Allahu akhbar' – 'God is great'.

A new day which smells and tastes like every other day: of dust.

An Attempt

One afternoon Leila pulls the burka over her head, puts on her high-heeled outdoor shoes and sneaks out of the flat; past the broken entrance-door, the washing hanging out, out to the yard. She picks up a little neighbourhood boy as escort and chaperone. They cross the bridge over the dried-up Kabul River and disappear under the trees on one of Kabul's few avenues. They pass shoe-blacks, melon-vendors and bakers, and men who just stand around and hang about. Those are the ones Leila hates, the ones with time on their hands, the ones who take time to gape.

The leaves on the trees are green for the first time in many years. The last three years it hardly rained in Kabul and the sun burnt the buds to cinders. Now, this first spring following the Taliban's flight, it has rained quite a lot, blessed rain, wonderful rain. Not enough to fill the Kabul River to its banks, but enough to make the few surviving trees sprout and turn green. Enough to allow the dust to settle now and again, the dust, the fine dust which is Kabul's curse. When it rains the dust turns to mud, when it's dry it whirls around, gets into the nose, causes inflammation of the eyes, sits in the throat and muddies up the lungs. This afternoon it rained and the wind freshened. But the moist air does not penetrate the burka. Leila is aware only of the smell of her own nervous breathing and her temples pulsating.

On a concrete block of flats in Mikrorayon no. 4 big signs have been hung with the word 'Courses'. The queues outside are long. There are literacy courses, computer courses and writing courses. Leila wants to sign up for an English course. Outside the entrance two men sit at a table to register new pupils. Leila pays the fee and joins the queue with hundreds of others who are trying to find their classroom. They descend some stairs and enter a cellar, which looks like a bomb shelter. The bullet holes form patterns on the walls. The premises were used for storing weapons during the civil war, right under a block of flats. Planks divide the various 'classrooms'. Each cubicle has a blackboard, a pointer and some benches. There are even desks in some of the cubicles. There is a low drone of voices; the heat starts to spread in the room.

Leila finds her section, 'slightly advanced English'. She is early; so are some gangly, loutish boys.

Can it be possible? Boys in the class? she wonders. She wants to turn and disappear but steels herself. She goes and sits at the back. Two girls sit quietly in the other corner. The voices from the other cubicles blend in one low buzz. Sharp teachers' voices penetrate the walls. Some time passes before their teacher turns up. The boys start scribbling on the blackboard. 'Pussy', they write. 'Dick, Fuck'. Leila regards the words uninterestedly. She has an English/Persian dictionary and looks the words up, under the table, so the boys won't see it. But she cannot find the words. She feels great distaste for the whole situation: alone, or nearly alone, with a gang of boys her own age, some of them even a bit older. She should never have come, she regrets it. What if some of the boys started talking to her? What a disgrace. And she has even taken off her burka. You cannot wear a burka in the classroom, she had thought. And now she has already exposed her face.

The teacher arrives and the boys quickly rub out the words. The hour is torture. They all have to present themselves, give their age and say something in English. The teacher, a thin, young man, points at her with the ruler and asks her to speak. She feels she is turning her soul inside out, in front of these boys. She feels dirty, exposed, her honour impaired. What on earth was she thinking of? She had never dreamt that there would be boys and girls in the same class, never, it was not her fault.

She dares not leave. The teacher would ask her why. But when the hour is over she rushes out. Throws the burka on and dashes off. Safely home she hangs the burka on the nail in the hall.

'Awful, there were boys in the class!'

The others stare open-mouthed. 'That's no good,' says her mother. 'You mustn't go there again.'

Leila would not even dream of going back. The Taliban might have disappeared but they were still present in Leila's head, and in Bibi Gul's and Sharifa's and in Sonya's. The women in Mikrorayon were glad the Taliban era was over, they could play music, they could dance, paint their toenails – as long as no one saw them, and they could hide under the safe burka. Leila was a true child of the civil war, the mullah reign and the Taliban. A child of fear. She cried inside. The attempt to break away, do something independent, learn something, had failed. During five years of Taliban reign girls' education had been forbidden. Now it was allowed, but she forbade herself. If only Sultan had allowed her to go to high school there would not have been a problem. There the classes were segregated.

She sat down on the kitchen floor to chop onions and potatoes. Sonya was eating a fried egg and nursing Latifa. Leila could not bear to talk to her. The stupid girl who had not even learnt the alphabet. Who did not even try. Sultan got her a private tutor to teach her to read and write. But nothing stuck, every hour was like the first one, and having learnt five letters in as many months, she gave up and asked Sultan if she could stop. Mansur had laughed scornfully from the outset at Sonya's private literacy course. 'When a man has everything and does not know what more to do, he tries to teach his donkey to talk,' he said aloud and laughed. Even Leila, who on the whole disliked everything Mansur said, had to laugh at the joke.

Leila tried to lord it over Sonya and reprimanded her when she said something stupid or was unable to manage, but only when Sultan was away. To Leila Sonya was the poor country bumpkin who had been lifted up into their relative wealth only because she was pretty. She disliked her for the many privileges Sultan gave her and because the two girls although the same age had such dissimilar workloads. She had nothing personal against Sonya, who sat around with a mild, absent expression, watching what was happening around her. She wasn't really lazy either; she had been a good worker at home, looking after her parents in the village. But Sultan would not let her work hard. When he was away, she often helped. Nevertheless, she got on Leila's nerves. She sat all day, waiting for Sultan, and jumped up when he returned. When he was away on business she dressed shabbily. When he was at home she powdered her dark face, blackened her eyes and painted her lips.

Sonya had made the transition from child to wife when she was sixteen. She cried before the wedding, but like a well-behaved girl, she soon got used to the idea. She had grown up without any expectations from life and Sultan had used the two-month-long period of engagement to his advantage. He had bribed her parents to enable him to spend time alone with Sonya before the wedding. The engaged couple are not supposed to see each other between the engagement party and the wedding day, a custom rarely observed. But it was one thing to go shopping together, quite another to spend nights together. That was unheard of. Her big brother wanted to defend her honour with a knife when he learnt that Sultan had paid the parents money to be allowed to stay overnight before the wedding night. But Sonya's indignant brother, too, was silenced with ready cash and Sultan got his way. In his eyes he did her a favour.

'I must prepare her for the wedding night, she is very young and I am experienced,' he told the parents. 'If we spend time together now the wedding night won't be so shocking. But I promise I will not assault her,' he said. Gradually he prepared the sixteen-year-old for the great night.

Two years on Sonya is satisfied with her drab existence. She wants nothing more than to sit at home, with a few visits to or from relatives, a new dress from time to time, every fifth year a gold bracelet.

Sultan once took her on a business trip to Teheran. They were away for a month and the women in Mikrorayon were curious to hear what she had experienced abroad. But when she returned, Sonya had nothing to relate. They had stayed with relatives and she had played with Latifa on the floor, as usual. She had only just glimpsed Teheran and had no wish to explore further. The only thing she remarked on were the bazaars; there were nicer things in the Teheran bazaars than in the Kabul bazaars.

The most important thing on Sonya's mind is to have children, or rather, sons. She is pregnant again and terrified it will be another daughter. When Latifa pulls her shawl off and starts playing with it, Sonya slaps her and ties it round her head. When the last-born plays with the mother's shawl, the next child will be a girl, so the saying goes.

'If I have a daughter, Sultan will take a third wife,' she says after the two sisters-in-law have been squatting some time in silence on the kitchen floor.

'Has he said so?' Leila is surprised.

'He said so yesterday.'

'He only says it to frighten you.'

Sonya is not listening. 'It must not be a daughter, it must not be a daughter,' she mutters. The one-year-old she is nursing is lulled to sleep by her mother's monotonous voice.

Leila is not in the mood for talking. She needs to get out. She knows she cannot sit at home all day with Sonya, Sharifa, Bulbula and her mother. I'm going mad. I cannot stand it any longer, she thinks. I don't belong here.

She thinks of Fazil and the way in which Sultan treated him. It was that which made her realise that the time had come to stand on her own two feet, to try the English course.

The eleven-year-old had worked every day carrying boxes in the bookshop, eaten with them every evening, and slept on the mat curled up beside Leila every night. Fazil is Mariam's oldest son, and Sultan and Leila's nephew.

Mariam and her husband could not afford to feed all their children, and when Sultan needed help in the shop they gladly accepted the offer of board and lodging with Sultan for their son. Payment was Fazil's daily twelve-hour labours. He was let off on Fridays to visit his mother and father in the village.

Fazil thrived. He tidied up the shop and carried cases during the day and fought with Aimal at night. The only person he could not get on with was Mansur who slapped him or hit his back with his clenched fist when he made mistakes. But Mansur could be kind too. Suddenly he might take him to a shop and buy him some new clothes, or even take him to a restaurant and buy him a nice lunch. On the whole Fazil enjoyed life, far removed from the muddy streets of his native village.

But one day Sultan said: 'I'm fed up with you. Go home. Don't show yourself in the shop any more.'

The family was stunned. Had he not promised Mariam to look after the boy for a year? No one said anything, nor did Fazil. But when he lay on his mat that night he cried. Leila tried to console him, but it was no good, Sultan's word was law.

The next morning she packed up his few belongings and sent him home. It would be up to him to explain to his mother why he had been sent home.

Leila was livid. How could Sultan treat Fazil like that? She might be next in line. It was time to think of something.

Leila hatched a new plan. One morning when Sultan and the sons had left, she pulled the burka over her head and disappeared out of the door. This time too she grabbed a little boy to accompany her. Today she chose another way, out of Mikrorayon, out of the appalling concrete jungle. On the outskirts of the neighbourhood the houses were so ruined they had remained unoccupied. Nevertheless, some families had taken shelter in the ruins and survived by begging from their almost equally poor neighbours, who at least had a roof over their heads. Leila crossed a little field where a herd of goats grazed the sparse clumps of grass while the goatherd dozed under the only remaining shade-giving tree. This was the border between town and village. On the other side of the field was the village Deh Khudaidad. But first she dropped in on big sister Shakila.

The gate was opened by Said, the oldest son of Wakil, the man Shakila had recently married. Said was missing two fingers from one hand. He had lost them when a car battery he was fixing exploded. But he told everyone that he had tripped over a mine. There was more status in being injured by a mine; he might have been fighting in the war. Leila did not like him, she found him simple and coarse. He could neither read nor write and spoke like a peasant, like Wakil. She shuddered at the thought of him. He gave her a crooked smile and grazed her burka as she walked past him. She shuddered once again. She shuddered at the thought of being yoked to him. Many of the family had tried to hook them up. Shakila and Wakil had both asked Bibi Gul for her.

'Too early,' Bibi Gul said.

'About time,' said Sultan. No one asked Leila and Leila would not have answered. A well-behaved girl does not answer questions about whether she likes so-and-so or not. But she hoped, hoped to escape.

Shakila arrived, hips swaying, smiling, beaming. All fear as regards her marriage to Wakil was unfounded. She was continuing to work as a biology teacher. His children worshipped her; she wiped their noses and washed their clothes. She made her husband fix the house and give her money for new curtains and cushions. She sent the children to school; Wakil and his first wife had not bothered much about that. When the oldest sons grumbled because they found it embarrassing to sit in the same classroom as little children, she just said: 'It will be a lot more embarrassing later if you don't go.'

Shakila was over the moon. At last she had a man. Her eyes sparkled. She looked in love. After thirty-five years as an old maid she had adjusted brilliantly to the role of housewife.

The sisters kissed each other on both cheeks, pulled the burkas over their heads and strode out of the gate, Leila in black, high-heeled shoes, Shakila wearing the white, sky-high, gold-buckled pumps, the wedding shoes. Shoes are important when neither body nor clothes, hair nor face can be exposed.

They skipped over puddles, avoided coagulated mud and deep ruts, while the gravel ground through the thin soles. The road was the road to school. Leila was en route to apply for work as a teacher. This was her secret plan.

Shakila had made enquiries at the village school where she worked. There was no English teacher. In spite of Leila having completed only nine years at school, she felt confident that she could teach beginners. When she lived in Pakistan she had attended English evening classes.

The school lies behind a mud enclosure. The wall is too high to see over. An old man sits by the entrance. He makes sure no intruders are admitted, especially men, as this is a girls' school and all the teachers are women. The play-ground was once a grass pitch, now it's a potato patch.

Round the patch cubicles have been built into the wall. The classrooms have three walls: the back enclosure and the two side walls. The playground side is open, so the school head can observe what is going on in all the class-rooms. In each cubicle there are some benches, tables and a blackboard. Only the older girls have stools and tables; the younger ones sit on the ground and follow what goes on on the blackboard. Many of the students cannot afford exercise books but write on little boards or bits and pieces of paper they have found.

Confusion reigns. Daily new pupils turn up who want to start school; the classes are getting bigger and bigger. The authorities' school campaign has been very visible. All over the country large banners have gone up depicting smiling children carrying books. 'Back to school' is the only text necessary, the picture tells the rest.

When Shakila and Leila arrive the inspector is busy with a young woman who wants to register as a pupil. She says she has completed three classes and wants to start the fourth.

'I cannot find you on our lists,' the inspector says, leaf-ing through the card index, which by chance has been left lying in a cupboard during the entire Taliban era. The woman is silent.

'Can you read and write?' the inspector asks.

The woman hesitates. In the end she admits she has never attended school.

'But it would have been nice to start in the fourth class,' she whispers. 'It is so embarrassing to be with the little ones in the first class.'

The inspector says that if she wants to learn anything she will have to start from the beginning, in the first class, a class consisting of five-year-olds up to teenagers. The woman would have been the oldest. She thanks the inspector and leaves.

Then it's Leila's turn. The inspector remembers her from before the Taliban. Leila had been a pupil at this school and the inspector would welcome her as a teacher.

'First you have to register,' she says. 'You must go to the Ministry of Education with your papers and apply for a job here.'

'But you don't have an English teacher, can't you apply for me? Or I can start now and register later,' asks Leila.

'Impossible. You must get personal clearance from the authorities, those are the rules.'

The yells from noisy girls penetrate the open office. A teacher swipes them with a branch to quieten them as they tumble into the classrooms.

Leila walks out of the gate feeling depressed. The sound of excited children fades. She plods home, forgetting that she is stumping along alone on high-heeled shoes. How will she get to the Ministry of Education without anyone noticing? The plan was to get a job and then tell Sultan. If he knew about it beforehand he would put his foot down, but if she already had a job he might let her continue. The teaching was in any case only a few hours each day; she would just have to get up even earlier and work even harder.

Her school certificate is in Pakistan. She feels like giving up. But then she remembers the dark flat and the dusty floors in Mikrorayon and she goes to the nearby telegraph office. She phones some relatives in Peshawar and asks them to retrieve her papers. They promise to help and will send them with anyone who is coming to Kabul. The Afghan postal service is not operating and most things are sent with people travelling.

The papers arrive in a few weeks. Next step is to go to the Ministry of Education. But how will she get there? She cannot go alone. She asks Yunus but he doesn't think she should work. 'You never know what kind of job they might give you,' he says. 'Stay at home and look after your old mother.'

Her favourite brother is of no help. Her nephew Mansur only snorts when she asks him. She is getting nowhere. The school year started ages ago. 'It is too late,' says her mother. 'Wait until next year.'

Leila despairs. 'Maybe I don't want to teach,' she thinks, to make it easier to bury the plans.

Leila is at a standstill; a standstill in the mud of society and the dust of tradition. She has reached the deadlock in a system which is rooted in centuries-old traditions and which paralyses half the population. The Ministry of Education is a half-hour bus ride away; an impossible half-hour. Leila is not used to fighting for something – on the contrary, she is used to giving up. But there must be a way out. She just has to find it.

Can God Die?

The everlasting boredom of the detention homework is threatening to overwhelm Fazil. He wants to leap up and howl, but restrains himself, as an eleven-year-old should who has been punished for not knowing his homework. His hand moves haltingly across the page. He writes in small letters so as not to take up too much room; exercise books are expensive. The light from the gas lamp throws a reddish glow over the paper, like writing on flames, he thinks.

In the corner his grandmother sits glaring at him with one eye. The other one was lost when she fell into an oven which was cemented into the floor. His mother Mariam is breast-feeding two-year-old Osip. He is exhausted and his writing frenzied. He must finish, even if it takes him all night. He can't bear the blow over the knuckles from the teacher's ruler. He can't bear the shame.

He must write ten times what God is: God is the creator, God is eternal, God is almighty, God is good, God is truth, God is life, God sees all, God hears all, God is omniscient, God is omnipotent, God rules all, God . . .

The reason for the detention work was his inability to answer correctly during the lesson on Islam. 'I never answer properly,' he moans to his mother. 'Because when I see the teacher I get so nervous I forget. He's always angry, and even if you only make a tiny mistake he hates you.'

From start to finish, everything had gone wrong when Fazil was asked to come up to the blackboard and answer questions about God. He had done his lessons, but when he got up to the blackboard he remembered nothing. He must have thought of something else while he was reading. The Islam teacher, the man with the long beard, turban, tunic and loose trousers, had turned on him with his black piercing eyes and asked: 'Can God die?'

'No.' Fazil trembled beneath his gaze. Whatever he said, it was bound to be wrong.

'Why not?'

Fazil is tongue-tied. Why can't God die? Can no knives pierce him? Can no bullets injure him? Thoughts rush through his head.

'Well?' the teacher says. Fazil blushes and stutters, but utters not a word. Another boy is allowed to answer. 'Because he is eternal,' he says promptly.

'Right. Can God talk?' the teacher continues.

'No,' says Fazil. 'Or rather, yes.'

'If you think he can talk, how does he talk?' the teacher asks.

Fazil is speechless yet again. How does he talk? With a thunderous voice, low, whispering?

'Well, you say he can talk, does he have a tongue?' the teacher asks.

Does God have a tongue?

Fazil tries hard to imagine what the correct answer might be. He does not think God has a tongue, but dares say nothing. It is better to say nothing, than to give a wrong answer and be laughed at by the whole class. Again another boy is allowed to answer.

'He talks through the Koran,' he says. 'The Koran is his tongue.'

'Correct. Can God see?'

Fazil realises the teacher is fiddling with the ruler and hitting the palm of his hand gently, as if practising the blows that will any moment rain over Fazil's knuckles.

'Yes,' says Fazil.

'How does he see? Does he have eyes?'

Fazil hesitates before saying: 'I've never seen God. How do I know?'

The blows rained down over Fazil until the tears flowed. He must surely be the stupidest boy in the class. The pain was nothing compared to the shame of standing there. Then he was given detention homework.

'If you cannot learn this, you cannot continue in the class,' he concluded.

Having written what God is ten times, he must learn it off by heart. He mumbles under his breath and repeats it aloud to his mother. Finally it sticks. The grandmother pities her grandchild. She has no education and thinks the homework is too difficult for the little boy. She holds a glass of tea in the stumps that remain of her hands and slurps.

'When the Prophet Muhammad drank, he never made a sound,' Fazil says sternly. 'Every time he took a sip he removed the glass from his lips three times and thanked God,' he relates.

The one-eyed grandmother steals a glance at him and says: 'Really, you don't say.'

The next part of the homework is about the life of the

Prophet. He has reached the chapter which deals with his habits, and he reads aloud, his finger tracing the letters, from right to left.

"'The Prophet Muhammad, peace be upon him, always squatted on the ground. There was no furniture in his house. A man's life ought to be like that of a traveller, resting in the shade, then continuing on his way. A house must be nothing more than a place to rest, a protection against cold and heat, against wild animals and a place where privacy is preserved.

"'Muhammad, peace be upon him, was in the habit of resting on his left arm. When he meditated, he liked to dig in the earth with a shovel or a stick, or he sat on the ground with his arms around his legs. When he slept he slept on his right side, and the palm of his right hand lay under his face. Sometimes he slept lying on his back; sometimes he crossed one leg over the other, always making sure that each part of the body was covered up. He hated lying face down and forbade others to do so. He did not like sleeping in a dark room or on a rooftop. He always washed before going to bed and recited prayers until he fell asleep. When he slept he snored quietly. If he woke at night to urinate, he washed his hands and his face when he had finished. He wore a loincloth in bed but usually took off his shirt. As houses were without latrines in those days the Prophet might walk several miles out of town in order to be out of sight and he chose soft ground to avoid being sprayed. He made sure he was out of sight behind a stone or a rise. He bathed behind a blanket or in a loincloth when bathing in the rain. When he blew his nose he always used a rag.'"

Fazil continues to read aloud about the Prophet's feeding habits. He liked dates, preferably mixed with milk or butter; he preferred the neck and side of an animal, but never ate onions or garlic because he disliked bad breath; before sitting down to a meal he took his shoes off and washed his hands; he used his right hand when he ate, and ate only from his side of the bowl, never reaching his hand into the middle of the bowl. He never used cutlery, and used but three fingers when he ate. Every time a morsel entered his mouth he thanked God.

And: he drank without making a sound.

He closes the book.

'Go to bed, Fazil.'

Mariam has made his bed up in the room where they were eating. Three siblings are already snoring away. But Fazil still has to mug up prayers in Arabic. He swots up on the incomprehensible words from the Koran and then collapses on to his mat, fully clothed. He must be at school at seven next morning. He shudders. First lesson is Islam. He falls asleep exhausted, sleeps restlessly and dreams that he is being examined and answers everything incorrectly. He knows the answers, but can't get them out.

High above his head heavy clouds gather over the village. After he has fallen asleep rain pours down. It falls on the mud roof and drums on the flagstones. Drops fasten themselves to the plastic sheeting covering the windows. A cool air current enters the room; grandmother wakes and turns over. 'God be praised,' she says when she sees the rain. She touches her face with the stumps, as in a prayer, turns over again and falls asleep. Around her four children breathe quietly.

When Fazil is woken at half-past five the next morning the rain has died down and the sun sends its first rays over the heights surrounding Kabul. When he has washed in the water his mother has put out, dressed and packed his rucksack, the sun is busy drying the rain puddles. Fazil drinks tea and eats breakfast before running off. He is cross and crabby and thinks his mother is not quick enough when he asks for something. His only thought is the Islam lesson.

Mariam spoils her oldest son. He gets the best food and the most care. She worries about not giving him food adequate for his brain. When, on rare occasions, she has money to spare it is he who gets a new piece of clothing. She has great hopes for him. She remembers how content she was eleven years ago. Her marriage to Karimullah was happy. She remembers the birth and the joy of having a boy. A big feast was held and she and her son received wonderful gifts. There were visits and much rejoicing. Two years later she gave birth to a girl; no more feasting or presents.

Her marriage to Karimullah lasted only a few years. When Fazil was three his father was killed in an exchange of fire. Mariam was a widow and thought life had come to an end. The one-eyed mother-in-law and her own mother, Bibi Gul, decided that she must marry Karimullah's younger brother Hazim. But he was not like his big brother, not as clever, not as strong. The civil war destroyed Karimullah's shop and they had to make do with Hazim's salary as a customs officer.

But Fazil, he is going to study and become famous, she hopes. Initially she thought he might work in her brother Sultan's shop. She thought a bookshop might be an enterprising environment. Sultan had taken on the responsibility of feeding him and Fazil had eaten better there than at home. She cried the entire day Sultan sent Fazil home. She worried he had misbehaved, but she knew Sultan's moods and realised that he no longer needed a crate-carrier.

Then her younger brother Yunus said he would try and get Fazil into Esteqlal, one of Kabul's best schools. Fazil was lucky and started in the fourth class. Everything had worked out for the best, Mariam realised. She thought about Aimal, Sultan's son, who hardly ever saw the sun, but worked from early morning till late at night in one of Sultan's shops, and was horrified.

She strokes Fazil's hair as he runs out of the house and down the mud path. He tries to avoid the puddles and jumps from tuft to tuft. Fazil must cross the village to get to the bus stop. He gets on at the front of the bus, where the men sit, and bumps along into Kabul.

He is one of the first into the classroom and sits down on his seat in row three. One by one the boys enter. Most of them are thin and shabbily dressed. Some wear clothes that are far too big, probably passed down from older brothers. There is a blissful mixture of style. Some still wear the Taliban-stipulated dress for men and boys. The trouser-bottoms have been added to with pieces of cloth sewn on as the boys grow. Others have produced seventies trousers and jerseys from basements and lofts, clothes used by their big brothers before the Taliban came to power. One boy has a pair of jeans. They look like a balloon, tied tightly round the waist. Others wear bell-bottoms. One boy's outer clothes are too tight and he has pulled his underpants up over the short jersey. A few boys have forgotten to zip up their flies. Having worn long tunics since childhood it is easy for them to forget this new unfamiliar mechanism. Some wear the same tatty cotton shirts as worn in Russian orphanages, and they have the same hungry, slightly untamed look. One boy wears a large, threadbare dress jacket, which he has folded up over the elbows.

The boys play and shout and throw things around the room; there is the sound of scraping as they drag the desks around. When the bell goes and the teacher enters all fifty are at their desks. They sit on high wooden benches fastened to the tables. The benches are designed for two, but in order to accommodate them all sometimes three have to share a bench.

When the teacher enters the pupils rise quick as a flash and greet him.

'Salaam alaikum.' – 'The peace of God be with you.'

The teacher walks slowly down the row of seats, making sure the boys all have the correct books and have done their homework. He inspects nails, clothes, shoes. If they are not completely clean at least they are not dirty. That would mean dismissal.

Then the teacher tests them, and this morning they all know their homework.

'Then we'll continue,' he says. '*Haram*,' he says in a loud voice and writes the unfamiliar word on the blackboard. 'Does anyone know what that means?'

A boy puts his hand up. 'Bad behaviour is *haram*.'

He's right. 'Bad behaviour, which is un-Muslim-like, is *haram*,' the teacher says. 'For example, killing someone without a reason. Or punishing someone without a reason. To drink alcohol is *haram*, to take drugs, to sin. To eat pork is *haram*. The infidel, the unbeliever, couldn't care less about *haram*. Much which is *haram* to the Muslim they look upon as good. That is bad.'

The teacher looks out over the class. He draws a diagram with the three ideas, *haram*, *halal*, *mubah*. *Haram* is whatever is bad and forbidden, *halal* is whatever is good and permitted, *mubah* is whatever is doubtful.

'*Mubah* is whatever is not good, but is not sinful either. For example, to eat pork rather than starve to death. Or to hunt; to kill in order to survive.'

The boys write and write. At the end the teacher asks his customary questions to see whether they have understood.

'If a man considers *haram* a good thing, what is he then?' No one answers.

'An infidel.' The Islam teacher answers his own question.

'And is *haram* good or bad?'

Nearly all the hands fly in the air. Fazil is too frightened; he is terrified of giving the wrong answer. He makes himself as small as possible on the third row. The teacher points to one of the boys, who stands up straight by his desk and answers: 'Bad!'

That was what Fazil had wanted to answer. An infidel is bad.

The Dreary Room

Aimal is Sultan's youngest son. He is twelve years old and works twelve hours a day. Every day, seven days a week, he is woken up at daybreak. He curls up again, until Leila or his mother forces him to get up. He washes his pale face, dresses, eats a fried egg with his fingers by dipping bits of bread into the yellow yolk and drinks tea.

At eight in the morning Aimal opens the door to a little booth in the dark lobby of one of Kabul's hotels. Here he sells chocolate, biscuits, soft drinks and chewing gum. He counts money and is bored. He calls the shop 'the dreary room'. His heart bleeds and his tummy churns every time he opens the door. This is where he must sit until he is fetched at eight o'clock in the evening, when it is already dark outside. He goes straight home to eat supper and go to bed.

Immediately outside his door are three tubs. The receptionist tries desperately to collect all the water dripping from the ceiling. Regardless of how many tubs he puts out, there are always large puddles outside Aimal's door and people avoid both them and the shop. The lobby is often blacked out. During the day the heavy curtains are pulled away from the windows, but the daylight cannot penetrate to the dark corners. In the evenings, if there is electricity, the lamps are turned on. If there is no electricity there are large kerosene lamps on the reception counter.

When the hotel was built in the 1960s it was the most up-to-date in Kabul. The foyer was bustling with men in elegant suits and women in short skirts and modern hairdos. Alcohol was served and western music played. Even the King came here, to participate in meetings and to eat dinner.

The sixties and seventies were characterised by Kabul's most liberal regimes; first the reign of 'man about town' Zahir Shah, then that of his cousin Daoud, who cut down on political freedom and filled the prisons with political prisoners, but who at a superficial level allowed partying and western, modern ways. The building contained bars and nightclubs. When the country started to slide, so did the hotel. During the civil war it was completely destroyed. The rooms facing town were riddled by bullets, grenades landed on the balconies and rockets tore down the roof.

After the civil war, when the Taliban took over, the renovation work dragged on. There were few guests and so no need for the wrecked rooms. The reigning mullahs didn't care about developing tourism; on the contrary, they wanted the smallest possible number of foreigners in the country. The roof fell in and the corridors buckled under the unstable framework.

Now that yet another regime wants to stamp its authority on Kabul, work has begun to fill in the holes and replace broken windowpanes. Aimal often watches the repair work or follows keenly the electricians' furious battles with the generator when electricity is needed to supply important meetings with microphones and loudspeakers. The lobby is Aimal's playground. He slides on the water, wanders around. But that, on the whole, is that. Completely boring, completely lonely.

Sometimes he talks to people in this gloomy hall: the men who sweep and wash, the receptionists, the door-man, the security people, a guest or two and the other stall-keepers. They rarely have customers. One man sells traditional Afghan jewellery from behind a counter. He too is bored all day. The demand amongst hotel customers for jewellery is not great. Someone else sells souvenirs, at a price that means no one buys anything or even returns to have a look.

Many shop windows are covered in dust, or covered by curtains or cardboard. 'Ariana Airlines' is written on a broken pane. Once upon a time Afghanistan's national air-line owned many aircraft. Classy air-hostesses served the passengers; whisky and brandy were on the menu. Many planes were destroyed during the civil war, the remainder were bombed to bits by the Americans in their hunt for Osama bin Laden and Mullah Omar. One plane alone escaped the bombs; it was standing at New Delhi airport on September 11. This is the plane that will resurrect Ariana; it still flies Kabul–New Delhi return. But one plane is not enough to reopen the hotel's Ariana office.

At one end of the foyer lies the restaurant which serves Kabul's worst food, but which has the town's nicest wait-ers. It is as though they must compensate for the tasteless rice, the dry chicken and the watery carrots.

In the centre of the lobby is a small enclosure; a couple of square metres. A low wooden fence marks the boundary between the lobby floor and the green carpet inside. Guests, ministers, caretakers, and waiters are constantly seen, side by side, squatting on the small rugs that lie on top of the green carpet. In prayer all are equal. There is also a larger prayer room in the basement, but most people make do with a few minutes on the carpet, in the middle of two groups of chairs and sofas.

All day long a TV, towering on a rickety table in the lobby, broadcasts noisy programmes. It is right outside Aimal's chocolate stall, but he rarely stops to watch. Kabul TV, the one and only Afghan channel, has nothing interesting to report. There are religious programmes, long discussions, a few news bulletins, and lots of traditional music against a backdrop of stills of Afghan scenery. The channel employs female newsreaders, but no singers or dancers. 'People are not ready yet,' say the management. Sometimes Polish or Czech cartoons are shown. Aimal rushes out but is often disappointed. He has seen them before.

Outside the hotel lies what was once its pride – a swimming pool. It was inaugurated with drums beating and flags flying one fine summer's day, and every Kabul citizen, or at least every male, was welcomed that first summer. The swimming pool met with a tragic end. The water quickly turned greyish brown; no one had thought of installing a filter system. As the pool got increasingly dirty, it was closed. Some people maintained they had contracted rashes and other skin diseases from the bathing. Rumours were that several had died. The pool was emptied and never used again.

Today a thick layer of dust covers the pale-blue bottom. Shrivelled rosebushes along the fence make a futile attempt to cover up the monstrosity. Next door is a tennis court. It is not in use either. The hotel's telephone directory still lists the number of the tennis trainer. But he is lucky; he found another job. His services were not in great demand this first spring of the new Kabul.

Aimal's days consist of restless wanderings between the shop, the restaurant and the shabby furniture. He is conscientious and keeps an eye on the shop in case someone should come. Once there was a run on the shop and items were flying off the shelves. When the Taliban fled town the corridors were heaving with journalists. The journalists had been living for months with the soldiers of the Northern Alliance, existing on rotten rice and green tea, and now they stuffed themselves with Aimal's Snickers and Bounty bars, smuggled in from Pakistan. They bought water at the equivalent of £3 a bottle, little round cream cheeses at £9 a box and jars of olives at a fortune per olive.

The journalists didn't mind about the prices. They had conquered Kabul and beaten the Taliban. They were dirty and bearded like guerrilla soldiers; the women were dressed like men and wore dirty boots. Many of them had yellow hair and pale-pink skin.

Sometimes Aimal stole away up to the roof where reporters were talking into large microphones in front of cameras. They no longer looked like guerrilla soldiers but had washed and combed their hair. The hall was full of funny types who joked and chatted with him. Aimal had learnt some English in Pakistan where he had lived as a refugee most of his life.

No one had asked him why he was not at school. None of the schools were operating anyhow. He counted dollars, used the calculator and dreamt of becoming a big businessman. Fazil was with him then and the two boys watched intently, wide-eyed, the extraordinary world that had invaded the hotel, while they raked in the money. But after a few weeks the journalists left the hotel, where many of them had slept in rooms without water, electricity or windows. The war was over, a leader had been installed and Afghanistan was no longer interesting.

When the journalists left, the newly elected Afghan ministers, their secretaries and aides moved in: dark Pashtoon from Kandahar, returned expatriates in tailor-made suits, and freshly shaven warlords from the steppes filled the sofas in the lobby. The hotel had become home to those who now ruled the country but who had no place to live in Kabul. None of them took any notice of Aimal or bought anything from his shop. They had never tasted a Bounty and they drank water from the tap. They would not dream of throwing away their money on Aimal's imported goods. Italian olives, Weetabix and a French soft cheese called Kiri, past their sell-by date, were not tempting.

Once in a while some journalist or other would find himself in Afghanistan, in the hotel and the shop.

'Are you still here? Why aren't you at school?' they would ask.

'I go in the afternoon,' Aimal would say if they came in the morning.

'I go in the morning,' he would say if they came in the afternoon.

He did not dare admit that he, like any other street urchin, did not go to school. Because Aimal is a rich little boy. His father is a rich bookseller, a father who is passionate about words and history, a father who has big dreams and big plans for his book emporium. But he is a father who trusts no one but his own sons to run the shops; a father who did not bother to register his sons when the schools in Kabul opened again after the New Year's cele-brations at the spring equinox. Aimal begged and pleaded but Sultan impressed on him: 'You are going to be a busi-nessman. The best place to learn that is in the shop.'

Aimal became increasingly unwell and unhappy. His face turned pale and his skin sallow. His young body stooped and lost its resilience. They called him 'the sad boy'. When he returned home he fought and bickered with his broth-ers, the only way to use pent-up energy. He regarded his cousin Fazil with envy. He had got in to Esteqlal, a school supported by the French government. Fazil came home with exercise books, pencils, ruler, compass, pencil sharp-ener, mud all up his trousers and masses of funny stories.

'The fatherless, poor Fazil can go to school,' Aimal com-plained to Mansur, his older brother. 'But I, I who have a father who has read all the books in the world, I have to work twelve hours a day. I should be playing football, have friends round,' he complained.

Mansur agreed. He did not like Aimal standing in the dark shop all day. He too begged Sultan to send his youngest to school. 'Later,' said the father. 'Later; now we must pull together. This is when we lay the foundations of our emporium.'

What can Aimal do? Run away? Refuse to get up in the morning?

When his father is away, Aimal ventures out of the lobby; he closes the shop and goes for a stroll round the car park. He'll maybe find someone to talk to or someone with whom he can kick a stone around. One day a British aid worker turned up. He had suddenly spotted his car, which had been stolen by the Taliban. He walked into the hotel to check it out. A minister, who alleged he had bought it legally, now owned the car. The aid worker had sometimes dropped by Aimal's shop since. Aimal always asked him how he was getting on with the car.

'Well, can you believe it. It's gone for good,' said the man. 'New crooks replacing the old ones.'

Very rarely something would break the monotony and the lobby would fill with people so the echo of his footsteps disappeared when he crept to the lavatory. Like the time the Minister for Aviation was killed. Like other out-of-town ministers, Abdur Rahman lived in the hotel. During the UN conference in Bonn, after the fall of the Taliban when Afghanistan's new government was being hurriedly assembled, Rahman commanded enough supporters to be named as the new minister. 'A playboy and a charlatan,' his opponents said of him.

The drama took place when thousands of *hadji* – pilgrims on their way to Mecca – were left standing at Kabul airport having been cheated by a tour operator. It had sold tickets for a non-existent plane. Ariana had chartered a shuttle plane to Mecca but there was not nearly room enough for everyone.

The pilgrims suddenly spotted an Ariana plane taxiing along the runway and they stormed it. But the plane was not going to Mecca; it was carrying the Minister of Aviation to New Delhi. The *hadji* in their white gowns were refused entry. In a raging mood, they knocked the pilot down and rushed into the plane, where they found the minister, who had made himself comfortable with some of his aides. The pilgrims pulled him into the aisle and beat him to death.

Aimal was one of the first to hear about the matter. The hotel lobby was teeming, people wanted details. 'A minister who was beaten to death by pilgrims? Who was behind it?'

One conspiracy theory after another reached Aimal's ears. 'Is this the start of an armed rebellion? Is it an ethnic rebellion? Do the Tajiks want to kill the Pashtoon? Is it personal revenge? Or just desperate pilgrims?'

Suddenly the lobby was even more hideous than normal. Buzzing voices, serious faces, excited people. Aimal wanted to cry.

He returned to the dreary room, sat down behind the table, ate a Snickers. Over four hours to go.

The cleaning man swept the floor and emptied the waste-paper basket.

'You look so sad, Aimal.'

'*Jigar khoon*,' said Aimal. 'My heart bleeds.'

'Did you know him?' asked the cleaning man.

'Who?'

'The minister.'

'No,' said Aimal. 'Or, yes. A little.'

It felt better that his heart bled for the dead minister than for his own lost childhood.

The Carpenter

Mansur runs panting into his father's shop. He is carrying a little parcel.

'Two hundred postcards,' he puffs. 'He tried to steal two hundred postcards.'

Drops of perspiration pour off his face. He has run the last stretch.

'Who?' asks his father. He places his calculator on the counter, enters a figure in the accounts book and looks at his son.

'The carpenter.'

'The carpenter?' Sultan asks, astounded. 'Are you sure?'

Haughtily, as though he has saved his father from a dangerous mafia gang, the son hands the brown envelope to the father. 'Two hundred postcards,' he repeats. 'When he was about to leave he looked rather embarrassed. But as it was his last day I thought nothing more of it. He asked if there was anything else he could do. He said he needed the work. I said I'd ask you. After all, the shelves are finished. Then I spotted something in his waistcoat pocket. "What's that?" I said. "What?" he said and looked confused. "In your pocket," I said. "That's something I brought with me," he said. "Show me," I said. He refused. In the end I pulled the packet out of his pocket myself. And here it is! He tried to steal postcards from us. But that one won't work, I was keeping an eye on him.'

Mansur has embroidered the story considerably. He was sitting dozing as usual when Jalaluddin was about to leave. It was the cleaning boy, Abdur, who caught the carpenter. Abdur saw him take the cards. 'Aren't you going to show Mansur what you have in your pocket?' he said. Jalaluddin just kept on going.

The cleaning boy was a poor Hazara, from the lowest ethnic group on the Kabul social ladder. He rarely spoke. 'Show Mansur your pockets,' he called after the carpenter. Only then had Mansur reacted and pulled the postcards out of Jalaluddin's pocket. Now he is yearning for his father's approval.

But Sultan continues to leaf slowly through the bunch of papers and says: 'Hm, where is he now?'

'I sent him home but told him he would not get off lightly.'

Sultan is silent. He remembers when the carpenter approached him in the shop. They were from the same village and had been practically neighbours. Jalaluddin had not changed since those days; he was still thin as a rake, with large, frightened, protruding eyes. He was possibly even thinner than before. And although he was only forty, he was already stooped. His family was poor, but well regarded. His father had also been a carpenter, but his sight failed a few years ago and he could no longer work.

Sultan was happy to give him work; Jalaluddin was

clever and Sultan needed new shelves. Up until now the bookshelves in his shop had been of the normal variety, where the books stand straight up and down with the title legible on the spine. The shelves covered the walls and in addition there were freestanding bookcases on the floor. But he needed shelves where he could display the books properly. He wanted sloping shelves, with a thin bar across, in order that the whole front cover of the book could be seen. His shop would be like a western shop. They agreed on a fee of £3 per day and Jalaluddin returned the next day with hammer, saw, ruler, nails and some planks. The storage room at the back of the shop was turned into a carpenter's workshop. Jalaluddin had hammered and nailed all day, surrounded by shelves and postcards. The cards were an important source of income to Sultan. He printed them in Pakistan for next to nothing and sold them at a large profit. Usually Sultan chose images he fancied, without ever thinking of crediting the photographer or painter. He found a picture, took it to Pakistan, and had it reproduced. Some photographers had given him pictures without asking for money. They sold well. The best customers were soldiers from the international peacekeeping force. When they were on patrol in Kabul they dropped in on Sultan's shop and bought postcards: postcards of women in burkas, children playing on tanks, queens from bygone days in daring dresses, the Bamiyan Buddhas before and after they were blown up by the Taliban, *buzkashi* horses, children in national costume, wild scenery, Kabul then and now. Sultan was good at choosing images and the soldiers often left the shop with a dozen postcards each.

Jalaluddin's daily wage was worth exactly nine postcards. In the back room they were stacked up, hundreds of each image, inside bags and out of bags, with rubber bands and without rubber bands, in boxes and cartons and on shelves.

'Two hundred, you say,' Sultan said thoughtfully. 'Do you think this is the first time?'

'I don't know. He said he was going to pay for them but that he had forgotten.'

'Yes, he can try and make us believe that.'

'Someone must have asked him to steal them,' Mansur stated. 'He's not smart enough to sell the cards on. And he certainly hasn't stolen them to hang them up on the wall,' he said.

Sultan swore. He had no time for this. In two days he was off to Iran, for the first time in several years. There were many things to do, but he would have to handle this one first. No one, but no one, was going to steal from him and get away with it.

'Keep the shop and I'll go to his house. We must get to the bottom of this,' said Sultan. He took Rasul with him, he knew the carpenter well. They drove out to the village Deh Khudaidad.

A dust cloud followed the car through the village. Then they came to the path leading up to Jalaluddin's house. 'Remember, no one needs to know about this, it is not necessary for the whole family to have the shame hanging over them,' Sultan said to Rasul.

At the village store on the corner, where the path led to Jalaluddin's house, stood a group of men, amongst them Jalaluddin's father Faiz. He smiled at them, squeezed Sultan's hand and embraced him. 'Come in and have a cup of tea,' he said cordially. He obviously knew nothing about the postcards. The other men also wanted a few words with Sultan – after all he had pulled himself up and achieved something in life.

'We only wanted to see your son,' said Sultan. 'Can you fetch him?'

The old man went off. He returned with his son following two steps behind. Jalaluddin looked at Sultan. He was shaking.

'We need you in the shop, could you come back with us for a moment,' Sultan said. Jalaluddin nodded.

'You'll have to come for tea another day,' the father called after them.

'You know what this is all about,' Sultan observes drily when they are sitting in the back seat of the car being driven by Rasul. They are on their way to Wakil's brother Mirdzjan, who is a policeman.

'I only wanted to look at them. I was going to give them back. I only wanted to show my children. They are so beautiful.'

The carpenter cowers in the corner, shoulders sagging, trying to make himself as small as possible. His fists are clenched together between his legs. Now and again he sinks his nails into his knuckles. When he talks he looks quickly and nervously at Sultan and resembles nothing but a frightened and dishevelled chicken. Sultan leans back in the seat and questions him quietly.

'I need to know how many postcards you took.'

'I only took the ones you saw.'

'I don't believe you.'

'It's true.'

'If you won't admit that you took more I'll report you to the police.'

The carpenter snatches Sultan's hand and showers it with kisses. Sultan snatches it back.

'Stop that nonsense; don't behave like an idiot.'

'In the name of Allah, upon my honour, I didn't take any more. Don't throw me into jail, please, I'll pay you back, I'm an honourable man, forgive me, I was stupid, forgive me. I have seven little children; two of my girls have polio. My wife is pregnant again and we have nothing to eat. My children are fading away, my wife cries every day because I don't make enough to feed us all. We eat potatoes and boiled vegetables, we can't even afford rice. My mother begs leftovers from hospitals and restaurants. Sometimes there is some boiled rice to spare. Sometimes they sell the leftovers in the market. These last days we haven't even had bread. And I also feed my sister's five children, her husband is out of work, and I also live with my old mother and father and grandmother.'

'The choice is yours. Admit that you have taken more and you'll be spared jail,' says Sultan.

The conversation goes round in circles. The carpenter bemoans his poverty and Sultan wants him to admit to a larger theft. He also wants to know to whom he has sold the cards.

They have travelled through Kabul and are out in the country again. Rasul drives them through muddy roads and past people hurrying to reach home before nightfall. Some stray dogs fight over a bone. Children run around barefoot. A burka-clad woman balances on the crossbar of her husband's bicycle. An old man is fighting a cart full of oranges; his feet sink into the deep ruts caused by the recent days' downpour. The hard mud road has been turned into an artery of shit, garbage and animal waste, forced into the road from alleyways and verges by torrential rain.

Rasul halts in front of a gate. Sultan asks him to go and knock on the door. Mirdzjan comes out, greets them all and invites them in.

When the men stomp up the stairs they hear the quiet

hiss of skirts. The women of the house hide. Some stand behind half-open doors, others behind curtains. A young girl peeps through a crack in the door to see who might be visiting them so late in the day. Outside the family no men must see them. The older boys serve the tea the sisters and mother have prepared in the kitchen.

'Well,' says Mirdzjan. He sits cross-legged wearing the traditional tunic with balloon trousers, the dress forced on all men by the Taliban. Mirdzjan loves it. He is small and podgy and feels comfortable in the loose-fitting clothes. Now he has to wear an outfit he likes little, the old Afghan police uniform which the police used before the Taliban. After hanging in the wardrobe for years it is now somewhat tight. It is also warm, as only the winter uniform, made of heavy homespun, has survived the storage. The uniforms are made to a Russian pattern, and are more at home in Siberia than in Kabul. Mirdzjan sweats his way through the spring days when the temperature can reach thirty degrees.

Sultan quickly explains their business. Mirdzjan lets them talk in turn, as though they were being cross-examined. Sultan sits at his side, Jalaluddin across from him. He nods understandingly and keeps a light, easy manner. Sultan and Jalaluddin are offered tea and cream toffees and talk over each other.

'For your own sake it is best that we sort it all out here, instead of going to the real police,' says Mirdzjan.

Jalaluddin looks down, wrings his hands, and stutters out a confession, not to Sultan but to Mirdzjan. 'I might have taken five hundred. But they're all at home. I'll give them all back. I haven't touched them.'

'Well I never,' says the policeman.

But that is not enough for Sultan. 'I'm sure you've taken many more. Come on! Who have you sold them to?'

'It is to your advantage to admit everything now,' says Mirdzjan. 'If it comes to a police interrogation, it won't be quite like this and there won't be any tea and cream toffees,' he says enigmatically and looks at Jalaluddin.

'But it is absolutely true. I have not sold them. In the name of Allah, I promise,' he says and looks from one to the other. Sultan insists, the words are repeated; it is time to go home. Anyone around after curfew is arrested. People have even been killed because the soldiers felt threatened by the passing cars.

They get into the car in silence. Rasul asks the carpenter to tell the truth. 'Otherwise this will go on and on, Jalaluddin,' he says. When they reach the carpenter's house he goes in to fetch the postcards. He returns quickly with a small bundle. The cards have been wrapped in an orange and green patterned scarf. Sultan unwraps them and looks admiringly at his pictures, which are now back with their rightful owner and will be returned to the shelves. But first they will be used as evidence. Rasul drives Sultan home. The carpenter is left standing shamefaced on the corner, where the path leads to his house.

480 postcards. Eqbal and Aimal sit on the mats counting. Sultan is trying to assess how many the carpenter might have taken. The postcards depict various subjects. In the back room there are hundreds upon hundreds. 'If the whole package has gone it will be difficult to assess, but if only about a dozen are missing from several of the packages, it is possible he has just opened a few packages and taken a few cards from each one,' Sultan reasons. 'We'll have to count tomorrow.'

The next morning, as they are counting, the carpenter suddenly appears at the door. He remains on the threshold

and looks more stooped than ever. Suddenly he rushes over
to Sultan and starts kissing his feet. Sultan drags him off the
floor and hisses: 'Pull yourself together, man. I don't want
your prayers.'

'Forgive me, forgive me, I'll pay you back, I'll pay you
back, I have hungry children at home,' says the carpenter.

'I'll say the same as yesterday, I don't need your money,
but I want to know who you have sold them to. How many
did you take?'

Jalaluddin's old father Faiz is there too. He too tries to
get down and kiss Sultan's feet, but Sultan catches him
before he gets down on the floor; he doesn't like anyone
kissing his shoes, especially not an elderly neighbour.

'You must know I've beaten him all night. I am so
ashamed. I've brought him up to be an honest worker, and
now! My son's a thief,' Faiz says and scowls at his son who
is cowering in the corner. The stooped carpenter looks
like a little child who has stolen and lied and is about to be
spanked.

Sultan calmly tells the father what has happened, that
Jalaluddin took postcards home with him and now they
want to know how many he took and who he sold them to.

'Give me one day and I'll make him admit to everything, if there is more to admit,' begs Faiz. The seams in his
shoes have come undone, he is not wearing socks and his
trousers are held up with a piece of string. The jacket
sleeves are shiny. He looks like his son, just a bit darker and
smaller and caved in. They are both thin and frail. The
father stands in front of Sultan, passive. Sultan does not
know what to do either. He feels embarrassed by the old
man's presence, a man who could have been his own father.

At last Faiz moves. He walks resolutely over to the bookcase where the son is standing. Like a flash his arm whips

out. And there, in the shop, he thrashes his son. 'You scoundrel, you cad, you are a disgrace to your family, you should never have been born, you're a loser, a crook,' his father cries whilst kicking and hitting him. He rams his knee into his son's stomach, his foot into his crotch, beats him over the back. Jalaluddin just stands there, stooped, protecting his chest with his arms, while the father lays into him. Then he suddenly breaks loose, and runs out of the shop. He's out in three long strides, and disappears down the steps and out on to the street.

Faiz's lambskin hat lies on the floor. It fell off in the heat of the battle. He picks it up, straightens it out and puts it back on his head. He stands up, bids Sultan farewell and walks out. Through the window Sultan sees how he totters on to his old bicycle, looks left and right and cycles stiffly and quietly back to his village.

When the dust has settled after the embarrassing scene, Sultan continues to count. He is unruffled. 'He worked here for forty days. Let's say he took two hundred cards every day; that makes eight thousand cards. I'm sure he's stolen at least eight thousand cards,' he says and looks at Mansur, who shrugs his shoulders. It had been agony to watch the poor carpenter being beaten by his father. Mansur couldn't give a shit about the postcards. He thinks they should forget the whole damn thing, now that they have got them back. 'He hasn't got the nous to sell them on, forget it,' he begs.

'It might have been done to order. You know all those stallholders who have bought postcards from us. Some of them haven't been for some time. I thought they might have bought enough, but look, they've bought cheap postcards from the carpenter. And he is stupid enough to have sold them for a song. What do you think?'

Mansur shrugs his shoulders again. He knows his father and knows that he wants to get to the bottom of it all. He also knows that he will be given the task. His father is off to Iran and will be away for a month.

'What if you and Mirdzjan make some enquiries while I am away? Truth will out. No one steals from Sultan,' he says, staring fixedly at Mansur. 'He could have ruined my entire business,' he says. 'Just imagine, he steals thousands of postcards and sells them to kiosks and bookshops all over Kabul. They sell them a lot cheaper than me. People will start going to them instead of to me. I'll lose all the soldiers who buy postcards – all those who buy books too. I'll get the reputation of being more expensive than anyone else. In the end I might have gone bankrupt.'

Mansur listens with half an ear to his father's predictions of doom. He is cross and irritated that he has been given yet another task to complete in his father's absence. In addition to having to register all the books, to fetch new crates of books sent from the printers in Pakistan, to sort out the red tape which is the consequence of owning a bookshop in Kabul, and to act as chauffeur and run his own bookshop, he now also has to take on the role of police inspector.

'I'll look after it,' he says abruptly. He could not very well say anything else.

'Don't be too soft, don't be too soft,' are Sultan's last words before he gets on the evening plane to Teheran.

When his father has gone Mansur forgets the whole thing. His sanctimonious period following the pilgrimage to Mazar is well and truly over. It lasted exactly one week. Nothing was improved by his praying five times a day. The beard got itchy and everyone told him he looked scruffy.

He didn't like the look of himself in the loose tunic. 'If I can't think permitted thoughts I might as well forget the whole thing,' he said to himself and gave up the piety just as quickly as he had started. The pilgrimage was nothing more than an outing.

The first evening of his father's absence he was invited out by some friends. He said he would come, not knowing they had bought Uzbek vodka, Armenian brandy and red wine at exorbitant prices on the black market. 'This is the very best available, everything is 40 per cent proof, actually the wine is forty-two per cent,' said the vendor. The boys paid forty dollars per bottle. Little did they realise that the vendor had drawn in two thin lines on the label of the French table wine: it was now increased from 12 to 42 per cent proof. It was all about strength. Most of his customers were young boys who, away from their parents' strict control, drank to get drunk.

Mansur had never tasted alcohol, Islam's most taboo substance. Early in the evening Mansur's two friends started drinking. They mixed brandy and vodka in a glass and after a few shots reeled around in the shady hotel room they had hired in order to escape their parents' wrath. Mansur had not yet arrived as he had to drive his younger brothers home, and when he turned up his friends were yelling and screaming and wanting to jump over the balcony.

Watching the scene, Mansur made up his mind: if alcohol made you so ill he might as well not touch it.

No one can sleep in Jalaluddin's house. The children lie on the floor and cry quietly. The last twenty-four hours have been the worst in their experience: to see their kind father being beaten by their grandfather and called a thief.

Everything had been turned upside down. In the courtyard Jalaluddin's father walks around in circles. 'How could I have had a son like that, bringing shame upon the whole family? What have I done wrong?'

The oldest son, the crook, sits on a mat in the one and only room. He can't lie down because his back is full of bloody streaks after having been beaten by his father with a thick branch. They had both returned home after the blows in the bookshop. First the father on his bicycle, then the son, walking all the way from town. The father had continued where he left off in the shop and the son had not resisted. While the flogging stung his back and the curses rained down over him, the family had watched in horror. The women had tried to get the children away, but there was no place to go.

The house was built round a courtyard; one of the walls was the fence to the path. Along two of the walls were platforms behind which rooms with big windows covered in oilcloth faced the courtyard – a room for the carpenter, his wife and seven children, a room for the father, mother and grandmother, a room for his sister, her husband and their five children, a dining room and a kitchen with an earthen kiln, a primus and a few shelves.

The carpenter's children slept on mats made up of a hotchpotch of rags and scraps of fabric. Some areas were covered in cardboard, others in plastic or sacking. The two girls with polio wore splints on one foot and used crutches. Two other children suffered from a virulent type of eczema; they were constantly scratching the scabs, which bled.

As Mansur's two friends were puking for the second time, the carpenter's children, on the other side of town, fell asleep.

*

When Mansur woke the first morning after his father had left, an intoxicating feeling of freedom overwhelmed him. He was free! He donned the sunglasses from Mazar and tore off at 100 kilometres per hour down Kabul's streets, past laden donkeys and dirty goats, beggars and disciplined German soldiers. He stuck a finger in the air at the Germans while he bumped and scraped over the endless holes in the tarmac. He swore and cursed and pedestrians jumped out of the way. He left behind district after district of Kabul's confusing mosaic of riddled ruins and tumbledown houses.

'He must take the consequences, that's character-building,' Sultan had said. Mansur pulls faces in the car. From now on Rasul can hump cases and deliver messages, from now on Mansur is going to enjoy himself until his father returns. Apart from the lift to the shops every morning, so his brothers won't grass on him, he's not going to do a damn thing. The only person Mansur fears is his father. In his presence he never dares protest, he is the only person he respects, at least to his face.

Mansur's aim is to get to know girls. That is not easy in Kabul where most families guard their daughters like treasure. He has a brainwave and starts an English course for beginners. Mansur's English is good as a result of his Pakistani schooling but he reasons that he will find the youngest and prettiest girls in the beginners' class. He's not wrong. After only one class he has spotted his favourite. Carefully he tries to talk to her. Once she even allows him to drive her some of the way home. He asks her to come to the shop, but she never does. One day the girl stops coming to the English course. Mansur cannot contact her. He misses her but first and foremost feels sorry for her sake, that she stopped coming; she wanted so much to learn the language.

The English student is quickly forgotten. Nothing is real and nothing is eternal in Mansur's life this spring. Once he is invited to a party in the outskirts of Kabul. Some acquaintances have hired a house and the owner is standing guard outside in the garden.

'They smoked dried scorpion,' Mansur tells a friend enthusiastically the next day. 'They crumbled it up into powder and mixed it with tobacco and got completely high, a bit angry too. Cool,' boasts Mansur.

Then one day Sultan sends a message that he will be home the next day. Mansur snaps out of his intoxication immediately. He has done none of the things his father asked him to do. Not catalogued the books, tidied the back room, made new order slips, fetched the book crates that by now have piled up at the transport depot. The matter of the carpenter and the investigations he has not even given a thought.

Sharifa fusses around him. 'What is it, my boy, are you ill?'

'Nothing,' he hisses.

She continues to nag. 'Keep your trap shut – go back to Pakistan,' Mansur shouts. 'Since you came everything has been shambolic.'

Sharifa starts to cry. 'How could I have such boys? What wrong have I done when they don't even want their mother around?'

Sharifa howls and yells at her children, Latifa starts to cry. Bibi Gul sways from side to side; Bulbula stares out into thin air. Sonya tries to soothe Latifa and Leila washes up. Mansur bangs the door into the room he shares with Yunus. Yunus is in bed snoring. He has hepatitis B and lies in bed all day swallowing medicine. His eyes are yellow and he looks paler and sadder than ever.

When Sultan returns the next day Mansur is so nervous that he avoids his sharp eyes. But he need not be so worried because Sultan is mostly preoccupied with Sonya. Only the following day, in the shop, does he ask his son if he has done all he asked him to do. Before Mansur has had time to answer the father is already issuing new instructions. Sultan's trip to Iran was very successful. He has linked up again with his old business associate and soon crate upon crate of Persian books will arrive in Kabul. But one thing he has not forgotten: the carpenter.

'Have you discovered nothing?' Sultan regards his son in astonishment. 'Are you undermining my work? Tomorrow you go to the police and report him. His father was going to give me the confession within a day and now a month has gone by! And if he's not locked up by the time I return from Pakistan, you are not my son,' he threatens. 'Anyone found helping themselves to my property will not be happy,' he says ominously.

The next morning, while it is still dark, two women carrying two children are found beating on the Khan family's door. Leila opens up drowsily. The women cry and remonstrate and after a time Leila realises that it is the carpenter's grandmother and aunt standing there with his children.

'Please, forgive him, forgive him,' they say. 'Please, in God's name,' they cry. The old grandmother is close to ninety; small and wizened with a face like a mouse. She has a sharp, hairy chin. She is the mother of the carpenter's father, who has been trying to beat the truth out of his son for the last weeks.

'We have nothing to eat, we're starving, look at the children. But we'll pay back for the postcards.'

Leila asks them in. The little mousy grandmother throws

herself at the feet of the women of the family who have been woken by the wailing and enter the room. They look deeply embarrassed at the misery, which has entered the room like a rush of cold air. The women have a two-year-old boy with them and one of the polio-stricken girls. The girl sits down on the floor with great difficulty. The stiff polio-leg with the splints sticks out beneath her. She sits solemnly and listens to the conversation.

Jalaluddin was not at home when the police came, so they took his father and uncle instead. They said they would come and get him the next morning. No one slept the whole night. Early in the morning, before the police came back, the two old women set off to beg Sultan for mercy and forgiveness on behalf of their relative.

'If he stole anything it was to save his family. Look at them, look at the children, thin as rakes. No proper clothes, nothing to eat.'

The Mikrorayon hearts melt, but the visit leads to nothing but pity. When Sultan has decided upon something there is nothing the women in the Khan family can do. And especially not if it has any bearing on the shop.

'We would love to help you, but we can do nothing. Sultan decides,' they say. 'And Sultan is not at home.'

The women continue to wail and cry. They know it is true but cannot afford to give up hope. Leila enters with fried eggs and fresh bread. She has boiled milk for the two children. When Mansur comes into the room, the two women rush over and kiss his feet. He kicks them away. They know that he, as his father's oldest son, has power in his absence. But Mansur has decided to do what his father asked him to do.

'Ever since Sultan confiscated his tools, he has not been able to work. We haven't eaten for many weeks. We have forgotten the taste of sugar,' the grandmother cries. 'The rice we buy is nearly rotten. His children are getting thinner every day; look, they are all skin and bone. Jalaluddin is beaten up by his father every day. I never thought I would raise a thief,' the grandmother says. The women in Mikrorayon promise to do their best to persuade Sultan, knowing all the time that nothing will help.

By the time the grandmother and the aunt have made their way back to the village with the two children, the police have already been to pick up Jalaluddin.

In the afternoon Mansur is called in as a witness. He sits on a stool by the chief constable's table, legs crossed. Seven men listen to the chief's interrogation. There are not enough chairs and two of them have to share one. The carpenter is squatting on the floor. They are a mixed bunch; some of the police wear thick, grey winter uniforms, some traditional clothes, others green MP uniforms. Nothing much happens at this station, so the postcard theft is an important matter. One of the policemen is standing by the door, without quite deciding whether he belongs in or out.

'You must tell us who you sold them to, otherwise you'll end up in the central prison,' the chief constable says. The words central prison send a chill around the room. Central prison – that's where all the real criminals go. The carpenter sags on the floor and looks hopeless. He is wringing his carpenter's hands; they are full of thousands of tiny cuts, scars criss-crossing his hands. In the strong sunlight that shines through the window, gashes and incisions from knives, saws and awls are easily visible. It is as though his hands represent him, the carpenter, not his face, and it is they who are now dully watching the seven men in the room; as though the matter does not concern him. After a while they send him away, to the tiny metre-square cell. A cell where he cannot stand up, but only crouch, squat or lie doubled up.

Jalaluddin's fate is in the hands of Mansur's family. They can withdraw or uphold the complaint. If they choose to uphold the complaint, he will be passed on along the system and it will be too late to acquit him. Then the police decide. 'We can hold him for seventy-two hours, then you'll have to make up your minds,' says the chief constable. He is of the opinion that Jalaluddin must be punished; poverty is no reason for stealing.

'Many people are poor. If we do not punish crime, society will become completely immoral. It is important to set an example when the rules have been broken.' The loud-spoken chief constable argues with Mansur, who has begun to question the whole affair. When he realises that Jalaluddin might be sent down for six years for the postcard theft, he starts thinking about his children, the hungry looks, the poor clothes. He thinks of his own life, how simple it is; he, who in one day can spend as much money as the carpenter's family does in one month.

An enormous bouquet of artificial flowers takes up half the table. The flowers acquired a thick layer of dust ages ago, but nevertheless brighten up the room. The police at Deh Khudaidad's police station obviously like colours; the walls are mint green, the lamp red, very red. On the wall hangs a picture of the war hero Massoud, as in all other official offices in Kabul.

'Don't forget, under the Taliban he would have had his hand cut off,' the chief constable emphasises. 'That happened to people who had committed lesser crimes than this one.' The constable relates the story of a woman who became a single mother when her husband died. 'She was very poor. The youngest son had no shoes and cold feet. It was winter and he could not go out of doors. The oldest son, scarcely a teenager, stole a pair of shoes for his little brother. He was caught red-handed, and his right hand was chopped off. That was taking it a bit too far,' the constable thought. 'But this carpenter has shown himself to be a bad lot. He's stolen several times. If you steal in order to feed your children, you only steal once,' he maintains.

The chief constable shows Mansur all the confiscated things lying in the cupboard behind him. Flick-knives, kitchen knives, pocket-knives, knives with large handles for hitting, pistols, torches, even a pack of cards have been collected. To gamble for money qualifies you for six months in prison. 'The pack of cards was confiscated because the losing player floored the winner and stabbed him with this knife. They had been drinking so he was punished for stabbing, drinking and gambling,' he laughs. 'The other player was let off, because he was now an invalid and that's punishment enough!'

'What is the punishment for drinking?' Mansur asks. He knows that according to Sharia law drinking is a gross sin and severely punished. The Koran recommends eighty lashes.

'To be honest, I normally close my eyes to such things. When there is a wedding I tell them that this is a holiday, but that everything should be in moderation and kept within the family,' says the chief constable.

'What about infidelity?'

'If they are married they will be killed by stoning. If they are unmarried the punishment is one hundred lashes, and they must marry. If one of them is married, and it is the man, and the woman is unmarried, he must take her for his second wife. If she is married and he is unmarried, the woman will be killed and the man whipped and put in prison,' the constable says. 'But I sometimes look through my fingers with that too. It might be widows, who need the money. Then I try to help them. Get them on an even keel again.'

'Yes, you're talking about prostitutes, but what about normal people?'

'Once we surprised a couple in a car. We, or rather the parents, forced them to marry,' he says. 'That was fair, don't you think? After all, we're not the Taliban,' says the constable. 'We must try to avoid stoning people. The Afghans have suffered enough.'

Mansur leaves the police station deep in thought. The chief constable gave him a three-day deadline. He can still pardon the sinner, but if it goes further, it'll be too late. Mansur is not in a mood to return to the shop, but goes home for lunch, a very rare occurrence. He throws himself down on a mat, and thank God, for the sake of peace, food is ready.

'Take your shoes off,' his mother says.

'Go to hell,' Mansur answers.

'Mansur, you must obey your mother,' Sharifa continues. Mansur does not answer but lies down on the floor, one foot in the air, crossed over the other. He keeps his shoes on. His mother pinches her mouth tight.

'We must decide what to do with the carpenter,' Mansur says. He lights a cigarette, and his mother starts to cry. Mansur would never, ever, light up in front of his father. But as soon as his father is out of the house, he not only takes pleasure in smoking but also in irritating his mother by smoking before, during and after the meal. The little room is thick with smoke. Bibi Gul has been complaining for a long time how impolite he is to his mother. But this time desire takes over, she stretches out her hand and whispers: 'Can I have one?'

Silence descends. Is grandmother starting to smoke?

'Mummy,' Leila cries and tears the cigarette out of her hand. Mansur gives her another one and Leila leaves the room in protest. Bibi Gul sits happily puffing away, laughing quietly. She even stops the rocking to and fro and holds the cigarette high up in the air, inhaling deeply. 'I'll eat less,' Bibi Gul explains.

'Release him,' she says after having enjoyed the cigarette. 'He's had his punishment, his father's beating, the shame, and anyhow he gave the postcards back.'

'Did you see his children? How are they going to manage without their father's income?' Sharifa supports her.

'We might be responsible for his children's death,' says Leila who has returned once her mother has stubbed out the cigarette. 'What if they get ill and cannot afford a doctor, then they'll die because of us, or they might die of starvation,' she says. 'And anyhow, the carpenter might die in prison. Many never make it through the six years. It's riddled with infection, tuberculosis and lots of other illnesses.'

'Show mercy,' says Bibi Gul.

Mansur phones Sultan in Pakistan on his newly acquired mobile phone. He asks for permission to release the carpenter. The room is silent; everyone is listening to the conversation.

They hear Sultan's voice shouting from Pakistan: 'He wants to ruin my business, undermine prices. I paid him well. There was no need to steal. He's a crook. He's guilty and the truth will have to be beaten out of him. No one, but no one will get away with destroying my business.'

'He might get six years! His children might be dead when he gets out,' Mansur shouts back.

'If he gets sixty years, I couldn't care less. He is going to suffer until he tells me who he has sold the cards to.'

'That's something you can say because your tummy's full,' Mansur yells. 'I cry when I think of those scraggy children of his. His family are finished.'

'How dare you contradict your father!' Sultan screams down the line. Everyone in the room knows his voice and knows that his face is puce with anger and his whole body shaking. 'What sort of a son are you? You are to obey me in everything, everything. What's wrong with you? Why are you rude to your father?'

Mansur's face shows the inner battle he is fighting. He has never done anything but what his father demands of him. That is, of the things his father knows about. He has never faced him in open confrontation; he quite simply does not dare incite his father's wrath.

'All right,' he says and puts the phone down. The family is silent. Mansur swears.

'He has a heart of stone,' Sharifa sighs. Sonya is silent.

Every morning and every evening the carpenter's family arrives. Sometimes it's the grandmother, other times the mother, the aunt or the wife. One or two of the children are always with them. They get the same answer each time. Sultan decides. When he gets home all will sort itself out. But they know that is not true; Sultan has already passed his verdict.

In the end they can take it no longer. They do not open the door but sit quietly, pretending they are not at home. Mansur goes to the local police station to ask for a post-ponement; he wants to wait for his father's return; he will take care of it. But the chief constable cannot wait any longer. The metre-square cell cannot house prisoners for more than a few days. Once again they ask the carpenter to admit that he took more postcards and to tell them whom he sold them to, but he refuses. Jalaluddin is handcuffed and led out of the little mud hut.

As the local police station has no car, it falls on Mansur to drive the carpenter to the central police station in Kabul.

Outside are the carpenter's father, son and grandmother. When Mansur arrives they approach him hesitatingly. Mansur hates every moment. In Sultan's absence he is having to act as the callous judge.

'I am only doing as my father has told me,' he excuses himself, puts on his sunglasses and sits in the car. The grandmother and the little son return home. The father mounts his rickety bicycle and follows Mansur's car. He is not giving up and wants to follow his son as far as he can. They see his upright silhouette disappear behind them.

Mansur drives slower than usual. It might be many years before the carpenter sees these streets again.

They reach the central police station. During the Taliban era this was one of the most hated buildings in Kabul. Here, at the Department for the Promotion of Virtue and Extermination of Sin, better known as the ministry of morality, the religious police had their headquarters. Men were brought here whose beards or trousers were too short, women who had walked down a street with men other than their relatives, women who had walked alone, women who wore make-up under the burka. For weeks on end they might languish in the basements before being moved to other gaols, or acquitted. When the Taliban left, the remand cells were opened and the prisoners freed. Cables and canes were found which had been used as instruments of torture. The men were beaten naked; women could drape a sheet around themselves when being tortured. Before the Taliban, first the brutal Soviet intelligence service, then the chaotic police force of the Mujahedeen had occupied the building.

The carpenter mounts the massive steps to the fifth floor. He tries to walk beside Mansur and looks pleadingly at him. His eyes seem to have grown during the week he was incarcerated. The beseeching eyes seem to bulge out of his head. 'Forgive me, forgive me. I'll work for you for nothing for the rest of my life. Forgive me.'

Mansur looks straight ahead. He must not buckle now. Sultan has given his verdict and he cannot contradict Sultan. He might be disinherited, thrown out of the house. He feels already that his brother has become Sultan's favourite. Eqbal can learn computing, Eqbal has been promised a bicycle. If Mansur opposes him now Sultan might sever all ties with him. However much he feels for the carpenter, he cannot risk that.

They wait for the interrogation and registration of the report. The system is that the person reported is imprisoned until innocence or guilt has been proved. Anyone can report anybody and have the person in question imprisoned.

Mansur puts his case to the interrogator. The carpenter squats on the floor. He has long, crooked toes and the nails have thick black edges. His waistcoat and jumper hang in shreds down his back. The trousers hang about his hips.

The interrogator behind the table carefully writes down the two declarations. He writes elegantly and uses carbon paper for a copy.

'Why are you so keen on postcards from Afghanistan?' the policeman laughs and finds the matter rather curious.

But before the carpenter can answer he continues: 'Tell me now whom you have sold them to; we all understand that you did not steal them to send to relatives.'

'I only took two hundred, and Rasul gave me some,' the carpenter starts tentatively.

'Rasul never gave you any postcards, that's a lie,' says Mansur.

'You will remember this room as a place where you had the chance to tell the truth,' says the policeman. Jalaluddin swallows and cracks his knuckles and breathes a sigh of relief when the policeman continues to interrogate Mansur about when, where and how the whole thing happened. Behind the interrogator, through the window, can be seen one of the heights outside Kabul. Little houses cling to the mountainside. The paths zigzag down the mountain. Through the window the carpenter can see people, they look like little ants walking up and down. The houses have been constructed with materials cannibalised from what can be found in war-torn Kabul: some sheets of corrugated iron, a piece of sacking, some plastic, a few bricks, bits and pieces from ruins.

Suddenly the interrogator squats beside him. 'I know that you have hungry children, and I know that you are not a criminal. I am giving you a last chance. Take it. If you tell me to whom you sold the cards I will let you go. If you don't tell me I'll give you several years in prison.'

Mansur is losing interest. This is the hundredth time the carpenter has been asked to admit who he sold the cards to. Maybe he's telling the truth. Maybe he hasn't sold them to anyone. Mansur looks at his watch and yawns.

Suddenly a name escapes Jalaluddin's lips, so quietly as to be nearly inaudible.

Mansur leaps up.

The man whose name Jalaluddin muttered owns a kiosk in the market where he sells calendars, pens and cards; cards for religious festivals, weddings, engagements and birthdays – and postcards with motifs from Afghanistan. He had always bought these cards from Sultan's bookshop, but he hadn't been there for some time. Mansur remembers him well because he always complained about the prices.

It's as if a cork has been unstopped; but Jalaluddin still trembles as he talks.

'He came over to me one afternoon when I was leaving work. We talked and he asked me if I needed money. Of course I did. Then he asked me if I could fetch him some postcards. At first I refused, but then he told me about the money I would get for it. I thought about my children at home. I'm not able to feed the children on a carpenter's salary. I thought about my wife who was starting to lose her teeth, she's only thirty. I thought of all the reproachful looks I get at home because I'm not able to earn enough. I thought of the clothes and the shoes I could not afford to buy my children, the doctor we cannot afford, the awful food we have to eat. So I thought if only I took a few, as long as I was working in the bookshop, I could solve some of my problems. Sultan won't notice. He has so many post-cards and so much money. And then I took some cards.'

'We'll have to go there and safeguard the evidence,' the policeman says. He gets up and orders the carpenter, Mansur and another policeman to come with him. They drive to the market and the postcard kiosk. A little boy is serving from behind the hatch.

'Where is Mahmoud?' the policeman asks. He is in plain clothes. Mahmoud is having lunch. The policeman shows the boy his identity card and says he wants to look at his postcards. The boy lets them in at the side of the kiosk, into a narrow area between the wall, the stack of wares and the counter. Mansur and a policeman tear the postcards from off the shelves; the ones Sultan has had printed are stuffed into a bag. They count several thousand. But which ones Mahmoud has bought lawfully and which ones he has bought from Jalaluddin it is hard to tell. They take the boy and the postcards to the police station.

A policeman is left behind to wait for Mahmoud. The kiosk is sealed. Mahmoud will not be selling any more thank-you cards today, or pictures of heroes and warriors either, for that matter.

When Mahmoud eventually arrives at the police station, still smelling of kebab, the interrogations start anew. Initially Mahmoud denies ever having set eyes on the carpenter. He says he has bought everything legally, from Sultan, from Yunus, from Eqbal, from Mansur. Then he changes tactics and says, yes, one day the carpenter did approach him, but he never bought anything.

The kiosk owner, too, must spend the night in detention. At last Mansur can get away. In the corridor the carpenter's father, uncle, nephew and son are waiting. They approach him, reach after him and watch terror-stricken when he hurries away. He can't bear it any more. Jalaluddin has confessed, Sultan will be pleased, the matter has been solved. Now that the theft and the resale have been proved, the criminal case can begin.

He remembers what the police interrogator had said: 'This is your last chance. If you confess we will let you go and you can return to your family.'

Mansur feels unwell. He rushes out. His thoughts are on Sultan's last words before he left. 'I have risked my life building up my business, I have been imprisoned, I have been beaten. I've worked my socks off to try and create something for Afghanistan and a bloody carpenter comes and tries to usurp my life's work. He will be punished. Don't be soft, Mansur, don't you start to buckle.'

In a run-down mud hut in Deh Khudaidad a woman sits and gazes into the air. Her youngest children are crying; they have nothing to eat yet, and wait the return of their grandfather from town. Maybe he'll have something with him. They rush at him when he enters the gate on his bicycle. But his hands are empty. The luggage carrier is empty too. They halt when they see his dark face. They are quiet for a moment before they start to cry and cling to him. 'Where is daddy, when will daddy come back?'

My Mother Osama

Tajmir holds the Koran up in front of his forehead, kisses it and reads a random verse. He kisses the book again, sticks it in his pocket and gazes out of the window. The car is on its way out of Kabul. It is headed east, towards the restless borderlands between Afghanistan and Pakistan, where there is still support for the Taliban and al-Qaida, and where, according to the Americans, terrorists are hiding out in the inaccessible mountain landscape. Here they comb the terrain, interrogate the local population, blow up caves, look for caches of weapons, find hiding places, and bomb and kill a few civilians, in their hunt for terrorists and the trophy they all dream of – Osama bin Laden.

This is the area where 'Operation Anaconda', the spring's major offensive against al-Qaida, took place, when international Special Forces, under US command, fought hard battles against Osama's remaining disciples in Afghanistan. Allegedly, several al-Qaida soldiers are still to be found in these border areas, areas where warlords have never recognised a central authority, but still rule according to tribal law. It is difficult for Americans and the central authorities to infiltrate villages that lie in the Pashtoon belt on either side of the border. Intelligence experts believe that if Osama bin Laden and the Taliban leader Mullah Omar are still alive and in Afghanistan, then this is where they are.

Tajmir is trying to find them. Or at least find someone who knows someone who has seen them, or thinks they have seen someone who resembled them. In contrast to his fellow traveller, Tajmir hopes they'll find absolutely nothing. Tajmir hates danger. He hates travelling into the tribal areas, where trouble can erupt at any moment. In the back of the car are bulletproof waistcoats and helmets, ready for action.

'What are you reading, Tajmir?'

'The holy Koran.'

'Yes, so I see, but anything special? I mean, like a "travel section" or something like that?'

'No, I never look for anything in particular; I just open it at random. Just now I got to the bit about whoever obeys God and his messenger will be led into the gardens of paradise, where streams trickle, whereas whoever turns their back will be afflicted by painful punishment. I read the Koran when I am frightened or sad.'

'Oh, yeah,' says Bob and rests his head against the window. He sees Kabul's filthy streets through squinting eyes. They drive into the morning sun and Bob closes his eyes against the glare.

Tajmir thinks about his assignment. He has been given the job of interpreter for a large American magazine. Previously, under the Taliban, he worked for a charity organisation. He was responsible for the distribution of flour and rice to the poor. When the foreigners departed after September 11 he was left in sole charge. The Taliban blocked all his efforts. The distributions were halted and one day a bomb destroyed the distribution depot. Tajmir thanked God that he had stopped the deliveries. What might have been the outcome if the place had been full of women and children in the desperate food queue?

But it now feels like an eternity since he worked with the emergency relief. When the journalists streamed into Kabul the American magazine picked him up. They offered to pay in one day what he was normally paid in two weeks. He thought about his poor family, left the aid work and started to interpret, in an imaginative and artful English.

Tajmir is sole provider for his family, which, in the scale of Afghan families, is small. He lives with his mother, father, stepsister, wife and one-year-old Bahar in a small flat in Mikrorayon, close to Sultan and his family. His mother is Sultan's elder sister, the sister who was married off to provide money for Sultan's education.

Feroza was the strictest of mothers. From the time Tajmir was a little boy he was rarely allowed to play outside with the other children. He had to play, quietly and calmly, in the little room under Feroza's observant eye. When he was older he was made to do schoolwork. He had to return from school immediately, was not allowed to go home with anyone or have anyone home to play. Tajmir never protested, it was never possible to argue with Feroza; because Feroza hit him and Feroza hit hard.

'She's worse than Osama bin Laden,' Tajmir tells Bob when he has to make excuses for turning up late or having to break off early. His new American friends hear terrible tales about 'Osama'. They imagine some sort of a shrew hidden beneath the burka. But when they met her, while visiting Tajmir, they saw a smiling little woman with searching, squinting eyes. A large gold medallion, inscribed with the Islamic creed, hung around her neck. She bought that with Tajmir's first American salary. Feroza knows exactly how much he earns, and he hands everything over to her. She gives him a bit of pocket money in return. Tajmir shows them all the marks on the walls where she has thrown shoes or other objects at him. He laughs now; the tyrant Feroza has become a funny story.

Feroza's burning wish was that Tajmir would grow into something important. Every time she had some spare cash she would enter him for a course: English classes, extra maths classes, computer courses. The illiterate woman, who was forced to marry to provide her family with money, was going to turn into an honoured and respected mother through her son.

Tajmir saw little of his father. He was a kindly and rather timid man and suffered from bad health. In the good old days he travelled as a salesman to India and Pakistan. Sometimes he would return with money, sometimes not.

Feroza might beat Tajmir but she never touched her husband, in spite of there being no doubt as to who was the stronger of the two. Over the years Feroza had grown into a buxom woman, round as a little ball, thick glasses balanced on the tip of her nose or hanging round her neck. Her husband, on the other hand, was grey and emaciated, weak and brittle like a dry branch. As the husband crumbled away Feroza took over the role of head of the family.

Feroza never had any more sons, but she never let go her hope of having more children. After having given up on becoming a mother again she went to one of Kabul's orphanages. Here she found Kheshmesh. Her family had left her outside the orphanage, wrapped up in a dirty pillowcase. Feroza adopted her and brought her up as Tajmir's sister. While Tajmir is the spitting image of Feroza – the same round face, the large stomach, the rolling gait – Kheshmesh is different.

Kheshmesh is a tense and unruly little girl, thin as a rake. Her skin is a lot darker than that of the other family members. Kheshmesh has a wild look about her, as though life inside her head is far more exciting than the real world. At family reunions, to Feroza's despair, Kheshmesh runs around like a frisky filly. Whilst Tajmir always obeyed his mother's wishes when he was a little boy, Kheshmesh is always getting dirty, always tousled, full of scrapes and cuts. But when she is in a quiet mood no one can be more devoted than Kheshmesh. No one gives their mother such tender kisses or strong hugs. Wherever Feroza goes, Kheshmesh is not far behind – like a skinny little shadow in the wake of her buxom mother.

Like all children, Kheshmesh quickly learnt about the Taliban. Once Kheshmesh and a friend were beaten up by a Taleb in the stairwell. They had been playing with his son who had fallen and hurt himself badly. The father had grabbed them both and beaten them with a stick. They never again played with the little boy. The Taliban were those people who never let her go to school with the boys in Mikrorayon, they were the people who forbade singing or clapping, stopped people dancing. The Taliban were those people who prevented her from playing outside with her dolls. Dolls and furry toy animals were banned because they portrayed living creatures. When the religious police searched people's homes, smashed up the televisions and cassette players, they might well confiscate children's toys if they found them. They tore off arms or heads, or crunched them underfoot, in front of the eyes of stunned children.

When Feroza told Kheshmesh that the Taliban had fled, the first thing she did was to take her favourite doll outside and show her the world. Tajmir got rid of his beard. Feroza sneaked out a dusty cassette player and wriggled around the flat singing: 'Now we'll make up for five lost years.'

Feroza never had any more children to look after. No sooner had she adopted Kheshmesh than the civil war started and she fled to Pakistan with Sultan's family. When she returned from the refugee existence, it was time to find a wife for Tajmir, not to look for abandoned baby girls in the hospital.

Like everything else in Tajmir's life, finding a wife was also his mother's prerogative. Tajmir was in love with a girl he met at English classes in Pakistan. They were sort of sweethearts, although they never held hands or kissed. They were hardly ever alone, but nevertheless, they were sweethearts, and they wrote each other notes and love letters. Tajmir never dared tell Feroza about this girl, but he dreamt of marrying her. She was a relative of Massoud, the war hero, and Tajmir knew his mother might fear all the problems that could involve. But regardless of who might be its object, Tajmir would never dare confide in his mother about his crush. He had been educated not to ask for anything, he never talked to Feroza about his feelings. He felt his subservience showed respect.

'I have found the girl I want you to marry,' Feroza said one day.

'Oh,' said Tajmir. His throat tightened, but not a word of protest escaped him. He knew he would have to write a letter to his pie-in-the-sky sweetheart and tell her it was all over.

'Who is it?' he asked.

'She is your second cousin, Khadija. You haven't seen her since you were small. She is clever and hard-working and from a good family.'

Tajmir merely nodded. Two months later he met Khadija for the first time, at the engagement party. They sat beside each other during the whole party without exchanging a word. I could love her, he thought.

Khadija looks like a Parisian jazz-singer from the twenties. She has black, wavy hair, parted on the side, cut straight across the shoulders, white powdered skin and always wears black eye make-up and red lipstick. Her cheeks are narrow and her lips wide, and she might have been posing for art photographers all her life. But according to Afghan standards she is not very pretty; she is too thin, too narrow. The ideal Afghan woman is round: round cheeks, round hips, round tummy.

'Now I love her,' Tajmir says. They are approaching Gardes, and Tajmir has given Bob, the American journalist, his entire life story.

'Wow,' he says. 'What a story. So you really love your wife now? What about the other girl?'

Tajmir hasn't a clue what has happened to the other girl. He never even thinks of her. Now he lives for his own little family. A year ago he and Khadija had a baby girl.

'Khadija was terrified of having a daughter,' he tells Bob. 'Khadija is always frightened of something and this time it was about having a daughter. I told her and everyone else that I wanted a daughter. That above all I wanted a daughter. So that if we did have a daughter no one would say, how sad, because after all that is what I had wished for, and if we got a boy no one would say anything because then everyone would be pleased no matter what.'

'Hm,' says Bob and tries to understand the logic of it all.

'Now Khadija is worried she won't conceive again, because we are trying but nothing's happening. So I keep on telling her that one child is enough, one child is fine. In the West many people have only one child. So if we never have any more, everyone will say we didn't want any more, and if we have some more then everyone will be pleased no matter what.'

'Hm.'

They stop in Gardes to buy something to eat. They buy a carton of 'hi-lite' cigarettes at ten pence a pack, a kilo of cucumbers, twenty eggs and some bread. They are peeling the cucumbers and cracking the eggs when Bob suddenly calls out: 'Stop!'

By the roadside about thirty men sit in a circle. Kalashnikovs lie on the ground in front of them and ammunition belts are strapped over their chests.

'That's Padsha Khan's men,' Bob cries. 'Stop the car.'

Bob grabs Tajmir and walks over to the men. Padsha Khan is sitting in the midst of them: the greatest warlord of the eastern provinces and one of Hamid Karzai's most vociferous opponents.

When the Taliban fled, Padsha Khan was appointed Governor of Paktia Province, known as one of Afghanistan's most unruly regions. As Governor of an area where there is still support for the al-Qaida network, Padsha Khan became an important man to American intelligence. They were dependent on co-operation on the ground and one warlord was no better nor worse than any other. Padsha Khan's task was to ferret out Taliban and al-Qaida soldiers. His remit was then to inform the Americans. To this end he was supplied with a satellite telephone, which he used frequently. He kept on phoning and telling the Americans about al-Qaida movements in the area. And the Americans used firepower – on a village here and a village there, on tribal chiefs en route to attend Karzai's inaugural ceremony, on a few wedding parties, a bunch of men in a house, and on America's own allies. None of them were connected to al-Qaida but they had one thing in common – they were enemies of Padsha Khan. The local protests against the headstrong Governor, who suddenly had B52s and F16 fighter planes at his disposal to settle local tribal scores, increased to such an extent that Karzai saw no other solution but to remove him.

Padsha Khan then started his own little war. He sent rockets to the villages where his enemies were holed up and warfare broke out between the various factions. Several innocent people were killed when he tried to regain his lost power. In the end he had to give up, for the time being. Bob had been looking for him for ages, and there he is, sitting in the sand, surrounded by a bunch of bearded men.

Padsha gets up when he sees them. He greets Bob rather coldly but embraces Tajmir warmly and pushes him down beside him. 'How are you my friend? Are you well?'

They had often met during Operation Anaconda, America's major al-Qaida offensive. Tajmir had interpreted, that was all.

Padsha Khan is used to ruling the region as though it were his own backyard, together with his three brothers. Only six weeks ago he allowed rockets to rain down over the town of Gardes. Now it is Khost's turn. A new Governor has been appointed, a sociologist who has lived for the last decade in Australia. He has gone to ground, for fear of Padsha Khan and his men.

'My men are prepared,' Padsha Khan tells Tajmir, who translates while Bob scribbles in his notebook. 'We are just now discussing what to do,' he continues and looks at his men. 'Do we take him or do we wait?' Padsha Khan goes on. 'Are you headed for Khost? Then you must tell my brother to get rid of the new Governor quick as a flash. Tell him to pack up and bugger off to Karzai!'

Padsha Khan uses his hands to mime packing up and sending away. The men look at him, then at Tajmir and then at blond Bob who is frantically noting everything down.

'Listen,' says Padsha Khan. There is no doubt who he thinks is the legitimate lord of the three provinces, the provinces the Americans are watching like hawks. The warlord uses Tajmir's leg to illustrate what he means, drawing maps, roads and frontiers on his thigh. Tajmir receives a slap on the thigh for every utterance; he translates automatically. The largest ant he has ever seen is crawling over his foot.

'Karzai is threatening to send in the army next week. What will you do about that?' asks Bob.

'What army? Karzai doesn't have an army. He has a few hundred bodyguards who are being trained by the British. No one can beat me on my territory,' says Padsha Khan, looking at his men. They wear worn-out sandals and ragged clothes, and the only polished and shining bit about them is their weapons. Some of the handles are covered in colourful rows of pearls, others have painstakingly embroidered borders. Several of the young soldiers have decorated their Kalashnikovs with stickers. One pink sticker bears the words 'kiss me'.

Many of these men fought on the side of the Taliban only a year ago. 'No one can own us, they can only hire us,' the Afghans say about themselves and their rapid change from side to side in war. Today they belong to Padsha Khan;

tomorrow the Americans might hire them. The most important thing to them now is to fight whomever Padsha Khan considers to be his enemy. The Americans' hunt for al-Qaida will have to wait.

'He's mad,' says Tajmir when they are back in the car. 'People like him are responsible for the fact that there is never peace in Afghanistan. To him power is more important than peace. He's mad enough to jeopardise the lives of thousands just so he can be in charge. I can't imagine why the Americans want to co-operate with a man like that,' he says.

'If they were to work only with people whose hands are clean they would not have found many in this province,' says Bob. 'They have no choice.'

'But now they no longer care about hunting the Taliban for the Americans, now their weapons are aimed at each other,' Tajmir protests.

'Hm,' Bob mumbles. 'I wonder if there will be any serious fighting,' he says, more to himself than to Tajmir.

Tajmir and Bob disagree fundamentally about what constitutes a successful trip. Bob wants action, the more the better. Tajmir wants to return home, as quickly as possible. In a few days he and Khadija celebrate their second wedding anniversary and he hopes to be home for that. He wants to surprise her with a wonderful present. Bob wants violent action in print; like a few weeks ago when he and Tajmir were nearly killed by a grenade. It didn't hit them, but got the car behind them. Or the time they had to take refuge in the dark because they were mistaken for the enemy on their way into Gardez and the bullets whizzed past them. Even though he is dead scared, those things make Bob feel he is doing an important job, while Tajmir curses ever having changed his. The only plus about these trips is the extra danger money; Feroza knows nothing about that, so he keeps that money for himself.

To Tajmir and the majority of Kabul's inhabitants, this part of Afghanistan is the one they identify with least. These areas are considered wild and violent. People live here who do not conform to national authority. Padsha Khan and his brother can be in charge of whole regions. It has always been like this. The law of the jungle.

They pass barren desert landscapes. Here and there they spot nomads and camels, which slowly and proudly sway their way across the sand dunes. In a few places the nomads have erected their large, sand-coloured tents. Women in billowing, colourful skirts walk between the tents. The women of the Kuchi tribe are looked upon as the most liberated in Afghanistan. As long as they kept away from the towns, not even the Taliban forced them to wear the burka. But these nomadic tribes have also suffered enormously in the past years. Owing to the war and the mines they have had to alter their centuries-old routes, and they now move about on much restricted territories. The drought of the last years has resulted in the death of much of their livestock, their goats and camels.

The landscape is increasingly empty; below them desert, above them mountain, all in a variation of brown. Up on the mountainside there are black zigzagging patterns, which turn out to be sheep, cheek by jowl, seeking food on the mountain ledges.

They approach Khost. Tajmir hates this town. Here the Taliban leader Mullah Omar found his most loyal supporters. Khost and the surrounding area hardly noticed that the country had been taken over by the Taliban. To them there was little change. The women had never gone out to work or the girls to school. The burka had been worn for as long as they could remember, not prescribed by the authorities, but by the families.

Khost is a town without women, at least on the surface. Whilst in Kabul during the first spring following the fall of the Taliban women were starting to throw off the burka, and one could, from time to time, see women in restaurants, in Khost women are rarely seen, not even hidden behind the burka. They lead a life closed in behind the backyard, they never go out, shop, or even visit. The law of purdah reigns, the total segregation of men and women.

Tajmir and Bob make their way to Padsha Khan's younger brother, Kamal Khan. He has occupied the Governor's residence, while the newly appointed Governor has placed himself under house arrest with the chief constable. The Governor's flower garden is flush with men loyal to the Khan clan. Soldiers of every age, from slender young boys to grey-haired men, sit, lie or walk around. The atmosphere is tense and rather exhausting.

'Kamal Khan?' Tajmir asks.

Two soldiers show them up to the commander, who is surrounded by men. He agrees to the interview and they sit down. A small boy arrives with tea.

'We are ready for battle. Until the spurious Governor leaves Khost and my brother is reinstated there will be no peace,' says the young man. The men nod. One man nods vigorously, he is the second in command under Kamal Khan. He sits on the floor, legs crossed, drinks tea and listens. All the time he is fondling another soldier. They are closely entwined and their entangled fingers lie in the lap of one of them. Many of the soldiers send Tajmir and Bob fawning looks.

In parts of Afghanistan, especially in the southeastern part of the country, homosexuality is widespread and tacitly accepted. Many commanders have young lovers and one often sees old men followed by a bunch of young boys. The boys adorn themselves with flowers in their hair, behind the ear or in a buttonhole. This behaviour is often explained by the strict purdah practised in the southern and eastern parts of the country. It is not rare to see a gaggle of mincing, swaying boys. They paint thick kohl lines round their eyes and their movements remind one of transvestites in the West. They stare, they flirt and they wiggle their hips and shoulders.

The commanders do not live as homosexuals only; the majority of them have wives and a large brood of children. But they are rarely at home and life is lived amongst men. Often major jealous dramas develop around the young men; many blood feuds have been fought over a young lover who divided his favours between two men. On one occasion two commanders launched a tank battle in the bazaar in a feud over a young lover. The result was several dozen killed.

Kamal Khan, a good-looking man in his twenties, maintains self-confidently that it is the Khan clan's right to rule the province.

'The people are on our side. We'll fight to the last man. It's not that we desire power,' Kamal Khan says disarmingly. 'It's the people, the people, who want us. And they deserve us. We're only following their wishes.'

Two long-legged spiders crawl up the wall behind him. Kamal Khan takes a little bag out of his waistcoat. In it are some tablets, which he swallows. 'I'm not well,' he says with eyes begging for sympathy.

These are the men who oppose Hamid Karzai. These are the men who continue to rule according to the law of the warlords, and who refuse to be dictated to from Kabul. If civilian life is lost, it matters little. It is power that matters, and power means two things: honour – that the Khan tribe maintains power in the province; and money – control of the flourishing traffic in smuggled goods and income from customs duty on items that are legally imported.

The reason why the American magazine is so interested in the local Khost conflict is not primarily because Karzai threatens to set the army on the warlords. That will probably not happen, because as Padsha Khan said: 'If he sends in the army people will be killed and he will get the blame.'

No, the magazine is interested because of the American forces in the region, the secret American Special Forces who are impossible to get close to, the secret agents crawling around in the mountains hunting for al-Qaida. Bob's magazine wants an article, an exclusive article, on 'The hunt for al-Qaida'. Most of all the young reporter wants to find Osama bin Laden. Or at least Mullah Omar. And cover the hunt. The Americans hedge their bets and work with both sides in the local conflict. The Americans give both sides money, both sides accompany them on missions, both sides are given weapons, communications equipment, intelligence equipment. They have good contacts on both sides; on both sides are former Taliban supporters.

The Khan brothers' arch-enemy is called Mustafa. He is the Khost chief constable. Mustafa co-operates with Karzai and the Americans. When one of Mustafa's men killed four Khan clan men during a shoot-out recently, he had to barricade himself in the police station for several days. The first four to leave the station would be killed, the Khans warned. When they ran out of food and water, they agreed to negotiate. They negotiated a postponement. That means little; four of Mustafa's men have a death sentence hanging over them, which can be implemented at any time. Blood is revenged with blood and the threat alone, before the killings have been carried out, is torture.

After Kamal Khan and younger brother Wasir Khan have described Mustafa as a criminal who kills women and children and who must be eliminated, Tajmir and Bob take their leave and are followed to the gate by two young boys who look like beautiful South Sea Island girls. They wear big, yellow flowers in their wavy hair, tight-fitting belts round their waists and they stare intensely at Tajmir and Bob. They don't know which of the two to look at, slender blond Bob or powerful Tajmir with the creamy face.

'Look out for Mustafa's men,' they say. 'You can't trust them; they'll betray you as soon as you turn your back. And don't go out after dark, they'll rob you!'

The two travellers make straight for the enemy. The police station is a few blocks away from the occupied Governor's residence and doubles up as a prison. The police station is a fortress. The walls are several metres thick. Mustafa's men open up the heavy iron gates, and they enter a backyard; there too the beautiful scent of flowers greets them, but from flowering trees and bushes, not from the men. Mustafa's soldiers are easy to tell apart from the Khans'. They wear dark-brown uniforms, small square caps and heavy boots. Many of them wear a scarf covering their nose and mouth and dark glasses. Not being able to see them makes them look more threatening.

Tajmir and Bob are led up narrow stairs and passages in the fortress. Mustafa sits in a room in the innermost part of the building. Like his enemy Kamal Khan, men and weapons surround him. The weapons are the same, the beards the same, the looks the same. The picture of Mecca on the wall is the same. The only difference is that the chief constable sits on a chair behind a table, not on the floor. In addition there are no flower-power young men there. The only flowers are a bunch of plastic daffodils on the chief's table, daffodils in fluorescent yellow, red and green. Beside the vase lies the Koran wrapped in a green cloth, and a miniature Afghan flag flies from a plinth.

'We have Karzai on our side and we will fight,' says Mustafa. 'The Khans have ravaged this region long enough, now we will put an end to the barbarism!' Round him the men nod agreement.

Tajmir translates and translates. The same threats, the same words. Why Mustafa is better than Padsha Khan, how Mustafa will make peace. He is really outlining the reason for there never being real peace in Afghanistan.

Mustafa has joined the Americans in many reconnaissance sorties. He recalls how they watched over a house which they were sure contained bin Laden and Mullah Omar. But they never found anything. The American reconnaissance work continues but they are hedged around by a lot of secretiveness, and Bob and Tajmir are not enlightened further. Bob asks if they can join them one night. Mustafa laughs. 'No, that's top secret, that's how the Americans want it. It won't help how much you beg, young man,' he says.

'Don't go out after dusk,' Mustafa commands them strictly when they leave. 'Khan's men will get you.'

Thoroughly warned by both sides, they visit the local kebab house, a large room where cushions have been laid out on long benches. Tajmir orders pilau and kebab, Bob asks for boiled eggs and bread. He is frightened of parasites and germs. They eat hastily and hurry back to the hotel before dusk falls. In this town anything can happen and one is well advised to take precautions.

A heavy grille in front of the gate to the town's only hotel is opened and locked behind them. They look out on Khost, a town where shops are closed, policemen are masked and the population sympathise with al-Qaida. A scowling look at Bob from a passer-by is enough to make Tajmir feel unwell. In this region there is a bounty on Americans. Fifty thousand dollars will be paid to anyone who kills an American.

They go up on to the roof to erect Bob's satellite telephone. A helicopter flies overhead. Bob tries to guess where it is heading for. A dozen of the hotel's soldiers have gathered around them; they look in amazement at the wire-less phone Bob talks into.

'Is he talking to America?' asks a long, thin rake, wearing a turban, tunic and sandals. He looks like the leader. Tajmir nods. The soldiers keep on watching Bob. Tajmir makes small talk with them; they are only interested in the phone and how it works. They have hardly seen a telephone before. One of them exclaims in a sad voice: 'Do you know what is our problem? We know everything about our weapons, but we know nothing about how to use a telephone.'

After the conversation with America, Bob and Tajmir descend. The soldiers follow.

'Are these the ones who will kill us once we have turned our backs?' Bob whispers.

The soldiers are each carrying a Kalashnikov. Some of them have fastened long bayonets to the rifles. Tajmir and Bob sit down on a sofa in the lobby. An extraordinary picture hangs above their heads. It is a large framed poster of New York with both the twin towers from the World Trade Center still standing. But it is not New York's real skyline; behind the buildings high mountains tower. In the foreground a large, green park with red flowers has been glued on. New York looks like a small town made of wooden blocks, under an enormous mountain range.

The picture looks as though it has been hanging there for ages: it is discoloured and slightly wavy. It must have been hanging there long before anyone realised that exactly this image would be associated in such a grotesque way with Afghanistan and the dusty town of Khost, and would deliver to the country more of what it did not need: more bombs.

'Do you know which town that is?' asks Bob.

The soldiers shake their heads. They have seen hardly anything but one- and two-storey mud huts and it must be difficult for them to understand that the picture depicts a real town.

'That is New York,' says Bob. 'America. Those two buildings are the ones Osama bin Laden's men flew the planes into.'

The soldiers leap up. They've heard about those two buildings. They point and gesticulate. That's what they looked like! To think they had passed the picture every day without realising it!

Bob has one of his magazines with him and shows them a picture of a man every American recognises.

'Do you know who that is?' he asks. They shake their heads.

'That is Osama bin Laden.'

The soldiers open their eyes wide and tear the magazine out of his hands. They crowd around it. Everyone wants to see.

'Is that what he looks like?'

Both the man and the magazine fascinate them.

'Terrorist,' they say and point and hoot with laughter.

There are no papers or magazines in Khost and they have never before seen a picture of Osama bin Laden, the man who is responsible for Tajmir and Bob's presence in Khost.

The soldiers sit down and produce a large lump of hashish, which they offer Bob and Tajmir. Tajmir smells it and declines. 'Too strong,' he says and smiles.

The two travellers go to bed. All night machine-guns crackle. Next day they wonder how to get about and what story to follow.

Scowling they wander the streets of Khost. No one invites them to join important missions or cave-hunt for al-Qaida. Every day they drop in on the arch-enemies Mustafa and Kamal Khan to hear whether there is any news.

'You'll have to wait until Kamal Khan gets better,' is the message from the occupied Governor's residence.

'Nothing new today,' the police station echoes.

Padsha Khan has disappeared without a trace. Mustafa sits, petrified, behind the fluorescent flowers. There is no trace of the American Special Forces. Nothing happens. Nothing but the crackling of guns every night and the helicopters circling overhead. They are in one of the most lawless parts of the world, and they are bored. In the end Bob decides to return to Kabul. Tajmir rejoices silently: away from Khost, back to Mikrorayon. He is going to buy a huge cake for the wedding anniversary.

He returns a happy man to his own Osama, the little round one with short-sighted eyes. The mother whom he loves above everything in the whole world.

A Broken Heart

For several days now Leila has been receiving letters. Letters that have caused her to freeze with fear, her heart to beat faster than normal and her mind to forget everything else. After having read them she tears them into little bits and throws them in the stove.

The letters cause her to dream. About another life. The scribbles give her thoughts a lift and her life some quivering excitement. Both are new to Leila. Suddenly there is a world inside her head she never knew existed.

'I want to fly! I want to escape!' she shouts one day while sweeping the floor. 'Out!' she cries and swings the broom around the room.

'What did you say?' Sonya asks and looks up from the floor where she is sitting gazing into space and moving her fingers over the pattern in the carpet.

'Nothing,' answers Leila. She cannot stand it any longer. The house is a prison. 'Why is everything so difficult?' she moans. She normally hates going out, but she feels she cannot stay inside. She goes to the market. Fifteen minutes later she returns with a bag of onions, and is received with suspicion.

'Do you go out just to buy onions? Are you so keen to show yourself off that you go to the bazaar when we really don't need anything?' Sharifa is in a cutting mood. 'Next time you should send one of the small boys.'

Shopping is really the work of men and old women. It is unseemly for young women to stop and bargain with shop-owners or men in the market. All shops and stalls belong to men and during the Taliban period the authorities banned women from going to market alone; now Sharifa, in her dark dissatisfaction, bans her too.

Leila doesn't answer. As if she were interested in talking to an onion-vendor! She uses the lot, just to show Sharifa that the onions really were needed.

She's in the kitchen when the boys return. She hears Aimal cluck behind her and shrinks. Her heart beats faster. She has asked him not to bring any more letters. But Aimal pushes a letter on her, and a hard package. She hides both under her dress and rushes to her casket and locks it all up. While the others eat she sneaks out and into the room where all her treasures are kept. With trembling hands she unlocks the casket and unfolds the piece of paper.

Dear L. You must answer me now. My heart burns for you. You are so beautiful, do you want to remove my sorrow or must I live in darkness for ever? My life is in your hands. Please, send me a token. I want to meet you; answer me. I want to share my life with you. With love from K.

The package contains a watch, a watch with blue glass and a silver-coloured strap. She puts it on but quickly takes it off again. She can never wear it. What could she say if the others asked her who gave it to her? She blushes. What if the brothers get to know about it, or her mother? Fear and loathing, what shame. Sultan and Yunus would both condemn her. By accepting the letters she commits an immoral act.

'Do you feel the same as me?' he had asked. She doesn't really feel anything. She is desperate; a new reality has been forced on her. For the first time in her life someone is demanding an answer from her. He wants to know what she feels, what she thinks. But she feels nothing; she is not used to feeling anything. And she tells herself that she feels nothing because she knows she must feel nothing. Feelings are a disgrace, Leila has been taught.

Karim feels. Karim has seen her once. That was the time she and Sonya delivered lunch to the boys in the hotel. Karim had caught only a quick glimpse of her, but there was something about her which made him realise that she was the right one for him: the round, pale face, the beautiful skin, her eyes.

Karim lives alone in one room and works for a Japanese TV company. He is lonely. His mother was killed by shrapnel, which landed in their backyard during the civil war. His father quickly took a new wife, whom Karim could not get on with, and who did not like Karim. She didn't care for the children from the first marriage and beat them when the father was not around. Karim never complained. His father had chosen her, not them. After he'd finished school he worked with his father in his pharmacy in Jalalabad but in the end he couldn't bear living with his new family. His younger sister was married off to a man in Kabul, and Karim followed them, and lived with them. He studied odds and ends at the university and when the

Taliban fled and hordes of journalists filled Kabul's hotels and guesthouses, Karim turned up and offered his English skills to the highest bidder. He was lucky and procured a job with a company who established an office in Kabul and gave Karim a long contract with a good salary. They paid for his room in the hotel. There Karim got to know Mansur and the rest of the Khan family. He liked the family, their bookshop, their knowledge, their level-headedness. A good family, he thought.

When Karim caught sight of Leila he was smitten. But Leila never returned to the hotel, in fact she had loathed being there that one time. Not a good place for a young woman, she thought.

Karim could not divulge his obsession to anyone. Mansur would only laugh and at worst ruin it all. Nothing was sacred to Mansur and he wasn't particularly fond of his aunt.

Only Aimal knew and Aimal kept his mouth shut. Aimal was Karim's go-between.

If he could get closer to Aimal, Karim thought, he might get to know the family through him. He was lucky; one day Mansur invited him home to dinner. It is normal to introduce friends to the family and Karim was one of Mansur's most respected friends. Karim did his utmost to be well received: he was charming, a good listener, and showered the food with compliments. It was especially important that the grandmother liked him because she had the last say where Leila was concerned. But the one he came to see – Leila – never showed up. She was in the kitchen cooking. Sharifa or Bulbula carried the food in. A young man outside the family very rarely gets to see the unmarried women. When the food was eaten, the tea drunk and they were about to go to bed, he caught another glimpse of her.

Owing to the curfew, dinner guests often stayed overnight, and Leila was making the dining room into a bedroom. She laid out the mattresses, took out rugs and cushions and made up an extra mattress for Karim. Her only thought was that the letter-writer was in the apartment.

He thought she was done and went in to pray before the others went to bed. She was there still, bent over the mattress, her long hair braided and covered by a simple shawl. He turned in the doorway, surprised and excited. Leila didn't even notice him. All night Karim cherished the memory of her bent over the mattress. The next morning he didn't see her, although she had prepared water for him to wash in, fried his egg and made his tea. She had even polished his shoes while he was sleeping.

The next day he dispatched his sister to the women of the Khan family. When someone finds new friends, it is not only he who is presented to the family, but his relatives also, and the sister is Karim's closest relative. She knew about Karim's fascination with Leila and now she wanted to get to know the family a bit better. When she returned home she told Karim what he already knew. 'She is clever and a good worker. She is pretty and healthy. The family is quiet and decent. She is a good match.'

'But what did she say? How was she? What did she look like?' Karim listened to the answers time and again, even the rather tame answer describing Leila. 'She is a decent girl, I've already told you,' she said in the end.

As Karim no longer had a mother, the younger sister was obliged to take on the role of suitor for him. But it was still too early; first she would need to get to know the family better, as there was no kinship between them. Without kinship, they were bound to say no the first time.

After the sister had visited, everyone in the family

started pulling Leila's leg about Karim. Leila pretended not to notice when they teased her. She pretended not to care, although she burnt inside. They must not get to know about the letters. She was angry because Karim had put her in danger. She crushed the watch with a stone and threw it away.

First of all she was terrified that Yunus would find out. Of all the family, Yunus was the one who most lived up to the strictest Muslim way of life, although not even he followed it completely. He was also the one she loved most. She worried that he would think badly of her, if he got to know that she had received letters. When she was offered a part-time job on the strength of her knowledge of English, he forbade her to take it. He could not accept that she would work in an office alongside men.

Leila remembers the conversation they had had about Jamila. Sharifa had told her about the young girl's death by suffocation.

'What about her?' Yunus exclaimed. 'You mean the girl who died when an electric fan short-circuited?'

Yunus did not know that the bit about the electric fan was a lie, that Jamila was killed because a lover had visited her at night. Leila revealed the full story.

'Awful, awful,' he says. Leila nods.

'How could she?' he adds.

'She?' Leila exclaims. She had misunderstood the look on his face and thought it was shock, anger and sorrow over the fact that Jamila had been suffocated by her own brothers. But it was shock and anger that she could have taken a lover.

'Her husband was rich and good-looking,' he says, still shaking with indignation after the revelation. 'What a disgrace,' he says. 'And with a Pakistani. This makes me more determined than ever to wed a young girl, young and untouched. And I'll have to keep her on a short rein,' he says firmly.

'But what about the murder?' Leila asks.

'*Her* crime came first.'

Leila, too, wants to be young and untouched. She is terrified of being found out. She does not perceive the difference between being unfaithful to your husband and receiving letters from a boy. Both are forbidden, both are equally bad, both are a disgrace if found out. Now that she is beginning to see Karim as a saviour, as a way of escaping from the family, she is frightened that Yunus won't support her if he should propose.

On her part, there was no talk of being in love. She had hardly seen him, only peeped at him from behind a curtain, and seen him from the window when he came with Mansur. What little she had seen was more or less passable.

'He's so young,' she said to Sonya a bit later. 'He's small and thin and rather childish looking.'

But he was educated, he seemed kind and he was without a family. Therefore he was her saviour, because he might get her away from the life that was otherwise hers. The best of all was that he had no large family, so she would not risk becoming a servant girl. He would let her study, or take a job. It would be just the two of them; maybe they could go away, maybe abroad.

It was not that Leila had no suitors – she already had three. All were relatives, relatives she did not want. One was the son of an aunt, illiterate and jobless, lazy and useless.

The second suitor was Wakil's son, a big lout of a son. He was unemployed; now and again he helped Wakil drive.

'You are lucky, you'll get a man with three fingers,'

Mansur used to tease her. Wakil's son, the one who blew off two fingers when he was fiddling with an engine, was not someone Leila wanted. Big sister Shakila pushed for this marriage. She wanted to have Leila around her in the backyard. But Leila knew that she would continue to be a servant. She would always be under her big sister's thumb and Wakil's son would always have to fall in with what his father demanded.

That will mean twenty people's washing, and not just thirteen like now, she thought. Shakila would be the respected lady of the house; Leila would remain the servant girl. Whatever happened she would never get away; once again she would be caught within the family, like Shakila; chickens, hens and children around her skirts all day long.

The third suitor was Khaled. Khaled was her cousin – a nice, quiet young man. A boy with whom she'd grown up and who, on the whole, she liked. He was kind and his eyes were warm and beautiful. But his family – he had an awful family. A large family of about thirty people. His father, a strict old man, had just been released from jail having been accused of co-operating with the Taliban. Their house, like most other houses in Kabul, had been plundered during the civil war, and when the Taliban arrived and imposed law and order, Khaled's father laid a complaint about some Mujahedeen in his village. They were arrested and imprisoned for a long time. When the Taliban fled, these men regained power in the village and avenged themselves on Khaled's father by sending him to jail. 'That will teach him,' said many. 'He was stupid to complain.'

Khaled's father was known for his unruly temperament. Moreover, he had two wives who were continually quarrelling and who could hardly be in the same room together. Now he was thinking of getting a third wife. 'They are getting too old for me, I must have someone who can keep me young,' the seventy-year-old had said. Leila could not bear the thought of joining this chaotic family; anyhow Khaled had no money so they would never be able to set up somewhere on their own.

But now destiny had generously bestowed Karim on her. His attentions give her the lift she needs and reason for hope. She refuses to give up and continues to look for opportunities to get to the Ministry of Education and register as a teacher. When it is clear that none of the men in the family is prepared to help, Sharifa takes pity on her. She promises to go with Leila to the Ministry. But time passes and they never go. They have no appointment. Leila loses heart, but then suddenly things look up, in an extraordinary way.

Karim's sister had told him about the problems Leila was having registering as a teacher. After many weeks' exertion, and because he knows the Minister of Education's right-hand man, he arranges a meeting between Leila and the new Minister of Education, Rasul Amin. Leila's mother allows her to go because she might now get the teaching job she has wanted for so long. Luckily Sultan is abroad, and even Yunus doesn't put a spanner in the works. Everything is going her way. She lies all night thanking God and prays that all will go well, the meeting with Karim and the Minister.

Karim is to fetch her at nine. Leila tries on and rejects all her clothes. She tries Sonya's clothes, Sharifa's, her own. When the men of the family have left, the women make themselves comfortable on the floor while Leila walks in and out in new outfits.

'Too tight!'

'Too patterned!'

'Too much glitter!'

'Transparent!'

'That one's dirty!'

There is something wrong with everything. Leila has few clothes in the range between old, worn, fuzzy sweaters and blouses glittering with imitation gold. She possesses nothing that is normal. When very rarely she buys clothes it is usually for a wedding or engagement party and then she always chooses the glitziest she can find. She ends up with one of Sonya's white blouses and a big, black skirt. It doesn't actually matter that much, as she throws a long shawl over herself which covers her head and the upper part of her body to well below the hips. But she leaves her face uncovered. Leila has given up the burka. She had promised herself that when the King returned she would take off the veil; Afghanistan would then be a modern country. The April morning when ex-king Zahir Shah set foot on Afghan soil, after thirty years in exile, she hung up her burka for good and told herself she would never again use the stinking thing. Sonya and Sharifa followed suit. It was easy for Sharifa; she had lived most of her adult life with her face uncovered. It was worse for Sonya. She had lived under the burka all her life and she hung back. In the end it was Sultan who forbade her to use it. 'I don't want a prehistoric wife, you are the wife of a liberal man, not a fundamentalist.'

In many ways Sultan *was* a liberal. When he was in Iran he had bought Sonya western clothes. He often referred to the burka as an oppressive cage, and he was pleased that the new Government included female ministers. In his heart he wanted Afghanistan to be a modern country, and he talked warmly about the emancipation of women. But within the family he remained the authoritarian patriarch. When it came to ruling his family, Sultan had only one model: his own father.

When at last Karim arrives Leila is standing in front of the mirror, wrapped in her shawl, with a light in her eyes that has never been there before. Sharifa walks out in front of her. Leila is nervous and her head is bowed. Sharifa sits in front, Leila behind. She greets him quickly. It is going well, she is still anxious but some of the nervousness has gone. He seems completely harmless, looks kind and rather funny.

Karim talks to Sharifa about this and that: her sons, the job, the weather. She asks about his family, his work. Sharifa would also like to take up her old job as a teacher. In contrast to Leila her papers are in order and she only needs to re-register. Leila has a multi-coloured collection of papers, some from the school in Pakistan, some from English classes she has attended. She has no teacher training and did not even complete high school, but there are no other candidates – if Leila doesn't go and teach, the school will have no English teacher.

Once at the Ministry they have to wait for several hours for their moment with the Minister. Around them are numerous women. They sit in the corners, along the walls, with burkas, without burkas. They queue up in front of the many counters. Forms are thrown at them and they throw them back, completed. Employees hit them when they don't move fast enough. They scream at people behind the counters, and they are screamed at in turn from behind the counters. A sort of equal rights reigns: men bawl at men and women yell at women. Some men, obviously employed by the Ministry, run around with piles of papers. It looks as though they are running in circles. Everyone shouts.

An ancient, wizened woman roves around; she is clearly lost but no one helps her. Exhausted, she sits down in a corner and falls asleep. Another old woman is crying.

Karim uses the waiting period to his advantage. At one stage, when Sharifa disappears to enquire about something at a counter with a long queue, he even catches Leila alone.

'What is your answer?' he asks.

'You know I cannot answer you,' she says.

'But what do you want?'

'You know I cannot have a desire.'

'But do you like me?'

'You know I cannot answer that.'

'Will you say yes when I propose?'

'You know it is not me who answers.'

'Will you meet me again?'

'I can't.'

'Why can't you be a bit nicer? Don't you like me?'

'My family will decide whether I like you or not.'

Leila is irritated that he dares ask about these things. Anyhow, it is Sultan or her mother who decides. But of course she likes him. She likes him because he is her saviour. But she has no feelings towards him. How can she answer Karim's questions?

They wait for hours. At last they are called in. The Minister sits behind a curtain. He greets them briefly. He takes the papers Leila hands him and affixes his signature to them without even glancing at them. He signs seven pieces of paper, then they are hustled away.

That is how Afghan society functions. You must know someone to get on in life: a paralysing system. Nothing happens without the correct signatures and sanctions. Leila got to the Minister; someone else must make do with the signature of a less prominent person. But because the ministers spend large parts of the day signing the papers of people who have bribed their way in, their signatures become progressively less valuable.

Leila thinks that having procured the Minister's signature, the road to the world of teaching will be child's play. But she must visit a host of new offices, counters and booths. On the whole Sharifa talks while Leila sits and looks at the floor. Why should it be so difficult to register as a teacher when Afghanistan is crying out for teachers? In many places there are buildings and books, but no one to teach, the Minister said. When Leila reaches the office where new teachers are examined, her papers are all crumpled, they have been handled by so many.

It is an oral examination, to test her suitability as a teacher. In a room two men and two women sit behind a counter. When name, age and education have been recorded, questions are asked.

'Do you know the Islam creed?'

'There is no god but God and Muhammad is his prophet,' Leila rattles off.

'How many times a day must a Muslim pray?'

'Five.'

'Isn't it six?' the woman behind the counter asks. But Leila doesn't allow herself to be knocked off her perch.

'It might be for you, but for me it is five.'

'And how many times do you pray?'

'Five times a day,' Leila lies.

Then there are mathematical questions, which she solves. Then a physics formula she has never heard of.

'Aren't you going to test my English?'

They shake their heads. 'You can say whatever you want,' they laugh sarcastically. None of them can speak English. Leila feels that they would rather neither she nor any of the other candidate teachers got a job. The exam is over and after long discussions between themselves they realise that one piece of paper is missing. 'Come back when you've got that paper,' they say.

Having spent eight hours in the Ministry they return home, despondent. Confronted with such bureaucrats not even the Minister's signature was enough.

'I give up. Maybe I don't really want to be a teacher,' says Leila.

'I'll help you,' Karim smiles. 'Now that I've started, I'm going to complete it,' he promises. Leila's heart softens a tiny bit.

The next day Karim goes to Jalalabad to confer with his family. He tells them about Leila, what sort of family she comes from and that he wants to propose to her. They agree, and now all that remains is to dispatch his sister. It drags on. Karim is frightened of being rejected, and he needs a lot of money for the wedding, for furniture, for a house. Besides, his relationship with Mansur starts to cool. Mansur has ignored him the last few days and greets him curtly with a toss of his head when they meet. One day Karim asks him if he has done something wrong.

'I must tell you something about Leila,' Mansur answers.

'What?' Karim asks.

'No, I can't say anything after all,' says Mansur. 'Sorry.'

'What is it?' Karim remains standing, open-mouthed. 'Is she sick? Is there something wrong with her?'

'I can't say what it is, but if you knew you'd never want to marry her,' Mansur says. 'I have to go now.'

Every day Karim pesters Mansur about what is wrong with Leila. Mansur only draws away. Karim begs and implores, he's angry, he's sour, but Mansur never answers.

Aimal had told Mansur about the letters. In reality he would not have minded Karim marrying Leila, on the contrary, but Wakil too had got wind of Karim's courtship. He asked Mansur to keep Karim away from Leila. Mansur had to do what his aunt's husband asked. Wakil was family, Karim was not.

Wakil even threatened Karim. 'I have chosen her for my son,' he said. 'Leila belongs to our family, and my wife wants her to marry my son. I want that too, and Sultan and her mother will approve. For your own sake, keep away.'

Karim could say little to the older Wakil. His only chance would be if Leila fought to get him. But was there something wrong with Leila? Was it true, what Mansur said?

Karim started to doubt the whole courtship.

In the meantime Wakil and Shakila visit Mikrorayon. Leila disappears into the kitchen to make food. After the couple have gone Bibi Gul says: 'They have asked for you for Said.'

Leila remains standing, paralysed.

'I said it was OK by me, but I would ask you,' says Bibi Gul.

Leila has always done what her mother wanted. Now she says nothing. Wakil's son. With him her life will be exactly as it is now, only with more work and for more people. In addition she will acquire a husband with three fingers, one who has never opened a book.

Bibi Gul dips a piece of bread in the grease on her plate and puts it in her mouth. She takes a bone from Shakila's plate, and sucks up the marrow whilst regarding her daughter.

Leila feels how life, her youth, hope leave her – without being able to save herself. She feels her heart, heavy and lonely like a stone, condemned to be crushed for ever.

Leila turns, takes three paces to the door, closes it quietly behind her and goes out. Her crushed heart she leaves behind. Soon it blends with the dust, which blows in through the window, the dust that lives in the carpets. That evening she will sweep it up and throw it out into the backyard.

Epilogue

All happy families resemble each other.
Every unhappy family is unhappy in its own way.

Leo Tolstoy, *Anna Karenina*

A few weeks after I left Kabul, the family split up. An argument resulted in a fight and the words that fell between Sultan and the two wives on one side, and Leila and Bibi Gul on the other, were so irreconcilable that it would have been difficult to continue living together. When Yunus came home after the quarrel Sultan took him aside and said that he, the sisters and mother were duty-bound to show him the respect he deserved, because Sultan was the oldest and they ate at his table.

The following day, before daylight, Bibi Gul, Yunus, Leila and Bulbula left the apartment taking only what they were wearing. None of them has been back since.

They moved in with Farid, Sultan's other ostracised brother, his nine months pregnant wife and three children.

'Afghan brothers are not nice to each other,' Sultan concludes on the telephone from Kabul. 'It is time we lived independent lives. When they live in my house, they should respect me, shouldn't they?' he asks. 'If the families don't have rules, how can we form a society that respects rules and laws, and not just guns and rockets? This is a society in chaos, it is a lawless society, right out of a civil war. If the families are not guided by authority, we can expect an even worse chaos to follow.'

Leila has heard no more from Karim. When his relationship with Mansur cooled it was difficult for Karim to contact the family. Besides, he became uncertain of what he really wanted. He was awarded a scholarship from Egypt to study Islam at the al-Azhar University in Cairo.

'He's going to be a mullah,' Mansur guffaws from Kabul on a crackly telephone line.

The carpenter went to jail for three years. Sultan was merciless. 'Scoundrels cannot be let loose on society. I am sure he stole at least seven thousand postcards. What he said about his poor family is all lies. I've calculated that he must have made pots of money, but he's hidden it.'

Sultan's huge textbook contract fell through. Oxford University drew the longest straw. Sultan didn't really care. 'It would have sapped all my strength, the order was simply too large.'

Otherwise the bookshops are flourishing. Sultan has been awarded gilt-edged contracts in Iran; he also sells books to the western embassies' libraries. He is trying to buy one of the unused cinemas in Kabul to set up a centre with bookshop, lecture room and library, a place where researchers can have access to his vast collection. Next year he promises to send Mansur on a business trip to India. 'He needs to learn responsibility; that will be character-building,' he says. 'Maybe I'll send the other boys to school.' In addition, Sultan has granted his three sons a holiday on Fridays; to do with what they like.

The political situation worries Sultan. 'Dangerous. The Northern Alliance was given too much power by Loya Jirga, there is no balance. Karzai is too weak; he is unable to rule the country. The best thing would be to have a government consisting of technocrats appointed by the Europeans. When we Afghans try to appoint leaders, everything goes wrong. Without cooperation the people suffer. And besides, our intellectuals have not returned. There is an empty space where they should have been.'

Mansur has forbidden his mother to work as a teacher. 'Not good,' is all he says. Sultan did not mind her working again, but as long as Mansur, her oldest son, forbade it, nothing came of it. Nor has anything come of Leila's second attempt to register as a teacher.

Bulbula got her Rasul in the end. Sultan chose to stay at home and forbade his wives and sons to attend the wedding.

Mariam, who was so terrified of giving birth to a daughter, had Allah on her side and produced a son.

Sonya and Sharifa are the only women left in Sultan's house. When Sultan and the sons are at work the women are alone in the apartment, sometimes as mother and daughter, sometimes as rivals. In a few months Sonya

will give birth. She prays to Allah that it will be a son. She
asked me if I could pray for her too.

'What if it's another girl!'

Another little catastrophe in the Khan family.

A MIGHTY HEART

The Brave Life and Death of my Husband Daniel Pearl

by Mariane Pearl

A Mighty Heart is the emotionally riveting account of one of the most terrifying stories of our time: unforgettable for its individuality and its horror; memorable for what it tells us about a man and a woman's determination to understand the world: and a deeply moving demonstration of love.

The tragic murder of *Wall Street Journal* reporter Daniel Pearl is well known. Why he was in Karachi; how he saw his role as an international journalist; why he was singled out for kidnapping; and where the incredible search effort led: Mariane Pearl asks these questions and follows every clue.

A journalist in her own right Mariane is, as was her husband, profoundly committed to the idea that a more informed public makes for a better world, and to the idea that risks have to be taken to uncover a story. A superb writer, she presents a truly illuminating tale – including her own crucial role in the investigative team, where she was responsible for negotiating unprecedented cooperation between the FBI and Pakistani Intelligence and able to forge alliances with an array of people, from the Karachi chief of police to George Bush.

A Mighty Heart is an extraordinary book – a fitting tribute to a dedicated reporter and a profound and heartbreaking love story.

'A most remarkable woman. The book is heart-wrenching and extraordinary' – John Le Carré

MY FORBIDDEN FACE

A poignant story of a young woman's life
under the Taliban

by Latifa

Latifa was born in Kabul in 1980 into an educated middle-class Afghan family, at once liberal and religious. As a teenager, she was interested in fashion and cinema and going out with her friends, and she longed to become a journalist. Her mother, a doctor, and her father, a businessman, encouraged her dreams.

Then in 1996, the Taliban seized power. From that moment, Latifa, sixteen years old, became a prisoner in her own home. Her school was closed. Her mother was banned form working.

With painful honesty and clarity, Latifa describes the way her world fell apart. Her story goes to the heart of a people caught up in a terrible tragedy in a brutalised country.

'This simply-told book makes the stories that we have seen from the outside much more horrifyingly real. It is good that this powerful story has been told from the inside' *The Times*

'A short, sobering excursion into a mad world' *Irish Independent*

'An important, brave story' *Independent on Sunday*

Now you can order superb titles directly from Virago

☐ A Mighty Heart   Mariane Pearl   £10.99
☐ Desert Dawn   Waris Dirie   £10.99
☐ My Forbidden Face   Latifa   £6.99

The prices shown above are correct at time of going to press. However, the publishers reserve the right to increase prices on covers from those previously advertised, without further notice.

Virago

Please allow for postage and packing: **Free UK delivery.**
Europe: add 25% of retail price; Rest of World: 45% of retail price.

To order any of the above or any other Virago titles, please call our credit card orderline or fill in this coupon and send/fax it to:

Virago, PO Box 121, Kettering, Northants NN14 4ZQ
Fax: 01832 733076   Tel: 01832 737526
Email: aspenhouse@FSBDial.co.uk

☐ I enclose a UK bank cheque made payable to Virago for £ . . . .
☐ Please charge £ . . . . . . to my Visa/Access/Mastercard/Eurocard

Expiry Date ☐☐☐☐   Switch Issue No. ☐☐

NAME (BLOCK LETTERS please) . . . .

ADDRESS . . . .

. . . .

. . . .

Postcode . . . . Telephone . . . .

Signature . . . .

Please allow 28 days for delivery within the UK. Offer subject to price and availability.

Please do not send any further mailings from companies carefully selected by Virago ☐